Welcome to

THE EVERYTHING® PARENT'S GUIDES

As a parent, you're swamped with conflicting advice and parenting techniques that tell you what is best for your child. THE EVERYTHING® PARENT'S GUIDES get right to the point about specific issues. They give you the most recent, up-to-date information on parenting trends, behavior issues, and health concerns—providing you with a detailed resource to help you ease your parenting anxieties.

THE EVERYTHING® PARENT'S GUIDES are an extension of the bestselling Everything® series in the parenting category. These family-friendly books are designed to be a one-stop guide for parents. If you want authoritative information on specific topics not fully covered in other books, THE EVERYTHING® PARENT'S GUIDES are the perfect resource to ensure that you raise a healthy, confident child.

Visit the entire Everything® series at *www.everything.com*

THE

EVERYTHING® PARENT'S GUIDE TO Sensory Integration Disorder

Dear Reader,

Maybe you've heard about sensory integration disorder from a doctor, a teacher, or a friend. Maybe you've read about it in a magazine or seen a story on television. Maybe you've hoped this new theory could explain the confusing way your child sometimes behaves. Or maybe you've just wondered whether the world really needs another disorder, with so many acronyms already being pinned on kids who are discipline-resistant.

The exciting thing about sensory integration theory is that it can help you understand your child better, whether he is struggling enough to need a diagnosis of sensory integration disorder or just has strong likes and dislikes that sometimes interfere with good behavior. Learning about sensory processing, motor planning, and extremes of sensitivity and alertness can make you a stronger, more perceptive parent, able to make the world a friendlier place for your child. And who wouldn't want to do that?

Since my son was diagnosed with sensory integration disorder nearly ten years ago, I've read and learned everything I could about it. I've picked the brains of occupational therapists, looking for ideas and tricks to help my jumpy boy. I've corresponded with other parents who have found this to be the key to helping their own children. The medical profession may be slow to embrace sensory integration disorder as an accepted childhood malady, but moms and dads know what's most important: Therapy and knowledge work. My hope is that this book will inspire you to join their ranks.

Terri Mauro

SENSORY INTEGRATION DISORDER

Get the right diagnosis, understand treatments, and advocate for your child

Terri Mauro

with technical review by Sharon A. Cermak, Ed.D., OTR/L, FAOTA

Adams Media
Avon, Massachusetts

For Rick, Elena, and Andy

• • •

Publishing Director: Gary M. Krebs
Associate Managing Editor: Laura M. Daly
Associate Copy Chief: Brett Palana-Shanahan
Acquisitions Editor: Kate Burgo
Development Editor: Rachel Engelson
Associate Production Editor: Casey Ebert

Director of Manufacturing: Susan Beale
Associate Director of Production: Michelle Roy Kelly
Cover Design: Paul Beatrice, Matt LeBlanc, Erick DaCosta
Design and Layout: Colleen Cunningham, Jennifer Oliveira, Brewster Brownville

• • •

An Everything® Series Book.
Everything® and everything.com® are registered trademarks of F+W Media, Inc.

Published by Adams Media, a division of F+W Media, Inc.
57 Littlefield Street, Avon, MA 02322 U.S.A.
www.adamsmedia.com

ISBN 10: 1-59337-714-2
ISBN 13: 978-1-59337-714-4
Printed in the United States of America.

J I H G F E D

**Library of Congress Cataloging-in-Publication Data
is available from the publisher**

Sensory Integration Disorder

▶ ***n.*** A disorder characterized by the inability to accurately process information coming to the brain from the senses, which results in inaccurate judgment of sensory information such as touch, sight, movement, taste, and sound.

Acknowledgments

So much of what I've learned about sensory integration has come from the professionals who have worked with my son, generously sharing their knowledge and collaborating with me to help him be his best. I'd like to thank his occupational therapists, especially Dinah Leiter, Susan Wisotsky, and Linda Lee, and his wonderful special education teachers—Shirley Winkler, Wendy James, Jean Labriola, Linda Weisholtz, Maryann Stanckiewitz, Ursula Zarife, and Angela Fatsis.

Other parents have also been an amazing resource for information about sensory integration. Thanks to all the members of the Eastern European Adoption Coalition's APR and PEP lists for advice given over the years, and to the members who volunteered to share their experiences with me directly for this book, especially Kathleen, Karen, Terrie, Jennifer, Jo Ellen, and Harriet. On a personal note, my thanks to my agent, Barb Doyen, for getting me into this; my husband Rick and children Elena and Andy, for helping me out; and my mother, the late Ruth Evens Sheen, who always knew I would write a book.

Contents

Introduction

Your child is a unique individual. Her strengths and weaknesses, interests and sensitivities are what make her the original, special person she is. You don't hesitate to find methods to help your child learn in ways that are best suited to her particular abilities and struggles. You look eagerly to find her talents and encourage them. You brag about her accomplishments, and you enjoy all those little quirks of personality that distinguish your child from the rest—her offbeat sense of humor, eagerness to please, strong sense of self, great personal style. So why is discipline treated as a one-size-fits-all affair?

If you assume that the only reason your child acts up is because he's up to something, and that the only reason he ignores you is out of disrespect, you may be failing to take into account those very same differences and special qualities that seem positive in other contexts. Just as his strengths and weaknesses can impact his education, talent, or personality, they can impact his behavior and obedience and his response to discipline.

Expecting every child to behave the same and respond to the same techniques is like expecting every child to be good at math and at playing the cello. Some kids can calculate like computers and play with finesse. Others prefer reading and drums. Adjusting your behavioral expectations and disciplinary techniques to the

person your child actually is, and not the person that society or parenting books or your mother-in-law tells you he should be, is more merciful for your child and more effective for you.

Sensory integration theory works from the dual assumption that not everybody processes the information from eyes, ears, noses, taste buds, skin, inner ear, muscles, and joints in the same way, and that the differences in those perceptions affect the ways in which children learn, develop, and behave. Children with sensory integration disorder may react in dramatic ways to information that seems dramatic to no one else, and their reactions may be misinterpreted as misbehavior. Learning about the way your own one-of-a-kind child handles sensory input and responds to it will help you understand her sometimes-puzzling behavior and design an approach that is singularly appropriate to your child. It will make you appreciate the ingenuity your child brings to getting through confusing and overwhelming experiences, and it may help you understand your own reactions a little bit better, too.

Occupational therapy using a sensory integration approach can help your child grow stronger in areas in which her brain doesn't handle sensory information very well. Think of it as a tutor for her sensory education. Think of it, also, as the most fun your child will have all week. The serious play your child does with a therapist, which you carry through to playtime at home, will gradually lead your child to react less strongly to things that alarm her senses and to stay alert without needing to engage in disruptive behavior. It will also improve her movement skills and give her an upbeat, low-stress, confidence-building good time.

Your child may never fit some ironclad mold of behavioral perfection. Would you even want that? It is your duty and honor as a parent to nurture those things that are special about him and to give him strength to meet his challenges. An understanding of sensory integration will help you do that in a way that honors your child's individuality and your own.

CHAPTER 1

Introduction to Sensory Integration Disorder

It's the little things, really. The tag in a shirt, the seam of a sock. The tilt of the head for a shampoo. The sway of a swing, the whirr of a fan. The modest effort needed to lift a spoon, push a pencil, close a door. The small effort required to tolerate bright lights, sharp flavors, strong smells. They seem like such little things to you. How can they be such a big deal for your child?

How Your Brain Builds Your World

When kids can't interpret the information that comes through their senses, when they can't find the right balance between over- and undersensitivity, when they can't combine the impressions created by their eyes and their ears and their joints and their sense of balance, those little things can loom terrifyingly large. Sensory integration disorder is a diagnosis that encompasses these sensory missteps; occupational therapy using a sensory integration approach seeks to bring problems back down to size.

All the things you see, hear, smell, taste, and feel start out as waves of light or sound, chemicals in your nose or on your tongue, or pressure against nerve endings in your skin. Those sensations are translated into electrical impulses that zip along neurons to your brain, which has the task of interpreting all that information and deciding what to do with it. Successful sensory integration involves the following:

- Receiving the sensory information successfully
- Interpreting the sensory information correctly
- Combining information from different senses to create a complete picture
- Deciding on a response based on information from all sources
- Executing that response by sending electrical impulses back out to the muscles and limbs

Essential

Sensory integration disorder is a relatively recent diagnosis, but the disorder isn't new. Think of kids you knew growing up who were easily spooked by touch or excessively rambunctious. Putting a label on the behavior doesn't stigmatize your child; the behavior stigmatizes your child, while the label gives her and others a way of understanding those odd fears and compulsions.

If all this goes smoothly, you don't even notice it's happening. If it doesn't go so smoothly, as may be the case for your child, it's awfully hard to ignore. Sensory integration disorder is the brain's inability to use the information that comes through the senses in an organized and effective way. Your child may have trouble:

- *Receiving* sensory information successfully if his brain needs a larger than normal amount of information before it reacts, or reacts too strongly to a small amount of information
- *Interpreting* sensory information correctly if not enough information gets through, or so much information gets through that it is overwhelming and can't all be interpreted
- *Combining* information from different senses if information from some of the senses isn't successfully received or correctly

interpreted, or information from different senses can't be put together

- *Deciding* on a response if he doesn't have a complete picture to base it on or if his brain hasn't developed and/or stored a plan for action
- *Executing* that response if his brain doesn't know what his muscles and limbs are up to already

It may seem to you sometimes that your child is in another world. He may seem to occupy an alternate dimension, where some things are bigger and scarier than they really are, and other things don't register at all. In a way, that's just what's happening. Your world and your child's world are different, built by your own unique brains out of building blocks provided by your senses. Those blocks may be as different as Legos and alphabet blocks. Yours clings tightly together in a pleasing predictable structure, while his rises precariously and topples at the slightest nudge.

The Seven Senses

What the muscles and limbs are up to, and which way is up, are vitally important elements of sensory integration. You may not think of them when you're counting out the five senses, but you'll be hearing a lot about these extra two senses—the proprioceptive sense and the vestibular sense—as you pursue treatment for your child with sensory integration disorder.

Each of these seven senses will be discussed more fully later in this book, along with the way sensory integration disorder can affect your child's ability to use them effectively. But as a brief introduction, you may suspect your child has trouble with the following:

- The proprioceptive sense, or sense of body position, if he regularly bumps into things accidentally or on purpose; has trouble planning simple sequences of movements; jumps or rocks; likes hard hugs

- The vestibular sense, or sense of balance, if he either fears or craves swinging on a swing set; becomes upset when tipped backward; fears heights or having his feet off the ground; loves to spin around or rock back and forth
- The tactile sense, or sense of touch, if he has extreme reactions to clothing, combing, haircutting, dental work; doesn't react enough to pain, cold, discomfort; avoids hugs, tickles and cuddles
- The visual sense, or sense of sight, if he can't stand bright lights; feels agitated around bright colors or busy rooms; can't pick items out of a detailed picture or background or see how a puzzle goes together
- The auditory sense, or sense of hearing, if he has extreme reactions to sirens, alarms, vacuum cleaners; can't calm down in noisy rooms; doesn't hear or respond to your calls if there are too many other sounds in the room
- The olfactory sense, or sense of smell, if he has trouble telling the difference between smells; can't readily identify odors; has extreme reactions to certain smells; has no reaction to other strong smells
- The gustatory sense, or sense of taste, if he craves very strong, sharp, or sour flavors; refuses all but bland foods; can't tell the difference between foods; eats or sucks on nonfood items

Since sensory integration involves receiving and interpreting information from the senses and combining the information to form a well-rounded and accurate picture, problems with one sense can cause problems with all sensory input and output. If your child is distracted by the way her clothing feels, it's going to affect her ability to listen and to see detail and to stay still. If your child feels off-balance, it's going to affect the way she sees things, coordinates her movements, and hears what you're telling her.

For this reason, it is important to look for patterns of behavior across senses, especially extreme over- or underreactions to sensory information; clumsiness and craving for jumping, crashing, spinning, swinging, and rocking; and an inability to distinguish important information from a lot of background distraction.

Fact

The tactile, proprioceptive, and vestibular senses are the "big three" for sensory integration problems. Other senses can't work properly if these three are not doing their jobs. For that reason, therapy with a sensory integration approach tends to focus on activities that target touch, balance, and body position. These will actually improve your child's abilities in all areas.

Preferences and Phobias

As you've read about the way sensory integration disorder can affect your child's ability to use information from his senses, you may have realized that some of it applies to you as well. You may have extreme reactions to certain foods or fabrics. You may find it hard to concentrate in a noisy room. Certain sounds or movements may bother you in ways you can't quite pinpoint. Indeed, most people have difficulty with sensory processing in overwhelming conditions (like those you would experience in a noisy or dark room). Even children who don't have problems significant enough to merit a diagnosis of sensory integration disorder may meet some of the criteria and benefit from games and activities designed to strengthen their sensing abilities.

Disorders of sensory integration have been divided into sensory modulation disorders and dyspraxia (motor planning) disorders. Disorders of sensory modulation can be thought of as a spectrum that runs from extreme oversensitivity to extreme undersensitivity, with a pleasant balance in the middle. You can probably relate to feeling just a little off center, knocked out of your comfort zone by sensations you can't seem to process correctly. If you look at the range of likes and dislikes among family members, friends, and the public in general, it's easy to see that not everybody is processing sensations in exactly the same way. When you like certain sensory experiences a little more or a little less than most people, or fear them a little more or a little less, you're spreading out along that spectrum. You probably think of these things as personal preferences, not as glitches of the nervous system, but often that's what's at the root of them.

Essential

Sensory problems are more common than you might think. *The Diagnostic Manual for Infancy and Early Childhood* estimates that 5 to 10 percent of children without other disabilities have sensory processing disorder. Among children on the autism spectrum, the rates are much higher, possibly as much as 88 percent.

Most adults—unlike most children—are able to make adjustments for their sensory variations. Chances are that you don't wear clothes or eat foods or seek out activities that make you feel uncomfortable. You make lifestyle choices that allow you to do the things you need to do to feel alert and safe and comfortable.

Why Kids Can't Just Adjust

You accept your own sensory preferences. When, from time to time, you have to do things that unsettle you, you're able to draw on past experiences and social expectations to force yourself to tolerate unpleasantness for limited amounts of time. Why, you may wonder, can't your child also find a way to handle this? Why does he have to make such a big deal over everything or fall apart over such little, unimportant things?

Unlike adults, children with sensory integration disorder don't have much control over or understanding of their strong preferences and phobias. They are ill-equipped to tolerate them for the following reasons.

Neurological Impairment

It's important to realize that while many individuals have a certain amount of trouble with sensory integration and sensory sensitivities some of the time, children with sensory integration disorder have brains that may work less efficiently in this area than those of other people. No specific cause for this has been pinpointed, but one or more of the following may be true:

- There is mild brain damage from birth
- There is some form of sensory deprivation in early life, such as that experienced by children in Eastern European orphanages
- The child was born premature
- There is a co-occurring problem, such as an autism spectrum disorder
- There is an environmental factor, such as alcohol consumed during pregnancy

There may be other environmental triggers, as is suspected with autism and attention deficit hyperactivity disorder (ADHD). Whatever the reason, your child with sensory integration disorder has a neurological impairment that makes him less able to deal with sensory integration and less able to find acceptable solutions to his distress.

Inefficient Neural Pathways

Sensations make their way to the brain by way of electrical impulses passed over synapses, or gaps, between neurons (nerve cells). Impulses follow a neural pathway of neurons and synapses from your eyes or fingertips to various outposts in the brain. The more each pathway is used, the stronger the chemical connection becomes, while pathways that are not used as much are not as strong or as fast.

Children are building those neural pathways when they play, investigate, figure things out, and seek new sensations. The more they try and see and hear, the stronger those pathways get, until activities that were once challenging are done smoothly, efficiently, competently, and with a great deal of satisfaction.

Don't assume that since weak or inefficient neural pathways are one reason for your child's inability to handle certain experiences, the best remedy is to force him to have those experiences over and over again. The fear and stress this would cause would wipe out any benefit and make those experiences even more difficult.

If your child has sensory integration disorder, however, all that playing and investigating and figuring things out can be a trial. Sensations that feel threatening or overwhelming will not be repeated, making the pathways weaker and the sensations more threatening or overwhelming. Experiences as basic as a tap on the shoulder or a swoop on a swing may always seem new and frightening. Pathways may form improperly and emphasize the wrong things; cause information to be lost along the way; or deliver information to the wrong place, magnify its importance, or undersell it. Your child's nervous system may not gain the sort of experience needed to problem-solve, adjust, and compensate that you probably take for granted.

Lack of Understanding

You know from observation, discussion, reading, and research when your own personal likes and dislikes differ sharply from the norm. But your child doesn't have that kind of awareness. He knows only what he feels, and he assumes that everybody else must feel the same. This can leave him confused and hurt when you don't seem to understand what he's doing and feeling. It's the way you might feel if someone came up to you and ordered you to fly, or else. You'd be baffled that the person didn't understand how impossible that was, and being bribed or threatened or yelled at would only make you more frustrated.

Things get worse when your child lacks the language needed to even try to explain herself. Depending on your child's age and developmental level, she may not have the words to express the discomfort and distress she's feeling. But more than that, she may not have the body language to do it. If your child has a poor internal picture of her body, it may be impossible for her to explain what feels right and what feels wrong. Tenacious defense of a tenuous comfort zone may be the only action she can conceive of.

When adults interpret sensory integration problems as deliberate behavioral choices, things can spiral out of control quickly. If a child legitimately cannot find a way within his neurological capabilities to do something a parent or teacher is insisting on—and lacks any sort of useful vocabulary for explaining why he can't—there is very little option but to explode in fear and frustration. Understanding that a child is trying his best and needs help to overcome challenges is an important first step in helping kids with sensory integration disorder.

Essential

Behavior is the best way some kids have to communicate. If your child's behavior puzzles you—if she seems eager to please and generally compliant, but stubbornly insists on her way from time to time with desperate passion—ask yourself what that behavior might be telling you about her sensory preferences and fears.

Lack of Choice

Adults routinely adjust for their sensory processing irregularities by carefully making choices that allow them to honor their nervous systems without intruding on others'. But children are rarely given that kind of choice. An adult who needs to move to feel comfortable and alert can most likely find a job that doesn't involve sitting behind a desk; kids are expected to sit in a schoolroom and be still, no matter what. An adult who finds certain foods unappetizing can choose not to eat them; kids are expected to eat what's put in front of them without whining or excuses. You expect your child to wear what you say, have her hair washed or cut in whatever way is convenient to you, sit still when you say, and move when given instructions. Refusal is seen as a conscious behavioral choice. For kids with sensory integration disorder, it's anything but.

From Discomfort to Discombobulation

It's one thing to dislike something, even to the point of strenuous avoidance, and another to melt into a screaming, unreachable tantrum when faced with that item or experience. Children with sensory integration disorder may have extreme reactions—intense fearfulness, unbreakable resistance, complete breakdowns, and obsessive drives. For them, poor sensory processing is not a source of discomfort or displeasure; it's a matter of life and death. In their fun house world, things are so disorganized and difficult to make sense of that they abandon everything to find a comfort zone, or abandon all hope of finding one. What looks to you like defiant or heedless behavior feels to your child like the necessities of survival.

Think of how you feel when you have a bad cold that stops up your ears and affects your balance. That sensation of mild vertigo impacts you in a number of ways. You may feel sick to your stomach. You may get a headache. You may decide to stay home, crawl in bed, and remain as immobile as possible until you feel like yourself. But what if you felt like that all the time, and had no explanation for it? Would you be able to operate at a normal brisk pace and optimal alertness? Or would your actions be slow and deliberate, your attention focused on keeping your body and brain together, your most ardent desire to lie down and make the world stop turning?

Your child with sensory integration disorder may be in that very position. Her body doesn't feel right. She may not be able to verbalize this because it is the only reality she's known. She may want very much to please you and to do things the way they're supposed to be done. But just as a desire to be back to normal isn't going to make your cold go away, a desire to please her parents isn't going to magically allow your child to process the world in an accurate way. At some point, she will always have to do what she feels is necessary to bring the world into some sort of manageable balance.

That may mean jumping up and down, hard, to activate a balky proprioceptive system. It may mean lying down or twirling around to handle vestibular input. It may mean screaming in fear when a faulty tactile sense indicates attack, or ignoring messages that a lazy auditory sense never delivers. It may, sometimes, just mean losing it and having a good tantrum. If you've ever descended into anger and self-pity over the flu, an accident, or an illness that robbed you of control, you know how she feels.

Occupational Therapists to the Rescue

The desire to help children caught in this bind started A. Jean Ayres, a California occupational therapist, doing research on sensory integration in the 1960s. Working with children whose learning and behavioral problems seemed to have no satisfactory explanation, she noticed that they had trouble accurately processing and modulating the information coming in from their senses. She worked on some techniques that would introduce needed sensory information, allowing for gradual improvement in the children's sensory abilities. That work has been continued and refined over the past forty years by other occupational therapists (OTs), who have made therapy with a sensory integration approach one of their techniques for helping children who cannot comfortably find their way in the world.

The job of OTs is to work on the skills (occupations) people need to function in their daily lives. For adults, that might involve regaining fine motor skills after an accident or stroke. For kids, it often involves learning the skills necessary for play and schoolwork and healthy relationships. These things are problems for kids with poor sensory integration function. Working either in private clinics or in schools, OTs seek to strengthen the children's abilities to handle the information coming from their senses while also giving them strategies to find their own comfort zones without being disruptive to others.

Fact

A. Jean Ayres wasn't just a pioneer of sensory integration theory—she was related to a child with sensory integration disorder. Her correspondence with her nephew, in which he describes his sensory challenges and she offers sympathy and advice, has been collected in the book *Love, Jean: Inspiration for Families Living With Dysfunction of Sensory Integration*.

Play is the way children gain information about their world, experiment with different sensory experiences, learn the way their bodies work and how to manipulate them, and gain an understanding of the give and take of social interaction. Consequently, play is the medium through which OTs using a sensory integration approach do their work. Such therapy is fun for kids, and it may look like nothing more than a session of swinging or game-playing or ball-pit lounging. But all the activities are carefully calibrated to increase children's ability to process, modulate, and integrate information coming in from the senses. Often, a puzzle or a board game is used as a distraction to keep the child from being overwhelmed by sensations that are usually frightening.

Naming the Disorder

Ayres used the term "sensory integration disorder" to describe the problems she was seeing in children. The term wasn't intended to describe a specific malady, just a way of understanding the difficulties the children were having. Finding a permanent name to hang on sensory integration problems has been something of an ongoing process. You may hear sensory integration disorder called sensory integration dysfunction or dysfunction of sensory integration (coined at least in part to change the acronym from SID, which came a little close to the acronym for sudden infant death syndrome). As therapists further research the sensory problems of children and refine their understanding, they're also trying to fine-tune the language used to describe them. "Sensory processing disorder" and "regulatory-sensory processing disorders" are two names that are being used more frequently now, with the latter broken down into a variety of subcategories, including sensory modulation, sensory discrimination challenges, and sensory-based motor challenges. The name changes may be confusing to parents, but they're helpful to therapists and researchers in pinpointing the specific needs of children and addressing them most efficiently.

Whatever name you use, a diagnosis of sensory integration disorder and therapy using a sensory integration approach can make your child more attentive at school, more manageable at home, and more comfortable in his own skin. Most parents would call that a miracle.

CHAPTER 2

Getting a Diagnosis

As with any disability, getting a diagnosis can be the first step to getting proper treatment. Unlike most disabilities, you may not hear about this one from a doctor first. A teacher, social worker, or therapist might mention it, or you may read a magazine article or a book and see your child in it. Because sensory integration disorder hasn't been fully accepted by many in the medical profession as a legitimate diagnosis, it's possible that you'll have to do your own investigating and then give your pediatrician a push.

Receiving a Referral

Generally, the process of getting an evaluation of sensory integration disorder may begin with your pediatrician or a specialist, either of whom might refer you to an occupational therapist. You may refer yourself, since in most states, a medical referral isn't needed for a child to receive OT services (which is in contrast to physical therapy services, which often require a referral). It is recommended, though, that you work with your child's pediatrician or medical specialist to be sure that medical conditions have been ruled out before a diagnosis of sensory integration disorder is applied. That referral can be hard to get if your child's doctor is a nonbeliever. A doubting pediatrician may dismiss your request by asserting that because there's no scientific proof that therapy with a sensory integration approach works, it's all quackery. Don't let that

discourage you. Hard facts and figures are difficult to come by in a field that is based mostly on observation and on a sensory profile that varies sharply from child to child, requiring an intensely personalized approach. While solid scientific evidence may be lacking, there is strong anecdotal evidence from parents that this approach has made a significant difference in their children's ability to function.

Should I change pediatricians if we disagree on sensory integration?
If that's your only disagreement, maybe not. However, an ideal parent-pediatrician relationship should allow for active input on your part. If your pediatrician regularly dismisses your observations and refuses to give serious and respectful consideration to any suggestions that you make, it's not unreasonable to look for a better fit.

If your child's doctor refuses to consider difficulty in sensory integration as a possible contributing factor for your child's struggles—or is quick to suggest attention deficit disorder (ADD) or attention deficit hyperactivity disorder (ADHD) and prescribe medication, although those diagnoses are also made largely by observation—consider switching to a pediatrician who is more willing to work with you on considering all options for your child's care. Ask around your community, especially among occupational therapists or parents whose children have successfully received a diagnosis of sensory integration disorder. You may be able to find a pediatrician who has an interest in sensory integration theory or a specialist who will make the referral to have your child evaluated by an occupational therapist. Then again, if your child is eligible for public early intervention or special education services, or you're not concerned about getting insurance coverage for the therapy, you may be able to do at least the preliminary referring yourself.

Early Intervention

Depending on the age of your child, your doctor might suggest an evaluation for sensory integration as part of the process of getting early intervention services. These services are called different things in different parts of the country, but they generally consist of education, speech, physical, and occupational therapy for children under the age of three. In the course of having your child evaluated for early intervention, you may be able to get at least an informal sensory integration assessment, and therapy may be included as one of the services offered. These services have two virtues. They are free (or inexpensive), and they consolidate your child's therapy in one place.

You can refer your child for early intervention services yourself. To find the agency responsible for these services in your area, go to the National Early Childhood Technical Assistance Center Web site (at *www.nectac.org*) and find your state. You'll find contact information including address, phone number, e-mail, and in most cases a Web address. The people who staff these agencies should be willing to talk with you about your concerns about your child's development, and they should give you information on what needs to be done to get your child evaluated for services. There may be a significant lag between when you start the process and when the evaluations can be performed, so don't wait in the hopes that your child's problems will magically resolve. If they do, you can always cancel.

The Sensory Integration and Praxis Tests (SIPT), the standard evaluation for sensory integration disorder, are designed for kids aged four and older. As a result, you may not get formal testing through an early intervention program. However, an occupational therapist with knowledge of and experience in sensory integration therapy should be able to include sensory integration in the observations made of your child and incorporate appropriate therapeutic activities in the intervention. Be sure to mention your sensory integration suspicions in any communications with the people who will be testing your child.

Your child's chronological age isn't the only thing that determines whether the SIPT are appropriate. Developmental age may also be a factor. If your child is age four or older but has severe trouble paying attention and following instructions, the therapist may decide against using formal testing.

School-Based Therapy

If your child is school age and eligible for special education services, he may be able to receive an occupational therapy evaluation including sensory integration evaluation as part of the individualized education plan (IEP) process. This will largely depend on whether the school therapist happens to be experienced in sensory integration. You will likely not get the same quality of evaluation and therapy in a school setting as you would in a private office that specializes in sensory integration, but the services are free, and they take place somewhere your child is already going to be.

Special education preschool is an option for three and four year olds, providing a few hours of instruction and therapy in a school setting. As with early intervention, this is something you may be able to initiate yourself, and it does not obligate you to put your child into special education for kindergarten and beyond. Check with your school district to find out what's offered and how you can refer your child for evaluation.

Fact

Although occupational therapists may work at your child's school, they are not necessarily employees of the school district. Many are independent contractors who work for an outside agency that provides services for schools. They are also likely to work in more than one school in the district and to be available to your child only on certain days and at certain times.

Private Therapy

Having your child evaluated by a private occupational therapist, with all the referral paperwork and insurance runaround that entails, will probably give you the most thorough information about your child's sensory processing abilities and disabilities, and the most intensive therapy. Unlike school therapists, private therapists have space for equipment that doesn't have to be crammed into a classroom or moved from school to school. They are not working under time and budget constraints in the same way that school or early intervention therapists are, and they can be more flexible in their goals than therapists bound by IEPs. And since you're paying them, they may be more responsive to your input and forthcoming with information than a therapist in the employ of a school district or early intervention service can reasonably be. You may find that the expense is worth it.

Essential

You need to be comfortable with your child's therapist, or you'll never have the kind of two-way collaboration needed to give your child the best shot at successful therapy. If anything bothers you during the evaluation process about the person, the office, the way you are spoken to, or the way your child is treated, look elsewhere.

If you want to find and contact a therapist on your own, the Sensory Processing Disorders Network (SPD Network) provides a listing of therapists and resources on their Web site (*www.spdnetwork.org*). Other parents are also an excellent source of referrals and recommendations. Local chapters of organizations that serve people with special needs, such as The ARC or the Autism Society of America, may be able to point you to knowledgeable therapists. Even if your child is too old for early intervention services, you might call the agency in your state and ask if there are therapists they'd recommend. Make sure before you start that any therapist you choose is an occupational therapist who is knowledgable about using a sensory integration approach.

The Value of Observation

Sensory integration disorder isn't something you can do a blood test for. There are no X-rays or EEGs that will allow a specialist to say, "Aha! There it is! Sensory integration disorder!" The tests that occupational therapists do to determine whether your child has sensory integration disorder mostly involve observing your child at play or engaged in playful activities. A therapist will probably sit down with your child at a table and ask him to play with some toys—stacking blocks, dressing a doll, drawing shapes—while following instructions, and identifying objects by touch and not by sight. These will be tasks that might show a difficulty in combining input from the senses to accurately interpret the environment and perform activities in an orderly fashion.

The therapist's observations aren't the only ones that count. You will be asked to share your observations as well. This may come in the form of a lengthy questionnaire, an interview between you and the therapist, or both. You may be asked to fill out a sensory profile in which you rate your child's ability in a number of areas. The therapist may also ask you questions while evaluating your child to find out what you think about various things your child is doing. Never forget that you are the expert on your child, and don't be afraid to ask questions or share information at any time.

The length and the detail of a sensory profile questionnaire can be intimidating. But no one is expecting you to recall things with complete accuracy or to offer perceptions that are beyond your abilities and knowledge. One of the reasons there are so many questions is so that impressions can be averaged. Just make your best choice, and ask questions!

If your child has had a lot of evaluations with specialists, one thing that may particularly strike you about an occupational therapy evaluation is how much the therapist actively tries to engage your child. Specialists often spend most of their time reviewing reports and talking to you. They tend to give your child a cursory look, with no attempt to communicate in a way that reveals his personality or special gifts. An occupational therapist, on the other hand, will get right down on the floor with your child, meet him wherever he is developmentally, and find out what really works. For parents beaten down by professional negativity, it's an encouraging sight.

Sensory Integration and Praxis Tests (SIPT)

If your child is age four or older and being evaluated by a private therapist, as opposed to a more generalized evaluation being done for special education services, the therapist will most likely administer the Sensory Integration and Praxis Tests (SIPT), a series of seventeen standardized tests designed to detect a wide range of problems with receiving, interpreting, and integrating sensory information. The therapist will have been trained in both giving the tests and interpreting them. Although the tests may look playful and nontechnical, you can't buy the official materials for giving and scoring the tests without listing your qualifications for using them. These are not informal games, but standardized tests in which your child's response will be measured against that of 2,000 children from across the United States, ages four to nine. The results, combined with parent interviews, parent-teacher questionnaires, and observation of the child in school and at home, will help determine whether or not your child has sensory integration disorder. They will also give the therapist the information needed to set appropriate goals and choose techniques that will be most effective.

Each of the tests takes about ten minutes to administer, with the entire series of seventeen taking a little more than two hours. Depending on your child's particular strengths and weaknesses, the therapist may administer only some of the tests or may split the testing into multiple sessions. The tests fall generally into four categories: motor planning, sensory integration, touch, and visual perception.

Motor Planning Tests

These tests will determine whether your child can move blocks or body parts according to simple verbal or visual instructions. "Praxis" means the ability to plan out the movements needed for a particular activity. The tests include the following:

- **Constructional praxis:** The therapist builds a simple structure with blocks and asks your child to build one just like it.
- **Design copying:** The therapist draws a simple shape and asks your child to copy it.
- **Oral praxis:** The therapist demonstrates some funny faces to make with the mouth, tongue, and lips, and asks your child to copy them.
- **Postural praxis:** The therapist strikes some unusual poses and asks your child to copy them.
- **Praxis on verbal command:** Your child is asked to do a simple movement activity, such as touching the top of his head.
- **Sequencing praxis:** Your child is asked to copy arm and hand sequences performed by the therapist.

Sensory Integration Tests

These tests demonstrate how well your child's brain and body are able to use the information from the senses:

- **Bilateral motor coordination:** Your child is asked to move her arms in ways that help the therapist assess how well the two sides of her body work together.
- **Motor accuracy:** Your child is asked to trace a line on a piece of paper so that the therapist can evaluate her eye-hand coordination.
- **Postrotary nystagmus:** The therapist assesses integration of the visual and vestibular systems. The therapist spins your child for twenty seconds, stops her, and then looks at her eyes. Most people have involuntary movements of the eyes

(nystagmus) for a period of time after the spinning stops, but individuals whose vestibular systems are not well integrated have them for a shorter time or not at all.

- **Standing and walking balance:** The therapist evaluates how well your child's proprioceptive and vestibular senses work together when your child stands and walks with eyes open and eyes closed.

Touch Tests

These tests examine your child's ability to process information that comes in through the tactile sense and kinesthetic (muscle and joint) sense and his awareness of where his body is in space. They include the following:

- **Finger identification:** The therapist touches one of your child's fingers and then asks your child which finger it was.
- **Graphesthesia:** With one finger, the therapist traces a shape on the back of your child's hand, then asks him to trace the same shape.
- **Kinesthesia:** The therapist moves your child's hand to a certain location and asks your child to put his finger in the same place.
- **Localization of tactile stimuli:** The therapist makes a light mark on your child's arm with a washable pen, and your child is asked to point, without looking, at the spot.
- **Manual form perception:** Your child is asked to identify a shape just by touching it, without being able to see it.

Visual Perception Tests

These tests seek to determine how efficiently your child can use her visual sense. They include the following:

- **Figure-ground perception:** Your child will be asked to pick out a picture hidden among others in a busy background.
- **Space visualization:** The therapist will see whether your child

can tell just by looking which of two pieces fits into a slot on a puzzle.

Other Occupational Therapy Tests

The occupational therapist may do other tests on your child besides the one for sensory integration. Names you may hear or see in a report include these:

- The Assessment of Motor and Process Skills (AMPS)
- The Berry-Buktenica Developmental Test of Visual-Motor Integration (VMI)
- The Bruininks-Oseretsky Test of Motor Proficiency 2 (BOT-2)
- The Gardner Test of Visual-Perceptual Skills (TVPS)
- The Peabody Developmental Motor Scales-2 (tests of gross motor development and fine motor development)
- Sensory Profile

These tests can tell the therapist if your child is meeting various developmental milestones and can suggest areas in which occupational therapy can help with living and learning skills. The SIPT are good indicators of whether your child has difficulty with sensory integration, but there may be other ways in which occupational therapy can help your child as well.

You may not be able to watch your child during the evaluation, especially if he is easily distracted by your presence. However, some occupational therapy offices have two-way mirrors so you can observe the proceedings without your child's knowledge. You may also be able to obtain a videotape of your child's testing to review at home.

What a Diagnosis Gets You

A diagnosis of sensory integration disorder is the first step toward getting treatment for your child. A private therapist will probably want that confirmation before starting therapy with a sensory integration approach. Assuming you have a doctor who is receptive to sensory integration theory, a diagnosis from an occupational therapist will facilitate that. An official diagnosis may also be necessary to get accommodations placed in your child's IEP for special education.

Neither "sensory integration disorder" nor any of the other names that are used to describe problems with the receiving, interpreting, and combining of sensory information are yet included in the *Diagnostic and Statistical Manual of Mental Disorders*. There are active efforts underway to gain this important recognition.

More than that, though, a diagnosis of sensory integration disorder can help you give your child the understanding he deserves. You may think of labels as bad things to apply to children, but there is immense comfort and relief in finding a diagnosis that actually fits your child and helps so many odd-shaped pieces fall into place. As your child grows and becomes more able to use language to explain and comprehend his difficulties, it will help him to know that there is a name for what he feels and that other people feel the same way.

What a Diagnosis Won't Do

Unfortunately, one thing a diagnosis of sensory integration disorder won't do is get you insurance coverage for the therapy your child will need. Since sensory integration disorder is not yet an official medical diagnosis, many insurance companies will not consider it as an acceptable reason for services.

That doesn't mean you'll necessarily be left to pay for everything out-of-pocket. There are codes and related diagnoses that the person in charge of billing at your occupational therapist's office might use to put therapy with a sensory integration approach into a category that your insurer will find acceptable. These may include developmental coordination disorder, motor apraxia (problems with movement skills), hypotonia (low muscle tone), delay in development (missing milestones), or encephalopathy (problems with brain function). When looking for private occupational therapists, be sure to discuss the issue of having occupational therapy evaluation and treatment covered by insurance, and make sure your chosen therapist has ways of working that out.

The ability to get therapy covered by insurance shouldn't be your only criteria for selecting a particular therapist, but it should definitely be a consideration. You may find that large or hospital-based practices will offer the most experience in selecting codes that will be acceptable to insurers. They will likely offer other advantages as well.

There are a few other things that a diagnosis of sensory integration disorder won't do:

- Cure your child instantly
- Give you a specific, easy-to-follow plan of action
- Convince skeptics in your family that there really is something wrong with your child
- Eliminate the possibility that other things may be wrong with your child
- Answer all of your questions

A diagnosis is empowering. It will help you understand your child. It will help you give your child assistance and therapy that will make a significant difference to her. But it's not a magic wand. For some kids, it may offer enough of a solution to bring problems that had seemed uncontrollable to a level that can be managed or overlooked. For some, it will be just one piece to a neurological puzzle that is far more complex. Anything that helps you understand your child a little better and parent more effectively is worthwhile. And in that context, a diagnosis of sensory integration disorder is very useful indeed.

What If You Can't Get One?

So your doctor doesn't believe in sensory integration disorder. There's no trained occupational therapist in your area. Your child's school occupational therapist doesn't know much about it. You can't afford to pursue a diagnosis or to pay for the therapy if you get one. You're certain that sensory integration is part of your child's puzzle, but tests don't confirm it. That doesn't mean you can't apply sensory integration theory to your child's behavior or do activities that will help bring his sensory system into balance. It just means that you're going to have to do all the work.

This book will show you how to understand your child better, care for him better, play with him better, advocate for him better, and appreciate him more. You'll learn how to assess the functioning of sensory systems, and what to do about malfunctions. You will be empowered to help your child in ways you never were before. It's not a diagnosis, but it's a start.

CHAPTER 3

Look-Alike Problems

Society is pretty sure of itself when it comes to labeling children with popular disorders. Take a jumpy kid anywhere, and you'll have someone ask you if he has ADHD. Kids who have trouble snapping to attention get tagged with ADD. Those who cling desperately to routine might be called obsessive-compulsive, and those who blow up at every little thing might be called oppositional-defiant. Kids who retract from parental affection might be called attachment disordered. For some kids, these popular diagnoses will be accurate. For others, the real reason for the behavior is sensory integration disorder.

ADD

Your child daydreams in class, makes mistakes on homework even when she understands the material, and acts like she doesn't hear you when you call her. Could she have attention deficit disorder (ADD), or is this a sensory integration problem? The answer will depend on whether inattention and distractibility are your child's only problem or whether the sensory glitches responsible for that behavior show up in other areas, too.

Making an ADD Diagnosis

To make a diagnosis of ADD, a pediatrician, psychologist, or neurologist will review information provided by parents and teachers and look for certain patterns of behavior, using guidelines set down in the *Diagnostic and Statistical Manual of Mental Disorders* (DSM). ADD may be indicated when a child frequently has trouble with the following:

- Attending to details
- Maintaining interest in an activity
- Listening when someone is talking to her
- Following instructions
- Completing a task
- Getting organized
- Concentrating on something hard
- Keeping track of belongings
- Ignoring distractions
- Remembering everyday routines

The doctor would expect to see problems in a majority of these areas—problems lasting more than six months; problems that impact behavior in a variety of settings, including home and school; problems that began before the age of seven; and problems that can't be explained by developmental delays, neurological problems, or another mental disorder.

The Sensory Integration Difference

If your child is hyposensitive in some areas—that is, he doesn't get enough information from his senses to really understand what's going on around him—he can appear to have many of the signs of ADD. If he's hypersensitive, on the other hand—getting so much information that it overwhelms him—he may also not be able to focus on any one thing and resemble a child with ADD. Looking at the ADD criteria above, your child with sensory integration problems may have trouble doing the following:

- Attending to details if he can't tell the difference between important and unimportant things in his field of vision
- Maintaining interest in an activity if sensory problems make

that activity difficult, confusing, or overwhelming

- Listening when someone is talking to him if his auditory sense can't distinguish between speaking and background noise
- Following instructions if there are too many steps and he can't visualize the outcome
- Completing a task if it is too tiring or complex
- Getting organized if he can't perceive patterns or similarities
- Concentrating on something hard if protecting his overstimulated or overtaxed sensory systems becomes more important
- Keeping track of belongings if he can't judge distances or physical locations
- Ignoring distractions if they're easier to process and integrate than the information he's supposed to be attending to
- Remembering everyday routines if they're not done in just the same way and at just the same time, without disruption

These sensory integration difficulties may look like ADD, but they don't exist all by themselves. If your child has problems with her auditory sense, she may have trouble listening when an adult speaks to her, but she'll also ignore loud noises or overreact to them severely, will often speak in a voice too loud or too soft, and will have a hard time distinguishing the difference between similar sounds. If your child has problems with motor planning—determining what motions need to be made in what sequence to complete an activity—she'll have trouble with instructions and following through on tasks, but will also be unable to hit a baseball or kick a soccer ball, will appear clumsy or poorly coordinated, and will have trouble with even simple motion tasks like pedaling a tricycle or spearing food on a fork and bringing the fork to her mouth. Whereas children with ADD will be otherwise performing at a normal developmental level, your child with sensory integration problems is likely to have developmental delays in inconsistent patterns over a wide range of skills.

ADHD

Your child runs on an unstoppable motor, zipping through life in turbocharged style. He's constantly running and talking and jumping and climbing, and if you had a dime for every time somebody asked if he had attention deficit hyperactivity disorder (ADHD), you'd be able to pay for a nice long vacation. But does your child really have ADHD, or is sensory integration disorder somehow responsible for all that activity?

Making an ADHD Diagnosis

To make a diagnosis of ADHD, a pediatrician will review information provided by parents and teachers and use DSM guidelines to identify certain patterns of behavior. ADHD is indicated when a child frequently has trouble with the following:

- Keeping his hands and feet to himself
- Staying in his seat
- Controlling behavior like running or climbing in places where that's not allowed
- Playing quietly
- Settling down
- Being quiet
- Letting an adult finish a question before answering it
- Taking turns
- Entering a conversation without interrupting
- Joining other children without intruding

As with ADD, the doctor would expect to see problems in a majority of these areas; problems lasting more than six months; problems that impact behavior in a variety of settings, including home and school; problems that began before the age of seven; and problems that can't be explained by developmental delays, neurological problems, or another mental disorder.

The Sensory Integration Difference

If your child is hyposensitive to proprioceptive and vestibular input—that is, she doesn't have a good sense of balance or gravity or how her limbs are arranged—the movements she makes to feel more comfortable may look like ADHD. Lack of sensitivity to differences in sound can cause problems as well. Looking at the criteria for an ADHD diagnosis, your child with sensory integration problems may have trouble with the following:

- Keeping her hands and feet to herself if she needs to move those body parts to register where they are
- Staying in her seat if sitting still makes her feel sleepy
- Controlling behavior like running or climbing in places where that's not allowed if it's hard to sustain movements without momentum
- Playing quietly if she can't sense the difference between soft and loud
- Settling down if her body feels unsettled and off-kilter
- Being quiet if she needs a lot of self-talk for planning and sequencing movements
- Letting an adult finish a question before answering it if she misses differences in tone that indicate the end of a question is still to come
- Taking turns if she strongly needs the input from a swing or a slide in order to feel comfortable and in control
- Entering a conversation without interrupting if her auditory system isn't sensitive to the flow of speech among other noises in the room
- Joining other children without intruding if she can't control her movements or judge how much force she needs to use

Ironically, although your child appears to be overstimulated, he may in fact be understimulated and engaging in frantic movement in order to stay awake, pay attention, and make his body comfortable. Think of how you feel when your foot is asleep. You need to move it hard and fast to clear the prickly feeling, and if you don't, you won't be able to concentrate on anything else. Your child may be experiencing the same problem when he runs, jumps, climbs, and crashes into things.

Fact

In a 2003 survey, the U.S. Centers for Disease Control and Prevention found that nearly 8 percent of American children had been diagnosed with ADHD, and medication was being used to treat half those cases. Boys were 2.5 times more likely to have been diagnosed than girls.

One question to ask when trying to tell the difference between ADHD and sensory integration disorder is this: What happens when my child actually does sit still? Children with sensory integration problems who need to move to stay alert may fall asleep if they stop, or seem to fall into a trance. They truly can pay better attention when they're wiggly.

Obsessive-Compulsive Disorder

Your child clings desperately to a particular piece of clothing or a rundown toy. He's stuck on one game, one type of food, one way of going through his daily routine. He has little rituals he goes through that make no sense to anyone but him. Could he have obsessive-compulsive disorder (OCD)? Sensory integration-related behaviors can appear to fit into this psychiatric disorder, but the reason behind the rituals may not be the same at all.

Making an OCD Diagnosis

To make a diagnosis of OCD, a mental health professional (such as a psychologist) will review information provided by parents and teachers and use DSM guidelines to identify certain patterns of behavior. OCD is indicated when a child is frequently troubled by obsessions, which are thoughts or mental images that meet the following criteria:

- They are unwanted, inappropriate, and disturbing
- They are unrelated to actual events and concerns
- The child tries to block them out with other thoughts or actions
- They come from her own mind and not someone's suggestion

The child frequently responds with compulsions, activities that meet the following criteria:

- They are done to combat obsessions, or according to unchangeable rules
- They are not realistic responses to actual events
- They are done to avoid a feared outcome

The mental health professional would expect to see these obsessions and compulsions taking up a large amount of the child's time and attention, causing problems with her daily school and home routine, and keeping her from normal relationships and activities.

The Sensory Integration Difference

If your child is hypersensitive to information coming in through her senses—that is, she perceives a threat from a touch or sight or sound that others would find harmless—she may set up routines and defenses for herself that could be mistaken for OCD. Additionally, if she has problems with planning out how to do a particular activity, she may become strongly attached to the one way of doing it that she has already worked out, or she may stick stubbornly to activities that are much simpler. In both cases, though, she will likely be open to other alternatives that achieve the same effect. She may be willing to change routines if you very patiently teach her how to do it differently.

A child with OCD is obsessed with things that aren't real and develops compulsions to deal with them, whereas a child with sensory integration disorder is bothered by real things in her environment and develops routines and defenses to deal with them. If you can change those real things, you can most likely change the behaviors.

It's estimated that 1 million U.S. children and teens have obsessive-compulsive disorder, about 1 in 200. Although the cause is not known, a genetic connection is suspected. Children who have one parent with the disorder are as much as 8 percent more likely to be diagnosed with it.

Reactive Attachment Disorder

Your child doesn't like to be touched or hugged. He doesn't seem to mind hitting you, though, or pushing or wrestling or bonking heads. Is this a case of reactive attachment disorder (RAD), the frightening diagnosis that describes children who are unable to bond with their parents? Or could sensory integration disorder be responsible for his standoffishness and aggression? It depends on whether your child is reacting to the physical sensations caused by touching and hitting or the emotional ones.

Making a RAD Diagnosis

To make a diagnosis of RAD, a mental health professional will talk to the child and the parents and use DSM guidelines to identify certain patterns of behavior. RAD is indicated when a child exhibits the following:

- Relationships that are not developmentally appropriate
- Resistance to close family relationships

- Excessive watchfulness and lack of trust that her needs will be met
- Excessive desire for control in relationships
- A mix of different responses to affection
- Indiscriminate affection or attachments to people outside the family

The mental health professional will want to make sure that the child does not have any developmental delay or disorder that might account for the behavior and will also look into the child's background to see whether, at some time, the child was abused, neglected, or cared for by so many different people that attachments did not form. Children from Eastern European orphanages are often diagnosed with attachment problems for these reasons. Since the benign neglect of orphanage life can also be a factor in sensory integration disorder, it's not surprising that the two can become confused. In reality, both diagnoses may be appropriate for some of these children.

The Sensory Integration Difference

You may be confused by the fact that your child seems to love you, enjoy your company, and engage you in conversation or play and yet withdraws so determinedly from your touch or embrace. This is actually a good sign. Children with attachment disorder are overwhelmed by the emotion involved in hugs and caresses, and they can't allow themselves to trust that the emotion is honest and reliable. Children with sensory integration disorder, on the other hand, have no trouble with the emotion part of the equation—they love and trust and want very much to please their parents. It's the tactile sensations they have trouble with. A child who is overly sensitive to touch may process your tender pat on the head or touch on the shoulder as painful or an attack. Even a gentle hug may provide too much sensory information and feel as overwhelming to your child as a smothering bear hug does to you. If your child is undersensitive to touch, on the other hand, he may not feel your gentle touch at all, and he may not realize that when he hits or pushes or shoves or leaps on top of you, he appears aggressive. To him, wrestling feels like good, affectionate contact.

Fact

It's possible for sensory integration disorder to coexist with one of these similar disorders. With neurological impairments, the lines between diagnoses are often very blurry, and it may be that more than one will fit. If a dual diagnosis is suspected, make sure therapy for sensory integration doesn't get lost in the rush to medicate or treat the other problem.

Many adopted children experience attachment as a process rather than a given. If your child seems to be open and friendly toward you emotionally, meet her at a place where she feels comfortable and work from there. If your child seems emotionally guarded or manipulative, that may be a sign that serious attachment work needs to be done. That work often involves therapy that may be difficult and disruptive for a child with sensory integration disorder, so it's worth making a distinction as early as possible.

Oppositional Defiant Disorder

Your child gives a whole new meaning to the word stubborn. He loses his temper over the least little thing, refuses to compromise or listen to reason, and doesn't seem to care how his actions make other people feel. Does this behavior reach the level of oppositional defiant disorder (ODD)? Or are his unreasonable responses an attempt to defend his sensory system from attack?

Making a ODD Diagnosis

To make a diagnosis of ODD, a mental health professional will talk to the child and the parents and use DSM guidelines to identify certain patterns of behavior. ODD is indicated when a child frequently does the following:

- Exhibits an inability to control his temper
- Fights with parents and other grownups
- Disobeys rules
- Refuses to comply with reasonable requests
- Behaves in a way that is annoying to others
- Gets annoyed by others
- Is unwilling to take responsibility for his behavior
- Is in a bad mood
- Behaves in a way that is vengeful and nasty

The mental health professional will expect to see that the behavior has been going on for more than half a year; impairs the child's ability to function in school, at home, and during social activities; and is not due to other psychoses or disorders.

The Sensory Integration Difference

If your child has sensory integration problems that cause her to feel threatened or upset by things that seem absolutely normal to other people, her behavior may appear to be oppositional and defiant. She knows that being tipped back to have her hair washed makes her feel off balance and frightened, and she will resist it the way you might resist being pushed off a building. As compared to the criteria for ODD, it may appear that your child does the following:

- Exhibits an inability to control her temper if a temper tantrum is the only way she can make unpleasant activities stop
- Fights with parents and other grownups if they don't take her sensory needs into account
- Disobeys rules if she needs to do other things to keep her body comfortable and in control
- Refuses to comply with reasonable requests if those requests don't seem reasonable to her

- Behaves in a way that is annoying to others if she can't modulate her movements and the volume of her voice
- Gets annoyed by others if they do things that feel overwhelming or threatening to her
- Is unwilling to take responsibility for her behavior if she does not understand that the things that seem right to her aren't right to others
- Is in a bad mood if she is constantly overwhelmed by strong sensations and receives no help in adjusting to them
- Behaves in a way that is vengeful and nasty if she reacts too strongly to things that bother her

Understanding your child's sensory integration problems and helping her find socially acceptable ways to deal with them will go a long way toward eliminating oppositional and defiant behavior. Eliminating the source of the problem will help as well. Whereas children with ODD may truly be engaging in their behaviors for no reason, your child with sensory integration disorder has reasons that make good sense to her. If they make sense to you as well, she won't have to fight so hard.

Anxiety Disorder

The top mental health problem in America isn't hyperactivity or depression or OCD: it's anxiety, with anxiety disorder afflicting an estimated 13 percent of children and teens. Cognitive behavior therapy, which in part helps kids visualize ways to gain control over their worries and understand how scary thoughts form, is effective 70 to 80 percent of the time.

If your child seems to worry too much about new routines and experiences, sometimes seems tired and irritable, or sometimes seems to zone out, she may have anxiety disorder. Children with sensory integration disorder may appear more anxious or withdrawn than other children, but their anxiety is tied to their inefficient sensory systems rather than a generalized feeling of worry.

Looking at lists of symptoms for neurological or psychiatric disorders can put any parent into a panic. Many children exhibit a few of the behaviors indicated, whether the diagnosis truly applies to them or not. But individual behaviors can have any number of causes and interpretations. Always look at the big picture, the whole child, before rushing to worry.

Making an Anxiety Disorder Diagnosis

To make a diagnosis of anxiety disorder, a mental health professional will talk to the child and the parents and use DSM guidelines to identify certain patterns of behavior. An anxiety disorder is indicated when a child frequently does the following:

- Worries excessively about things going on in her life
- Can't stop worrying if she tries
- Feels restless or on edge
- Tires easily
- Easily loses her train of thought
- Is cranky or tense
- Has trouble falling asleep or staying asleep

The mental health professional would look to see that there is not another mental disorder causing the anxiety, the anxiety is distressing to the child and interfering with normal life, and there is no medical condition or medication causing the problem.

The Sensory Integration Difference

If your child has sensory integration problems that make her feel physically uncomfortable, or if she has developed routines she can follow to avoid feeling that way, her behavior may resemble anxiety disorder. In reference to the criteria for anxiety disorder, it may appear that she does the following:

- Worries excessively about things going on in her life if she spends a lot of time thinking about how she can avoid distressing situations
- Can't stop worrying if she tries if no one understands what her concerns are
- Feels restless or on edge if she is understimulated and needs to move to stay alert
- Tires easily if she is understimulated and has trouble staying alert
- Easily loses her train of thought if she is distracted by unwanted sensations
- Is cranky or tense if she is not able to avoid uncomfortable sensations
- Has trouble falling asleep or staying asleep if she needs a lot of proprioceptive input, as from rocking, to comfort herself

When you start to understand what causes discomfort for your child with sensory integration disorder and what she needs to do to regulate her sensory system—and start taking some of the responsibility for helping your child do that—the behaviors that mimic anxiety disorder should go away.

Developmental Coordination Disorder

Your child can't walk five steps without tripping over his own feet. He has trouble catching a ball, buttoning a shirt, or tying his shoes. You think he's just clumsy, but a doctor has suggested he might have developmental coordination disorder (DCD). How does this differ from the kind of motor planning problems seen with sensory integration disorder?

Making a DCD Diagnosis

Unlike sensory integration disorder, developmental coordination disorder is in fact in the DSM. A doctor using those guidelines to diagnose it would look for coordination problems that do the following:

- Impair participation in normal life and school activities
- Are below the child's chronological age
- Are significantly below what is expected for the child's intelligence
- Are not due to medical conditions such as muscular dystrophy or cerebral palsy
- Are not due to a pervasive developmental disorder

Signs of developmental coordination disorder are particularly noticeable in the delay of motor milestones, lack of ability in sports, and problems with handwriting.

The Sensory Integration Difference

There is a large overlap among dyspraxia from a sensory integration perspective and developmental coordination disorder. Delay of motor milestones, lack of ability in sports, and problems with handwriting are commonly seen in both children with sensory integration disorder with dyspraxia and developmental coordination disorder. If your child has sensory-related motor planning problems, low muscle tone, and inadequate information from his proprioceptive and vestibular systems, clumsiness and lack of coordination can be major problems. However, it's unlikely that these would be your child's only problems. One distinction lies in the nature of the disorder. Children can have poor coordination for many reasons; children with sensory integration disorder with motor planning problems (developmental dyspraxia) have an underlying problem of difficulty interpreting information received from their tactile, vestibular, and proprioceptive senses that is believed to contribute to their difficulty in motor planning.

Chapter 4

Just a Piece of the Puzzle

Often, sensory integration difficulties come as a subset or a companion to other disorders that can be even more challenging and life altering. Brain damage in any area could trigger sensory problems as well as other more serious ones. If you have a child with one of these disabilities, consider whether sensory integration disorder could be a factor within the larger diagnosis.

Autism Spectrum Disorder

Falling under the umbrella of autism spectrum disorder are such developmental delays as autism, Asperger syndrome, pervasive developmental disorder, childhood disintegrative disorder, and Rett's syndrome. What these disabilities have in common is an impaired ability to communicate, from total isolation at the severe end of the spectrum to social awkwardness at the lighter end. They also share a difficulty with sensory processing.

Sensory Behaviors

Many so-called "autistic behaviors" have a strong sensory component. Although they may seem to be signs of detachment from reality, when looked at from a sensory perspective they may be seen to have an important function in helping the child deal with faulty

sensory information. Occupational therapy may be effective in lessening the behaviors or in giving the people who work with the child a framework for understanding them.

Stereotypical Movements

The hand-flapping, rocking, jumping, and other apparently purposeless movements often performed by children with autism are also seen in children with sensory integration disorder. From a sensory integration perspective, these motions are not purposeless at all, instead, they provide intense input to the vestibular and proprioceptive senses. The same may be true of children with autism spectrum disorders. Rather than try to stop the movements outright, occupational therapists with a sensory integration approach might work to provide the child with more acceptable opportunities for proprioceptive input throughout the day.

Avoidance of Eye Contact

Refusal or reluctance to make eye contact is a key feature of children on the autism spectrum. It seems symbolic of a refusal or inability, to communicate or to recognize the presence or importance of others. The same resistance to eye contact is seen in children who are overstimulated by input from the visual sense. They may find a direct gaze too intense, or be too distracted by the many features and movements of the other person's face to pay attention to words. Occupational therapy with a sensory integration approach might work to make children more comfortable with visual stimuli, rather than on enforcing eye contact.

Resistance to Touch

Children on the autism spectrum often do not like to be touched, rejecting hugs and other forms of affection. Tactile oversensitivity is common among children with sensory integration disorder, and the methods used to treat it are often helpful to children on the autism spectrum. These might include activities involving deep pressure and the brushing protocol described in Chapter 7. Children on the autism spectrum may particularly prefer touch that they can personally control over touch that comes to them unexpectedly.

Oversensitivity to Sound

Extreme overreactions to loud sounds such as sirens or alarms are common in children on the autism spectrum, as well as with children with sensory integration problems around the auditory sense. Occupational therapy with a sensory integration approach can help reduce sensitivity to sounds and suggest other ways to relieve the stress of an auditory overload.

Perseverative Play

Children on the autism spectrum tend to concentrate solely and obsessively on one particular activity and to be highly resistant to change. That activity may be something as simple as lining up toys or dangling keys. Sensory integration problems that impact motor planning can play a part in this, making a series of movements that have been worked out and organized more appealing than trying something different. Occupational therapy to improve motor planning, as well as play that very slowly and gently moves the child toward variations, can be more effective than simply insisting on change.

Fact

Motor planning refers to the sequencing of smaller actions needed to perform a larger activity. A task that seems easy to you may be complicated for your child if he can't break it down into the necessary small movements and put them in the right sequence. This can affect his ability to follow directions, obey orders, and make transitions.

The Big Picture

Not all children with sensory integration disorder have autism spectrum disorders. Even children who show the autistic behaviors mentioned above are not necessarily autistic. However, children who are on the autism spectrum most likely have some degree of sensory integration disorder and can benefit from therapy with a sensory integration approach—or at least an understanding of sensory integration informing their treatment.

Fetal Alcohol Spectrum Disorder

Fetal alcohol spectrum disorder (FASD) is an umbrella term used to describe the range of brain damage caused by prenatal alcohol exposure, encompassing what is sometimes described as fetal alcohol effects (FAE), fetal alcohol syndrome (FAS), and alcohol-related birth defects (ARBD). Children on the fetal alcohol spectrum can appear to have a wide range of different disabilities. ADHD, autism, Asperger syndrome, seizure disorder, obsessive-compulsive disorder, attachment disorder, oppositional-defiant disorder, and other developmental, neurological, and psychiatric disorders can all be coexisting or look-alike disabilities for alcohol-exposed children. A significant sensory thread runs through these disorders, and children with FASD can generally add sensory integration disorder to their long list of challenges.

Sensory Behaviors

No two children with FASD are alike. The severity and symptoms of prenatal alcohol exposure will vary with the amount of alcohol consumed, the part of the pregnancy in which it was consumed, and what part or parts of the brain were damaged as a result. Many children on the fetal alcohol spectrum may show behaviors very similar to those described above under autism spectrum disorder. These other behaviors common to children with FASD may also be improved by occupational therapy with a sensory integration approach.

Hyperactivity

Children with FASD often have trouble controlling their movements and seem to be always moving. It is possible for them to have

ADHD as a coexisting condition, but this excess movement sometimes more closely resembles the behavior of a child with sensory integration disorder who is seeking out movement to stimulate his vestibular and proprioceptive senses. Occupational therapy that concentrates on those senses, along with accessories like weighted vests or wiggly seat cushions, may be helpful for the child with FASD and do much to calm the behavior.

Essential

Early diagnosis and treatment are essential for children on the fetal alcohol spectrum, especially those who lack the distinctive facial features of fetal alcohol syndrome and therefore appear to be less affected. These children, whose impairments are no less severe but less easily recognized, often do worse in the long run due to lack of understanding, reasonable expectations, and accommodations.

Inattentiveness

Similarly, the inattentiveness sometimes seen in children with FASD may be more like the sensory integration challenge of a child who is either overstimulated by sensory information and can't concentrate on any one thing, or understimulated and can't be roused by anything other than very powerful information. Children with FASD may boomerang between hyperactivity and inattentiveness, as the bold sensory input they seek in order to become more alert propels them all the way into overstimulation. Helping children better manage their levels of alertness is a major component of occupational therapy with a sensory integration approach.

Low Muscle Tone

Children exposed to alcohol prenatally are often floppy, without adequate muscle tone to keep their joints firmly set. As discussed in more detail in Chapter 15, low muscle tone, or hypotonia, can cause a child to tire easily, move in rapid and uncontrolled ways, have a hard time sitting still, and struggle with tasks such as writing or eating with utensils that require a great deal of fine motor control. While hypotonia does not always go away with age and therapy, there are strategies and tools that occupational therapists can use to help children deal with it more appropriately.

Poor Stress Tolerance

Like many children with sensory integration problems, children on the fetal alcohol spectrum may have trouble in overly noisy or visually busy environments; places where restraint in physical movement is required and enforced; and situations in which expectations are out of line with their sensory needs. Stressful situations often lead to meltdowns, overreactions, and loss of control. Therapy to increase tolerance of sensory information, and strategies that reduce stress, can keep this from becoming an everyday occurrence.

Fact

Children with FASD, as well as children with sensory integration disorder, can be thought of as having a finite amount of self-control available to them on any given day. The various challenges they face draw from that self-control reservoir. Anything that reduces stress will help increase self-control, and vice versa.

The Big Picture

Again, not every child with sensory integration disorder has fetal alcohol spectrum disorder. One factor that may contribute to sensory integration disorder is some sort of brain damage, and alcohol is only one of the potential causes. If you believe that this could be the cause of your child's problem, or you have adopted a child whom you suspect may have been exposed to alcohol prenatally, occupational therapy with a sensory integration approach may be an important step in helping him to grow and develop.

Seizure Disorder

When you think of seizures, you may think of what used to be called a grand mal seizure (now more commonly referred to as a tonic-clonic seizure) and picture a child on the floor, jerking uncontrollably and losing consciousness. But there are other types of seizures that can occur in childhood, and some greatly resemble the kind of behaviors children with sensory integration disorder might exhibit.

A child who stares into space and can't be instantly brought to attention may be underresponsive to the sights and sounds in her environment due to sensory integration problems, or may be having an absence seizure (sometimes called a petit mal seizure). A child who is making what seem to be odd, repetitive, purposeless movements may be trying to jump-start her proprioceptive or vestibular senses, or may be having a complex partial seizure.

Overlap between these two disorders is possible. A child can have a seizure disorder and also have sensory integration disorder, or he might have one that is mistaken for the other. Either way, an increased knowledge and understanding of your child's sensory strengths and weaknesses will help sort the different behaviors out and make it clear when there are changes that might indicate seizures.

For information on childhood seizures, seek out a copy of *Seizures and Epilepsy in Childhood: A Guide for Parents*, by John M. Freeman, M.D., Eileen P. G. Vining, M.D., and Diana J. Pillas. It's filled with easy-to-understand information and provides confidence that your child and your family can function with this disability.

Post-Traumatic Stress Disorder

Children with post-traumatic stress disorder (PTSD) have experienced an extremely upsetting or life-threatening event, and they continue to periodically relive the experience in their minds with full emotional involvement. Since information that comes through our senses is so often tied to specific memories and emotions, the cues for an episode of PTSD are often sensory. In addition, children with PTSD may become hyperreactive to things like noise or touch. The intense stress of this disorder can actually cause changes in the brain, which may make problems with sensory integration more likely.

If your child has been through a trauma, don't be afraid to talk with her about it. You may feel it's healthier for your child to forget about it, but she probably won't; she'll just hold the bad feelings in, and that will hurt more. Be a compassionate but nonjudgmental audience, and refrain from telling her to cheer up and feel better. For kids with PTSD, as with children with sensory integration disorder, having someone who will listen and understand is a major element of recovery.

Post-Institutionalized Children

Problems with sensory integration are common among children living in and adopted from orphanages in Eastern Europe. Sometimes, it occurs as a result of undiagnosed fetal alcohol exposure, abuse, or post-traumatic stress disorder. The sensory deprivation of orphanage life also contributes to inefficient neural pathways that are unable to adequately process and integrate sensory information. When these children come to their adoptive homes and are exposed to a huge array of new and unfamiliar experiences and sensory information, they may be unable to deal with it and either be overstimulated to the point of hyperactivity or shut down and appear to lack interactivity and alertness.

Parents who are adopting children from overseas orphanages should start their new little ones off with just a small amount of sensory stimulation and slowly build up to the degree that would be normal for a child who had grown up in a family. Don't start in immediately with lots of get-togethers and toys and television. Occupational therapy with a sensory integration approach may also be an important part of helping these children adjust and become secure and confident family members.

Fact

The Post Adoption Information Web site (at *www.postadoptinfo.org*) provides information about issues for children adopted from Eastern European orphanages. The PEP-L e-mail support list for adoptive parents of children from Eastern Europe is also a good place to discuss sensory integration issues with other parents. Join the e-mail list by visiting the Eastern European Adoption Coalition Web site, at *www.eeadopt.org*.

Learning Disabilities

Sensory integration disorder can contribute to learning disabilities by keeping children from developing the skills they need to read and write efficiently. When information from the visual and auditory sense is not processed correctly, children may avoid activities that involve close visual work or require careful listening. Low muscle tone, poor motor planning, and problems with the vestibular and proprioceptive sense can make writing, or even early activities like coloring, more challenging than your child may want to pursue. Early intervention services that incorporate sensory integration can go far in helping children avoid learning problems in the future.

In addition, sensory integration disorder can resemble learning disabilities, blurring lines and making appropriate treatment difficult to administer. A child with sensory integration disorder may have no problem understanding and working a math problem, but he may balk at completing a worksheet that is visually overstimulating or that leaves no room for his poorly coordinated handwriting. Your child might be able to read words and understand them, but he becomes lost in a page of print with close-set lines. Organizational problems linked to poor motor planning may make your child's grades lower due to missed assignments and lost homework.

Sensory integration may also be a factor for children with nonverbal learning disorders (NLD). These children may do fine with reading, writing, and calculating, and they generally have excellent rote memory and verbal skills. However, they have difficulty with the more abstract aspects of language—things like figures of speech, irony, sarcasm, body language, and facial expressions. They may also have motor and visual processing problems that overlap with sensory integration disorder and that make them appear clumsy, impulsive, and uncoordinated.

Nonverbal learning disorders aren't as well known as most learning disabilities, and it can be hard to find information about them. If you suspect that this may be an issue for your child, a good place to start is the NLDline Web site, online at *www.nldline.com*.

Tools and strategies employed and taught by occupational therapists will likely help a child with learning disabilities, regardless of whether sensory integration problems are a cause, a coexisting condition, or a look-alike diagnosis. There is enough overlap between these disorders, in any case, to make a sensory integration approach useful. Understanding the way your child's sensory integration strengths and weaknesses impact every part of his life will help you give your child the best and most thoughtful support.

Chapter 5

Occupational Therapy Using a Sensory Integration Approach

If you're expecting to see some sort of proper clinical setting when you walk into a sensory integration therapy room, you'll be in for a surprise. Rather than couches or tables or sophisticated equipment, you're likely to find gym mats on the floor, a ball pit in a corner, swings descending from the ceiling, a bin of rice, bikes, and scooters. Your first impression may be that you've stumbled into the playroom by mistake.

Fun and Games

The business of childhood is play, and it's the business of occupational therapists to make that play as effective, entertaining, and stimulating as possible. There's no better way to do that than to get right down on the floor and get into it.

To your child, an occupational therapist (OT) appointment will seem like a rolling, jumping, playing good time. The therapist will follow your child's lead while subtly adjusting activities to meet the goals you've set together. Sensory integration therapy involves providing a lot of the kind of input that calms the child whose nervous system needs calming, or arouses the child whose nervous system needs arousing. Children may enjoy some of the activities and be fearful of some of them, and the therapist will make adjustments to reduce anxiety while supporting gentle progress.

Generally, an OT will work with your child one-to-one

for an hour or so a week. This time may be broken up into several sessions, depending on your child's needs, his attention span, the therapist's schedule, and your schedule. If the therapy is being done in school or as part of an early intervention program, there may be some group sessions, but there should always be plenty of individualized time as well. The therapist should be able to tell you how much group time there will be and how it will be utilized.

Whether you're able to watch your child during therapy may be determined by the layout of the facility, the therapist's preference, how distracted your child is by your presence, and your desire to hang around during the therapy time. Some offices may allow you to watch through a window or two-way mirror. The therapist might call you in to show you a particular thing your child has accomplished or something to work on at home. At the end of each session, the therapist will likely bring your child out to you and tell you a little bit about how things went.

If you feel your child has a weakness in a particular area and are frustrated that the therapist doesn't seem to be dealing with it, don't hesitate to ask about it. There may be skills the therapist wants to work on first in order to lay the groundwork for the skills you want targeted, or to overcome fears your child has.

If your child gets therapy at school, of course, you will be less involved. However, some school OTs send home notebooks in which observations can be exchanged and reports given, and you can always call to check on progress or request a meeting. It may be possible to sit in on a session at school or to bring your child before or after school for a session so that you can observe. If your child is getting the therapy as part of early intervention, it may actually take place in your home. When the therapy takes place at an office, you may be able to observe sessions, or there may be a support group that you can participate in with other parents during that time.

Goals for school occupational therapy are stated in the child's individualized educational plan (IEP). The OT will provide a report on your child's status and set goals for the following year. If you have concerns about therapy goals, share them with the OT before the IEP meeting or discuss them with the child study team members at the meeting.

The Therapist's Playground

As you look around the room in which your child will have his occupational therapy, you should see numerous pieces of large play equipment, mats on the floor, some ride-on toys, a ball pit and maybe a trampoline, a table for doing fine-motor work, and at least one swinging object suspended from above. The therapist will use these items to improve your child's sensory processing and integration in many different ways. Therapy may concentrate on the vestibular, proprioceptive, and tactile senses—balance, body position, and touch—but includes other senses as well, both for therapeutic purposes and as distraction from potentially stressful activities.

While much of the equipment used may be specialized for therapists, some items may resemble what you'd see at a children's gymnastics class. Other items may be toy store purchases put to therapeutic use. OTs are a creative lot, and they often adapt things to their purposes in an effort to keep kids entertained and intrigued.

Swinging Things

A rope suspended from a hook in the ceiling can hold a wealth of activities for your child. The hook on the other end of the rope attaches to interchangeable swinging items to give your child a variety of different experiences. Among the things you may see dangling from that rope in a therapist's office, or in some cases suspended from a metal frame, are these:

- Flat platform
- Inner tube
- Fabric sling
- Net
- Bolster
- Ladder
- Chin-up bar
- Fabric sack
- Disk just big enough to sit on

Your child may swing on these items while sitting, standing, or lying on her tummy. She may swing while playing a game, catching a ball, or answering questions. The swinging may be vigorous or gentle. The therapist will adjust this activity to your child's comfort level and need for sensory stimulation. At different points during the session, the OT may unhook one item from the rope and hook on another.

Balance Boosters

Swinging isn't the only tool in the therapist's playroom for improving balance. Other items that concentrate on giving good input to the vestibular sense include the following:

- **Balance beam:** It may be narrow or wide, high or low to the ground, made of wood or foam.
- **Seesaw:** Your child may sit on this alone with the therapist pushing one end, share it with another child, or walk on it to practice holding balance on a shifting surface.
- **Balance board:** This is a platform atop a curved base that rocks back and forth. Depending on the child's level of coordination and fear, that platform may be small—just the right size to stand on—or large enough to be set down, sat, crawled or walked on.

- **T-stool:** As the name suggests, this kind of stool has one seat and one leg. Your child will have to constantly adjust his body position to stay balanced.
- **Rotation board:** Your child can rotate this round disk while sitting or standing by turning his body. There may be handles on the sitting models, or a game on the standing version that involves moving a ball around.
- **Fitness ball:** There may be various sizes and colors of these giant inflatable balls that your child can sit on or lie on. A ball may be used as a seat for table work, or your child may lay on it face down and the therapist may roll it forward and backward.

The OT may also engage your child in balance activities like hopping, skipping, jumping, or standing on one foot. Sometimes these can be facilitated with special stepping stones or pathways on the floor, or sometimes they will be done as part of a game like Simon Says. There are many ways to lure your child into doing an activity she would otherwise feel uncomfortable doing or distract her from her discomfort while she's doing it. In this way, the sense of balance can be improved without causing stress for your child.

School therapists often have limited equipment and space. Some work in many schools and have to carry equipment with them, and some have to use rooms limited in space and layout. If your child's IEP goals cannot be met due to space or equipment restrictions, advocate for a more appropriate setting.

Jumps and Jolts

Activities that involve changes in position and hard jolts to the joints are helpful for both the sense of balance and the sense of body position. They can increase your child's level of calmness or alertness in addition to being delightful to him. You'll likely notice lots of equipment in the therapist's playroom to provide that much-needed input, including these:

- **Bouncing balls:** These inflatable balls have a handle to allow your child to sit on them and bounce around the room. There may be different sizes available for children of different sizes or who are more or less brave about bouncing high off the floor.
- **Trampoline:** This may be a one-person size on a metal frame or a larger inflatable version. Two boards with a spring between can also provide a satisfactory jumping experience without overwhelming a child who might be frightened by the movement.
- **Crash pit:** A soft surface—often a number of big foam blocks inside a stretchy fabric sack—is a great place for your child to throw himself to get lots of pressure on his joints without getting hurt.
- **Ball pit:** Children who dive into a ball pit and thrash around get great input to their sense of balance and body position, and those who prefer a more gentle experience still get good information for their sense of touch. Ball pits may be very large or just big enough for a child or two.

Finding multiple uses for things is common in sensory integration therapy. The colorful balls in the ball pit are good for more than stimulating the sense of touch and body position. They are also appealing to your child's visual sense. The therapist may use them to improve color recognition by having your child select balls of a certain color to throw out of the pit or back into it during cleanup. Throwing the small hand-sized balls through a hoop or into a bin also strengthens eye-hand coordination.

These tools may be combined with swings for some very intense input, with your child jumping off a swing and into a ball pit. Your child may also be encouraged to jump off a low platform or set of steps; slide down a slide feet or head first; or throw and catch a ball while jumping on a trampoline or playing in a ball pit.

Path of Most Resistance

Crawling through and pressing against things that provide resistance are also good for improving your child's sense of body position and improving muscle tone. Some of the things you may see in the therapist's playroom for accomplishing this are the following:

- **Body sack:** Your child can step into this bag of stretchy fabric, have the opening fastened shut, and then walk, jump, push out or up, roll around, or do therapist-led activities.
- **Resistance tunnel:** This is a tight stretchy tube that your child crawls through, often pushing a ball before him.
- **Stretchy bands:** Like rubber bands on steroids, these half-foot-wide strips or circles of colorful thin rubber can be stretched or pulled by your child to provide lots of good muscle work and input into the sense of body position.

Other activities that provide your child with deep pressure, weight bearing, and resistance might include carrying a large ball, block, or bolster across the room; being rolled up in a blanket or mat and pushing out of it; having a ball, block, or bolster placed on top of your child, to enjoy the deep pressure or to push it off; or pushing hands or feet against a therapist's hands.

Fact

Besides being a therapy tool, stretchy bands of rubber can be a useful accessory in your child's classroom. They can be stretched across the legs on your child's desk chair, giving his feet something to fiddle with. Pressing against the band or down on it doesn't make much noise or trouble but gives your child good calming pressure against his legs.

Keeping in Touch

Activities that target the tactile sense, or sense of touch, are also a major component of an occupational therapy session with a sensory integration approach. Many of the activities listed above, like a ball pit or resistance tunnel, also have a strong tactile element. Some other activities that focus more directly on the tactile sense include these:

- **Tub of rice:** Just thrusting her hands into a tub of rice may be a comforting sensory experience for your child. The therapist can also put items in the rice for your child to find.
- **Sand box:** Like rice, sand can be a rich sensory experience for your child as she plunges her hands or her feet into it.
- **Water play:** Water is a sensory experience all its own, and therapy may include manipulating different objects in a tub or table filled with liquid.
- **Textured stepping stones:** Your child may remove her socks and shoes and take a walk along plastic stones or a special pathway that offers a variety of sensory experiences—bumpy, rough, prickly, smooth—as she steps and jumps along.
- **Finger paint:** If your child is overly sensitive to touch, she may not much like the feeling of finger-paint, but the therapist will work with her to increase her tolerance and ability to have fun with the slimy, slippery substance.
- **Bubble wrap:** Popping those plastic bubbles gives your child good tactile input and some stimulating input for the auditory sense, too.
- **Links and chains:** Toys that snap together into long strands require some force, some coordination, and a good feel for where the openings and connections are.
- **Clay or putty:** Getting your child comfortable with the feel of these malleable substances is another task the occupational therapist may tackle.

Puzzles, games, and toys of all types can also be useful in working on your child's sense of touch. Children who are particularly sensitive to touch may approach these activities with great reserve, while others will throw themselves into it with excess gusto. Modulating those reactions and finding novel ways to engage a child with an inaccurate sense of touch is one of the major tasks of occupational therapy using a sensory integration approach.

Fine Motor Strategies

In addition to specifically targeting sensory integration issues, the occupational therapist may work with your child to improve fine motor skills. Just as "fine" can mean sharp and exact and "gross" can mean large and all-encompassing, "fine motor" means movements that are small and require careful coordinated control—writing, cutting, or picking up small objects—and "gross motor" means movements that are large and involve coordination of multiple body parts—running, jumping, skipping, or throwing. Your child may be delayed in one or both of these areas, and sensory integration therapy will, even indirectly, help with both.

Children with sensory integration disorder are often delayed in skills like writing or using eating utensils, and techniques that take a sensory integration approach to those abilities can be very effective. Your child will likely sit at a table with the therapist to do this work, and some of these items may be employed:

- **Pencil weight:** A weight slipped around the barrel of a pencil can give your child additional information about where his hand is as he writes, improving accuracy and making him more comfortable.
- **Vibrating pen:** Although it makes funny squiggly letters instead of neat ones, a vibrating pen gives your child good information about the movements that he's making to form those letters.
- **Wikki Stix:** Pieces of string made stiff with wax, these toys can be formed into letters and shapes to increase your child's fine motor control. The slightly sticky feel may be pleasing to

kids who crave different tactile experiences.

- **Wind-up toys:** Turning the knob on a wind-up toy requires fine motor control and offers a big pay-off to motivate your child.
- **Tops:** The spinning toys also require fine motor coordination to function and give a child a pleasing result to his action.
- **Geoboards:** These flat plastic boards with pegs offer a canvas on which your child can stretch colored rubber bands to make designs. The stretching requires fine motor strength and planning.
- **Lace-up cards:** Getting a lace through a hole in a piece of cardboard takes good planning and control.
- **Pick-up sticks:** Your child picks out one thin stick from a pile and removes it without disturbing the others.

All these activities, plus others that include cutting, coloring, hole-punching, and picking up items with chopstick-like tweezers, will strengthen your child's fine motor ability while also providing strong sensory input. Don't be surprised if your child brings home artwork from school that he did in OT. Making designs with different substances is a great tactile workout, too.

Gross Motor Strategies

Like fine motor skills, gross motor skills can benefit from a sensory integration approach. Most of the activities described for balance, body position, and tactile stimulation will also strengthen your child's ability to do gross motor activities like walking and jumping. Another activity that can strengthen gross motor skills while also targeting sensory integration issues is playing with ride-on toys. Some of the wheeled wonders you may see in the therapist's playroom are these:

- Large and sturdy tricycles
- Tricycles with a handle on the back so that the therapist can push a child who is not strong enough to pedal

- A low plastic seat with wheels that your child moves by scuffling his feet along the floor in front of him and steers with handles attached to the seat
- A wheeled platform that looks like a fat skateboard that your child can sit on and move with his feet, or lie face-down on and move with his hands

The therapist may set up an obstacle course for your child to wheel her way through—requiring turns around traffic cones and sending her through tunnels—or have her pick up a puzzle or game piece at one end of the room and "drive" it to the other to put it in place. Obstacle courses that your child travels on foot are also a good gross motor and sensory integration challenge, and may involve many of the items described above. If your child comes upon an obstacle she can't handle, the therapist can quickly step in to help or change the challenge.

Improving Processing

Other senses get a workout in a sensory integration session, too. The therapist may use scented markers to bring an olfactory component to fine motor work. Puzzles involve visual as well as tactile perception, and they are frequently used alone or as part of other activities.

Be sure to let the occupational therapist know if your child has any food allergies. It's not unusual for crackers, sweets, or even peanut butter to be used as part of a therapy session, and your therapist will want to avoid anything that will harm your child.

The therapist may use a mirror to let your child see himself for the visual interest or so he can see how he is performing oral motor tasks like eating, sucking through a straw, or making funny faces. Blowing on whistles involves the auditory sense while strengthening the tactile sense around the mouth, and following soap bubbles as they float around targets the visual sense. Your child may be given snacks to engage his sense of taste and smell. If your child has particular issues around one of these senses, it will certainly be addressed in therapy. But all the senses can be used as motivation for work in areas of need and to promote good integration between them.

No Quick Fixes

Occupational therapy with a sensory integration approach is fun. It's creative and intuitive, carefully planned but flexible enough to adjust to a child's moods and changing needs. It will make your child more comfortable with her body and more willing to try new things. With time, it may be able to effectively resolve some of your child's problems with sensory integration. Other problems may always remain, but therapy will help your child find more acceptable ways to deal with them. At the very least, it will be someplace your child goes every week to do physical activities in an accepting, encouraging, celebratory environment, receiving praise and success for things she may struggle with under normal circumstances. That alone is a self-esteem and confidence booster that can't be undervalued.

You will most likely note improvement in your child, but it may not be dramatic—just a general increase in control and tolerance. The information you gain about your child's sensory strengths and weaknesses and what you can do for them at home will help as well. Still, as a parent, you need to understand that therapy for sensory integration is not a magic wand. It will not instantly make your child move better, eat better, write better, or behave better. There's no timetable and no guaranteed cure. It's important to keep your expectations realistic.

CHAPTER 6

The Sensory Diet

Occupational therapy using a sensory integration approach can do much, over time, to improve your child's ability to process and use information coming in through her senses, but your child struggles with sensory integration every day, every hour, every minute. What can be done to help her cope with her challenges as she's grappling with them in the real world? One tool your occupational therapist can arm you with is a sensory diet, a stimulation-rich routine that gives your child what she needs to cope right now.

You Aren't Just What You Eat

Think of the way you look after your child's nutritional needs. You don't expect him to be able to create a balanced diet for himself from the moment he learns to wield a spoon. You prepare meals for him that contain all the nutrients he needs to be strong and healthy. You provide snacks when he needs a little extra fuel, drinks when he's overheated. You monitor his weight and try to make choices appropriate to his continued health.

A sensory diet involves devoting the same kind of care and attention to your child's sensory needs. You know that, left to his own devices, he may make decisions about what his body wants and needs that will be damaging and disruptive. So you make sure he has a steady stream of the kind of movement and sensation that will

calm and organize him, making him more alert and able to deal with the demands of his day. Small "meals" of intense input to his sense of touch, balance, and body position, fed to him throughout the day, can keep him from seeking out "junk food" stimulation like rocking, jumping, bumping, crashing, and yelling. Constant sensory "snacks" can prevent a plunge into understimulation and oversensitivity.

Most children can make do with the movement they get during recess and gym class, along with activity after school. But children with sensory integration problems may require a much steadier intake of action than that. Like a child with diabetes needs to be constantly monitored for hypoglycemia or hyperglycemia and have immediate access to insulin or sugar if her blood sugar level falls out of balance, a child with sensory integration disorder needs to be constantly monitored for hypostimulation or hyperstimulation, and have immediate access to movement and relief from uncomfortable circumstances.

The concept of the sensory diet was introduced by Patricia Wilbarger and Julia Wilbarger in their 1991 book *Sensory Defensiveness in Children Aged 2–12: An Intervention Guide for Parents and Other Caretakers*. The Wilbargers also developed the Wilbarger protocol, a method that combines brushing and deep pressure to reduce a child's tactile sensitivity.

The need for a sensory diet is most marked if your child has trouble maintaining a comfort level of alertness and sensory balance throughout the day. A sensory diet may be necessary if you, your child's teacher, or your child care provider frequently sees behaviors like these in your child:

- Frequently zones out
- Seems sleepy when should be attentive

- Needs frequent movement
- Understands things sometimes, sometimes does not
- Often appears agitated
- Has trouble settling down after recess, physical education, or movement activities
- Displays uncontrollable silliness or laughing
- Is clumsy and uncoordinated
- Has trouble following organized movements during group activity
- Gets into shoving matches with other students
- Slides out of chair
- Sucks on fingers or shirt
- Frequently rests head on desk

Kids who have this degree of trouble keeping a balance between over- and understimulation will benefit from a consistent and comforting stream of input to their senses of balance, body position, and touch. The occupational therapist will work with you to develop a diet customized to your child's particular strengths, weaknesses, and sensory cravings.

Putting a Plan Together

Your child's occupational therapist may suggest a sensory diet, or you may go to the therapist with your concerns and request one. Either way, your occupational therapist is the one who should work with you and your child to plan the diet. Your job will be to implement it faithfully and to arrange for it to be implemented for your child at school or child care. You will want to give the occupational therapist plenty of information about your child's day and seek input from the teacher or child care provider as well. You can certainly do the activities listed in this chapter with your child on an informal basis, and that will be more helpful than nothing. But a plan developed by a therapist will be more effective for your child and more likely to be respected and followed by others.

The overall effect of a sensory diet should be to make your child more alert. You should see a decline in hyperactivity and hypersensitivity. If your child seems to be more agitated, hyperactive, or easily upset, let your occupational therapist know that the diet needs to be adjusted. Stop doing it until those changes are made.

The therapist will devise a plan through which your child will be given short breaks throughout the day for intense sensory input. A typical plan might schedule those breaks every half hour to two hours. Some activities might be offered continuously throughout the day, like a water bottle with a straw for sucking on or a fidget toy to play with. The therapist might recommend having your child jump on a trampoline before starting an activity that demands sustained attention. You might be advised to give your child deep pressure during these frequent intervals or provide deep pressure to his skin with a plastic surgical-style scrub brush.

Following Through

It might seem overwhelming to imagine finding the time, space, and patience to really pursue such a rigorous diet. You should see enough of a difference in your child's behavior and comfort level, however, to make it worthwhile. Once you get into a routine, it will not seem as time-intensive as it looks on paper. A brief interval is all it takes to make an impact.

Keep in mind that much of this is simply a matter of providing comfort and stimulation before your child has a meltdown, rather than after. The time saved by avoiding tantrums, disobedience, and tears will more than compensate for the time spent providing sensory meals for your child. The activities are fun for your child and will give him positive experiences with you and his caretakers that make him feel less stressed.

Getting Cooperation

Making sure your child gets her sensory diet when she's away from you may be a challenge. If your child is in a self-contained special education class, there may be an aide who can help with fulfilling the requirements of her sensory diet. You may be able to get the diet specified in her IEP so that everyone will be clear on the necessity of following through with it.

If your child is not in a self-contained class or the teacher doesn't have an aide who can take the time to attend to just your child, there may be times when your child can be excused to go to the occupational therapy room and get his diet requirements met there. However, you want to be sure that this doesn't take time away from your child's classroom learning; you don't want your child to miss important information in the class. You can work with the teacher and therapist to strategize ways that your child may be able to get the input he needs without disrupting the class—carrying a box of books to the office, for example, or helping to put things away on a high or low shelf. A lot of things that will be done in your child's sensory diet may be fun for the rest of the class to participate in, too, and the teacher or child care provider may find an advantage in increased movement breaks for everyone.

Minimum Daily Requirements

The choices that form your child's sensory diet will vary based on his level of comfort with vestibular, proprioceptive, and tactile stimulation. The idea is to strike a good balance between things that are calming and things that are stimulating so that your child maintains a good level of alertness. Activities targeting your child's vestibular sense (his sense of balance) might include these:

- Jumping jacks
- Rocking in a rocking chair
- Doing a dance
- Stretching and shaking

- Riding in a wagon
- Bouncing on a trampoline
- Marching around the room
- Copying head movements
- Going up and down steps
- Jumping rope
- Doing somersaults and headstands
- Standing on one foot
- Playing on swings

Activities targeting your child's proprioceptive sense (his sense of body position) might include the following:

- Doing sit-ups and pull-ups
- Doing silly walks
- Playing Simon Says, with lots of stretching, bending, and jumping
- Rolling a large ball or bolster over your child
- Making a sandwich of your child between two heavy items
- Playing catch with a heavy ball
- Pressing palms of hands together
- Pushing another child on a swing
- Vacuuming or sweeping the floor
- Eating something chewy
- Playing clapping games
- Wearing a weighted backpack or vest
- Doing a "wheelbarrow," with you holding his feet and him walking on his hands
- Jumping rope
- Wrestling
- Jumping on a trampoline
- Playing tug-of-war
- Getting a bear hug
- Playing with a vibrating toy

Activities targeting your child's tactile sense (his sense of touch) might include these:

- Popping bubble wrap
- Rubbing skin with lotion or towels
- Art projects that involve touching different substances
- Playing with water
- Plunging hands into tub of rice or dried beans
- Having shapes and letters drawn on back
- Blowing bubbles or balloons
- Squeezing soft balls or tubes
- Playing in sandbox
- Giving high-fives
- Drinking through a straw
- Eating crunchy foods
- Blowing on a whistle

Sensory diet activities don't have to be a "Stop everything!" interruption to the day's events. While it may be best at school or in a public place to go off with your child and have a little movement break away from other distractions, under most circumstances you can weave the diet activities into your child's normal routine, playing games or doing chores or tackling craft projects.

Special Circumstances

If every day of your child's life were exactly the same as every other day, identical minute-by-minute and hour-by-hour, staying on a sensory diet would be a fairly clear-cut endeavor. As with a food diet, though, there are days and events that can knock that strict and successful routine off the track. School vacations, parties, worship services, trips, visitors, and a thousand other variations can prompt a rethinking, at least temporarily, of the way in which your child's sensory diet is delivered.

Changing Plans

Unfortunately, departures from routine are times when your child most particularly needs his calming and organizing sensory input. Don't assume that a family vacation means a vacation from your child's sensory needs. Instead, think ahead to determine how you will be able to implement your child's sensory diet under unusual and restricted circumstances. Think of this just as you would the challenge of dealing with a child's food restrictions and dietary needs in differing environments.

There are really very few situations in which you can't go to a private place with your child as necessary to give the input required for his sensory diet. Find a spare room at a party, sneak outside the church mid-service, or find a secluded corner of an amusement park. Bring things you can use to administer appropriate sensory input in the course of an activity. Silly Putty, for example, is something your child can play with quietly and without being disruptive. Following through on this may call on all your ingenuity, but your child's peace of mind and body are worth it.

Unforeseen Circumstances

Sometimes routine-breaking events aren't planned for at all. Unexpected occurrences like fire alarms, ambulances, injuries, or illness may increase your child's need for calming sensory input, or impair her ability to participate in a sensory diet. Work with your occupational therapist to devise emergency provisions for times when the ordinary course of therapy doesn't apply. Make sure that everyone who works with your child knows what to do under such departures from the norm.

Going Off the Menu

While it is best for your child's sensory diet to be designed and supervised by an occupational therapist, that may not be possible for your child. Perhaps he isn't able to work with an occupational therapist at this time, or maybe the school therapist can't comply with your request due to time or administrative factors. That doesn't mean you can't pursue activities that address your child's sensory needs throughout the day. Finding out what works for your child, and then teaching him how to do those things for himself, will be a large part of your task as the parent of a child with sensory integration disorder. A sensory diet will help with that, but you can also pursue those activities informally instead.

I've asked my occupational therapist for a sensory diet, and she hasn't followed through. What can I do?
Keep asking. It's an important part of your child's therapy and an entirely reasonable thing for you to request. If it helps, try putting together a plan yourself using the information in this chapter and then ask your OT to look at it and make any changes.

Rather than setting up a formal plan, with therapeutic breaks at specific intervals, keep a running list of things that seem to calm or stimulate your child. Share that list with the people who work with him throughout his day. Make equipment available so that help can be provided informally whenever he seems to need it. Work with his teacher to determine which things can be most easily administered. You'll find more ideas for dealing with school and play times in later chapters of this book. You may also find that activities you would try with your child under any circumstances can help with alertness and sensory balance.

Good Sports

Sports can be a challenge for children with sensory integration disorder who have problems judging distances or figuring out how to put together movements, but if your child enjoys sports, they're a great way to ensure that he gets lots of vestibular and proprioceptive input.

Children who have trouble with team sports because their abilities are slow or unreliable may still get benefit out of more individual pursuits. Bowling provides lots of good work for muscles and joints, with the carrying and throwing of the weighted ball. Swimming provides resistance to the arms and legs and the soothing touch of water. Gymnastics is full of activities that involve balance and jumping and putting pressure on arms and legs. Dancing may also give your child good sensory information in an enjoyable, low-stress form.

Gymnastics can be overstimulating for some children with sensory integration disorder. If your child loves gymnastics class but is often in trouble for wandering away from the group or an inability to transition between activities, see if the gym will allow you or a volunteer to serve as a one-on-one aide to keep her on track.

Keeping Active

Whether you do them as part of a sensory diet or just part of your family time, the activities you choose with your child can contribute to her sensory well-being. Take long walks together, seeking a route that offers some uphill and downhill trekking. Add some touch to the trip by having your child pick up nature items that you find along the way and talking about how they feel. Wearing a weighted vest or backpack during walks can make them more productive for your child.

At home, bring your child into the kitchen and have her knead dough or help you bring items down from shelves and put them back. Household chores like sweeping, vacuuming, and washing dishes offer lots of work, bending, and stretching that may feel good to your child. Be creative in finding sensory-rich activities for your child in the natural flow of family life. Aside from the sensory benefit, they will make your child feel like a valued member of the household.

Don't Set It and Forget It

What works today may not always work. Stay involved with your child's sensory diet and keep track of his sensory needs. Some strategies may lose their effectiveness after a certain period of use and need to be rotated out. Others may no longer be necessary as your child's sensory system becomes stronger. Work with your child's therapist to make sure that his sensory diet is well balanced and suited to his current needs.

As your child ages and becomes less needy, she may naturally switch from a formal sensory diet to the sort of athletic and at-home activities mentioned above. Be ready to serve as a resource for her in making that switch. The key is for her to be able to stay comfortable and alert throughout the day, however that needs to happen. A sensory diet is just one important tool in your toolbox.

Chapter 7

The Parent As Therapist

Therapy performed by a therapist will be important for your child with sensory integration disorder. Having a formal sensory diet devised by the therapist will also be a significant part of his treatment plan. But there are a lot of hours in the day and a lot of ways you can use them to help your child's sensory system. Other home based, parent-directed therapies focus on things like reducing oversensitivity to touch and sound; increasing muscle tone and movement control; and using play to overcome fears and obsessions.

Brushing and Joint Compression

You may have heard parents in support groups or online message boards mention "brushing" their children with sensory integration disorder. If so, you've probably wondered what that could possibly mean. The brushing referred to is properly called the Wilbarger protocol, developed by occupational therapists Patricia Wilbarger and Julia Wilbarger as a way to reduce oversensitivity to touch. It involves rubbing a soft plastic brush, the kind surgeons use to clean their hands, along your child's skin in a specific way. Done many times throughout the day on a specific schedule, it eventually reduces your child's sensitivity to touch and makes him more able to deal with things like clothing, tags, sock seams, and hugs.

While the protocol seems harmless—rub the brush against your own skin, and you'll see that it doesn't hurt and feels a little stimulating—it must be done in the prescribed way or it could actually be harmful for your child. For this reason, it must be done under the supervision of your occupational therapist. If your therapist doesn't bring the subject up, don't hesitate to ask whether this would be a good option for your child. Have the therapist instruct you in what direction to move the brush, how frequently to do the treatments, and what sort of reaction on your child's part might signal a problem with the therapy.

Fact

Your occupational therapist will probably provide you with the sort of brush you'll need to do the Wilbarger protocol with your child. You may also be able to pick one up at a medical supply store. If not, they can be ordered from occupational therapy Web sites like *www.theraproducts.com* and *www.abilitations.com.*

Along with brushing, the Wilbarger protocol includes joint compressions (pushing) and traction (pulling). These must also be done in a particular way and in a particular sequence to ensure that they are as helpful as possible. However, you may find in playing with your child that games that include pushing against the joints—pushing against your child, palm to palm, or sole of foot to sole of foot, for example—have a calming effect. Ask your therapist how to do joint compressions along with brushing, and get instructions on the proper way to do it.

Therapeutic Listening

Listening to music may be naturally calming for your child, or, depending on his particular taste in tunes, intensely stimulating. Therapeutic listening programs take that inclination one or more steps further and use sound and music to promote specific goals. Most of these programs are things you can do at home with your child, on a prescribed schedule or whenever the need arises.

Auditory Integration Therapy

Perhaps the most intense of the bunch, auditory integration therapy works on the theory that the inability to receive certain frequencies of sound impairs the brain's ability to process what the ears hear. During the therapy, your child will listen to music that has been doctored to accent certain frequencies and block others. Your child will listen to the prepared music on a schedule—maybe twice a day, maybe twenty—for a predetermined period of time. Her behavior will be monitored to make sure that the therapy isn't proving unintentionally upsetting to her. While some programs require that the therapy be given in an office, many allow parents to administer the sound sessions at home. You may need to purchase or rent special equipment to give the proper degree of intensity to the sound.

Music Therapy

Although auditory integration therapy may be helpful for many children, it may seem too intense, too costly, or too unproven for your family. Another way to use sound to help your child is through special compilation CDs with music chosen to garner particular sensory responses. With titles like *Baroque for Modulation*, *No Worries*, *Soothing the Senses*, and *The Mozart Effect*, they employ mostly classical music of varying tempos to help kids feel calm, alert, organized, and ready for the challenges of the day. Your occupational therapist may have a favorite disc or two to recommend, or you can find good choices on occupational therapy Web sites like *www.sensoryresources.com and www.sensorycomfort.com.*

Computerized Therapy

Increasingly, specialized software and equipment are allowing you to bring into your home therapeutic options that once would have required an office visit. Programs such as Fast ForWord focus on auditory processing as it applies to language; these may be both helpful and fun for children who have trouble distinguishing different sounds and interpreting them correctly. Others use specialized helmets and other monitoring devices to deliver biofeedback training right to your home computer. These programs focus on improving attention and concentration, and they may improve motor planning and classroom behavior.

Essential

Versions of popular computer-based programs offered by other companies can help you take advantage of an office-based therapy when you can't make it to an office, or let you try out a particular approach before investing in it. Many parents considering Scientific Learning's therapist-monitored Fast ForWord try the less expensive, parent-monitored Earobics from Cognitive Concepts first.

As with auditory integration therapy, these programs require commitment to follow through with a routine, and they may involve a significant financial commitment as well. They are not right for every child and may need to be monitored by a professional. If you've read about a program that sounds interesting for your child or heard another parent rave about it, ask your occupational therapist if she is familiar with it. She may have had some experience with the program, good or bad, and will have a better idea as to whether it is safe and reasonable for your child. Ask the provider whether it's possible to try a demo or limited version before making a full commitment.

Educational Kinesiology

The notion that certain types of movements can cause the brain to become more focused and process information better is called educational kinesiology (from the Greek *kinesis*, or "movement"). A program called Brain Gym, devised by educators Paul E. Dennison and Gail E. Dennison, offers a variety of fun exercises for children that draw on these movements and use them to give young brains a charge. The movements generally involve crossing the midline of the body—for example, bringing the right hand across to the left side of the body, and the left across to the right. The exercises can be done in certain sequences, before particular activities, or on a regular schedule.

Your child's occupational therapist may have some Brain Gym materials, or your child's teacher may use them to give the class some exercise throughout the day. If the information on how to do the exercises isn't available to you from these sources, you can order a teacher's guide from the Brain Gym Web site (at *www.braingym.com*), which will tell you how to work with your child to implement the exercises most effectively, and a simpler guide for your child. The site includes other materials that may be helpful, including Vision Gym to improve visual processing, and tapes and posters to get your child more actively engaged in the Brain Gym exercises.

Play Therapy

If they do nothing else, activities that further your child's sensory integration therapy will give a purpose to your play and increase the time you spend together in close physical contact. Chapter 6 describes small activities you can do informally with your child, if not as part of a formal sensory diet plan. The chapters that follow include activities that target specific problems with specific senses. Here are a few other ways to make playtime count.

Floortime

The Floortime Foundation offers a game plan for getting down on the floor with your child and following his lead while gently directing him to variations that will expand his emotional development. While the focus of Floortime is not specifically on sensory integration, the techniques can be used to help your child increase his comfort level and overcome fears. *The Child with Special Needs: Encouraging Intellectual and Emotional Growth* gives good advice on using the technique to deal with processing problems and other special needs and challenges—including bedtime struggles and toilet training—that may be issues for your child.

Spending time down at your child's level can pay off in a number of ways. You'll have a great opportunity to really observe him, see where his strengths and weaknesses lie, and note the things he does with ease and the things he has to concentrate hard on. Play allows you to provide sensations and experiences your child needs in a nonthreatening context and can help build warmth and trust between you that will pay off as you try to help him extend his comfort boundaries.

You can learn more about Floortime in *The Child with Special Needs: Encouraging Intellectual and Emotional Growth* by Stanley I. Greenspan, MD, and Serena Wieder, Ph.D., with Robin Simons, and on the Floortime Foundation's Web site at *www.floortime.org*. The foundation also sells DVDs in which Drs. Greenspan and Wieder describe the approach and demonstrate it with young children.

Resist the temptation to take over playtime or make everything a strictly therapeutic experience. Directing you in play and having you follow her every order can be an empowering experience for your child. Even if your child's play is repetitive and limited in imagination, go along with it. Small gestures to change the play may be worth more than putting yourself in charge of it.

Deep Pressure

Children will often seek out what they need without even knowing they're doing it. Think of how many activities that occur naturally as a part of play involve deep pressure to your child's body and joints—

burrowing under sofa cushions, building a close and cozy fort with pillows, crawling into boxes or through tunnels, or wrestling. Since deep pressure is comforting to kids with a variety of sensory integration problems, encourage your child to pursue it in play and provide plenty yourself during your playtime together.

William Steig's children's book *Pete's a Pizza* tells the story of a dad who makes a pizza with his son, tossing the boy up in the air for the dough, and then applying toppings to his giggling body. Read this book with your child, and then try to make a pizza out of him.

In addition to massaging and roughhousing, pretend play can be a good way to work in some deep pressure. A good game to try is making your child into a sandwich. Press your hands firmly along his body to apply the condiments, then wrap him in a blanket or sandwich him between heavy cushions to complete the dish. Let your child help you come up with more ideas for games that involve squeezing and pressing. You may want to pretend he's a turtle, hiding under a shell of cushions, or a baby bear tightly tucked into a cave for the winter.

The Parent As Researcher

Although occupational therapists are great resources for information on programs and therapies to try with your child, the Internet has made it easy for parents of children with special needs to communicate with each other and share resources that have worked for their families. It's possible that you may hear of some promising new therapy or technique even before your therapist does. You may be in the best position to scout out information, seek out practitioners in your area, and obtain brochures and Web site printouts that describe the procedures.

You'll still want to check with your occupational therapist before embarking on alternative therapies with your child, and some programs require permission from your child's doctor as well. But an important part of your job as a "parent therapist" will be to keep your eyes and ears open and follow up on interesting ideas. Here are three non-home-based therapies you may want to investigate.

Therapy on Horseback

The idea of putting your floppy, hyperactive, or easily frightened child on the back of a horse may seem unthinkable. But horseback riding can be a positive, therapeutic activity for children with sensory integration disorder. Some may be able to ride on their own and find that the rocking, rising, and falling of the horse's body offers good input to their sense of balance and body position. Others may need a therapist's attention to be safe atop a horse and get the maximum benefit from the experience.

Hippotherapy

Hippotherapy—formed from the Greek word for horse, *hippos*—isn't really a riding program. It's the use of a horse as a piece of therapy equipment. A therapist will work closely with your child, manipulating her into different positions that utilize the movement of the horse to attain various goals. Hippotherapy may be administered by physical or occupational therapists who have special training in the methods used. The therapeutic goals for hippotherapy will likely be more intense and involved than for therapeutic riding.

Therapeutic Riding

Therapeutic riding will look much more like a horseback riding lesson, with your child sitting in a saddle and riding around a ring. There may be volunteers leading the horse and someone else helping your child stay on as the therapist or instructor gives commands that involve stretching, pointing, playing games, answering questions, and learning how to work with the horse.

In addition to developing the focus needed to ride and direct a large animal, therapeutic riding can improve muscle tone and strength through the torso.

During therapeutic riding, your child may interact with another rider and may engage in activities like throwing and catching balls or leaning over to pick up objects. All this will be done with someone holding on to him, so don't worry about falls!

Both hippotherapy and therapeutic riding are designed for children with disabilities, and both require a doctor's permission before your child will be accepted. Frequently, both have a waiting list.

The North American Riding for the Handicapped Association certifies riding programs for both hippotherapy and therapeutic riding. To find a center that offers these therapies in your area, search the NARHA Web site at *www.narha.org*. You can also contact local stables or call hospitals or universities in your area that offer programs for children with special needs.

Therapy in the Water

While water can serve to calm children with sensory integration disorder, it can also be intensely stimulating for them—so stimulating for some that they're unable to observe normal safety precautions because they're so intent on interacting exuberantly with all that wonderful fluid. You may have trouble keeping your child safe in ordinary swimming sessions or keeping her from splashing and bumping other children in mainstream swim classes. Both aquatic therapy and special-needs swim lessons can take advantage of the special properties of water while taking care of your child's safety.

Aquatic Therapy

Aquatic therapy with a therapist who is trained to work with children with special needs may be a good way to get your child water playtime and therapeutic movement in an environment that will be safe for him. Aquatic therapy may focus on movements that strengthen your child and improve muscle tone and strength. The therapist will use the weightlessness bestowed by the water to help your child do things that would be difficult on land. To find a pool that offers aquatic therapy, check with agencies in your area that serve children with special needs, or contact hospitals with extensive children's programs. If they don't know of any programs, they may be able to direct you to someone who does.

Special-Needs Swim Lessons

If you're less interested in therapy than in helping your child learn to swim, call some public pools in your area and inquire about swim lessons for children with special needs. You may be able to find someone who gives one-on-one lessons that will provide your child with plenty of hands-on assistance as she becomes comfortable with the water and learns to maneuver through it. Although it won't be as intensely therapeutic as aquatic therapy, any sort of water play may have benefits for your child's sense of touch, balance, and body position.

Yoga

Yoga practitioners have developed techniques for working with children with ADHD, learning disabilities, and autism. Anything that centers on body position, balance, and focus may also be useful for children with sensory integration disorder. To see if there's a practitioner in your area, check out the Web site *www.specialyoga.com.*

Rock Climbing

Many gymnastics centers have added rock-climbing walls to their facilities, and this offers a great opportunity for children with sensory integration issues to get lots of good stretching, weight-bearing, balancing, and attention-focusing work in a package that's fun and exciting. Since safety may be a particular issue for your child, check with rock-climbing gyms in your area to see if they offer classes for children with special needs or would be willing to work with your child on a one-to-one basis.

Your Greatest Responsibility: Understanding

Doing therapeutic activities with your child at home is important. Researching opportunities for your child to pursue special therapeutic activities outside your home is important, too. But the most important thing you can do for your child is the one you do every day just in the course of being a good parent, and that is understanding your child's special needs and accommodating them. Never discount the value that simple understanding has to your child. The benefit of that is far over and above any therapeutic work that you do, and if you do nothing else, you will still be helping. Interpreting behavior by its sensory basis and not as a deliberate and punishable offense will give your child the space and freedom from stress that she needs to do the work of bringing her sensory systems into line.

CHAPTER 8

The Tactile Sense

From the top of a sensitive scalp to the tip of a ticklish toe, your child's skin is filled with neurons eager to bring news of the outside world to her brain. The tactile sense, or sense of touch, relays news about temperature, texture, shape, size, number, pressure, and much more. When operating efficiently, the tactile sense helps your child do everything from buttoning a shirt to enjoying a hug. When tactile sensations aren't processed well or integrated with other sensory information, though, they can cause profound discomfort.

When Little Things Bug a Lot

Remember "The Princess and the Pea"? Maybe when you read that fairy tale about a young woman so sensitive to touch that she could feel a tiny pea through a stack of mattresses, it reminds you of some little one you know. While your child may not be able to feel a lump under the bed, she may feel other seemingly little things with extraordinary sensitivity. What's going on when your child complains about the seam in her socks or the movement of loose clothing against her body or the brush of a kiss against her cheek?

Sounding the alert over a dangerous situation is one of the tactile system's most basic purposes. It's important for your child to be able to feel when a stove is hot or a knife is too sharp. These things are meant to elicit a big, attention-getting reaction. As most children grow and develop, their nervous systems develop ways to inhibit that reaction when it's not really needed, but for children with sensory integration disorder, the tactile sense may remain on high alert. To your child, a scratchy tag may feel as painful as a knife, a pat on the head as dangerous as a blow.

Sensory Discrimination

Just as your child's nervous system may be unable to discriminate between what's safe and what's dangerous, it may be unable to discriminate between what's important and what's not important. Rather than filter out all the information that doesn't need to be dealt with consciously—the constant feel of clothes against the skin, furniture against the body, air brushing past the face—it all comes crashing in, leaving your child distracted and preoccupied by things you ignore. He may be unable to concentrate on things that would be helpful to feel, like the way shoelaces need to move together to tie a shoe or the way a button slides through a hole.

Your child may react to all this by avoiding new experiences and clinging to safe and comfortable ones that she has already found a way to process. She may seek to rigidly control all tactile input, finding that experiences she initiates herself are less threatening than ones that come to her, unpredictably, from others.

Out of Touch with Feelings

Some children whose tactile sense doesn't work right have the opposite of too much information—they don't seem to feel or respond to much of anything. Your child may feel light touch not at all, normal touch as a tickle, and only really register deep touch, hard hugs, and firm squeezes. If your child can't feel when his face is dirty, his shoes are on backward, his diaper is wet, or his knee is scraped, he may be more underwhelmed by touch than overwhelmed by it. As with children who feel too much, though, his behavior will be directed by a search for sensory comfort. The better you can meet that need, the less he'll need to act up.

What Not to Wear

Clothes are a frequent source of trouble for children with sensory integration disorder. If your child has an overreactive tactile sense, you may have despaired over getting her to vary from one safe and trusted outfit, even if it's a swimsuit in winter or a sweat suit in summer. Collars and ties, starchy dresses, dress-up shoes—these may be out of the question for your child, and the subject of many screaming tantrums.

Essential

Picking your battles is one of the smartest strategies for parenting a child with sensory integration disorder. There is very little reason to force unpleasant sensations on your child. In almost every situation, finding an option your child can tolerate will be easier than finding a way to change your child.

Your first instinct may be to see this as a power struggle and insist that your child do as you say. You may have good reasons for wanting him to dress in a way that's appropriate to the weather or to the occasion. But if your child's reaction is prompted by sensory integration problems, it's not a battle worth fighting. Your child has a right to wear clothes that don't feel painful or distractingly uncomfortable, and his overall behavior may improve if he's not constantly bothered by irritating fabrics and styles. Spend your time and energy finding outfits that will suit the both of you.

Tags and Collars

You may at one time have felt a particularly sharp tag at the back of your shirt collar and cut it out to feel more comfortable. Understand that your child may feel that same way about any sort of tag at all, even one that may seem inoffensive to you. Cutting the tags out of shirts, or looking for shirts that don't have tags, is an easy fix for a situation that may truly be causing your child misery.

Even collars without troublesome tags can be a trouble spot for your touch-sensitive child. He may not be able to tolerate a tight or restricting collar or may actually prefer something tight and snug to something that rubs against his skin. Collars with scratchy trim or stitching inside may be intolerable. A little judicious shopping should help ensure that your child does not have to deal with anything less than a comfortable collar. If you find a style your child likes, buy a bunch.

Waistbands

Waistbands are another part of your child's clothing that can become a major issue. She may feel uncomfortably squeezed by a tight waistband, or she may enjoy the feeling of a tight hug around the middle. Let your child's preference be your guide when choosing pants, skirts, tights, underwear, or dresses that bind at the waist. If your child protests a particular garment, look to see whether a waistband tag, scratchy trim, or a too-tight or too-loose fit might be causing the problem.

Beyond collars and waistbands, virtually anything about the fit of your child's clothes can be an issue. Don't let it become one. If she likes the feeling of very tight, snug clothes, see if she'll wear a bodysuit and leggings under other, more presentable garb. And if he insists on wearing loose sweat clothes everywhere, buy them in a variety of acceptable colors and styles and let it be. A perfectly dressed child who can't behave is going to be more eyebrow-raising in the long run than a casually dressed kid who's comfortable in his own skin.

Fabrics

Certain fabrics may feel unpleasant to your child, and it doesn't have to make sense to you to be real to him. If your child balks at certain garments, see if you can find something in common among the fabrics. Allowing your child's fabric preference to guide you can prevent a lot of dressing-time battles.

Shoes

Does your child kick off his shoes at the first possible opportunity? Does he do it even when it's inappropriate, like in class or at story time in a bookstore? Consider that even the best-fitted, most comfortable shoes may rub him the wrong way. Just the feel of anything on his feet may be unbearable (in fact, some children prefer to wear shoes because they don't like the feeling of things like carpet or grass on the soles of their feet). If you find shoes your child is comfortable wearing, consider letting him wear them with any outfit, whether or not it seems appropriate. For around the house, try slipper socks or anything else your child will tolerate.

Alternatively, your child may be so nonsensitive that she truly can't feel when her shoes are on the wrong feet or her socks are bunched up at the toes. This may appear to be a case of sloppiness or carelessness, but your child may legitimately not be able to tell the difference. It's a good idea to check for yourself before your child leaves the house, or to give her some verbal or physical help in putting shoes on.

Too Sticky, Too Slimy

Touching certain substances, like finger paints or play dough, may be intensely unpleasant for your child with tactile sensitivities. And since the sense of touch extends into the mouth, these aversions may include certain textures of food. If your child balks at a particular food or activity, an overactive sense of touch could be to blame. Rethink this as a legitimate sensory preference and not a behavioral challenge, and try finding alternatives that are acceptable to both of you. Glue sticks and paint bottles with sponge tops can be good alternatives for kids who don't want to touch glue or paint, and different food choices can be made available.

Slimy substances can also be bothersome to children who are underreactive to things they touch. Slippery, oozy materials or foods may not create strong enough input to trigger much of a reaction, and that may make your child uncomfortable—to have hands covered by or mouth full of something that can't quite be felt or identified. It may be helpful to put something with more tactile oomph in slithery substances—glitter or rice in finger paints, or fruit in Jell-O or pudding.

Fact

Children who are undersensitive to the feeling of things in their mouths may have speech problems because of it. Much of forming consonants and phonemes involves putting the tongue in a particular position against the teeth or the roof of the mouth, and kids who can't feel when that happens won't be able to speak clearly.

Feeling No Pain

If your child overreacts to touch, you'll never be in doubt when something hurts him. He'll deliver that news loud and clear. But if your child underreacts to touch, you may have to be the pain police. He may have stomach problems and not feel them or an ear infection and not be aware of it. This can lead to serious consequences if problems go untreated.

Tune into your child's pain capacity by observing how she reacts to things that would start another child crying. Does she fall and jump right back up again? Does she find things like hitting her head against the wall or the floor entertaining? Do you need to follow signs like slowed behavior, sluggishness, or fever to diagnose illness because she never says anything about feeling sick? Consider that your child may have trouble processing pain, and use this as a cue to keep a very close eye on her.

When your child has an experience that should be painful, model for him what an appropriate response would be. Make a big deal over the illness or injury and how much it must hurt. Point out scenes in movies or books where children use pain as a warning or respond to pain with tears or complaints. Your child may never feel pain in a normal way, but he may be able to learn responses that will keep him safe by letting others know when he's been hurt.

If you know that your child does not feel pain, you will want to keep him under much closer supervision than a child who can monitor this for himself. In case of accident or injury, your child will not be able to give the kind of information doctors may need to treat him.

The Tickle Threshold

Some children with tactile sensitivities may find even the slightest touch to be unbearably ticklish. Your child may shy away from gentle touch and be miserable if you try to play tickle games. Kids on the other end of the spectrum may feel even firm touch as ticklish and often crave the rough-and-tumble of a rigorous tickling session. Depending on where your child's preference falls, you will need to modulate your touch so as not to get either an uncomfortable child or an uncontrollably giggling one.

Don't assume that because your child laughs, she enjoys tickling. Giggling can be an involuntary response to tickling and does not necessarily indicate merriment. Check the other clues your child gives. Does she seek out tickling? Does she ask for more, or does she wriggle away? Use the answers to these questions to guide you both in your play time with your child and in everyday situations where touch may feel ticklish.

Don't Touch Me!

Touch can be a treacherous thing for your child with poor tactile processing. If your child is overly sensitive, he may feel even a tap or a pat as a hit or a shove. Touch may be painful, or it may be a more intense experience than he can handle. Your child may resist hugs and seem hostile and standoffish, but in fact he needs your love and affection as much or more as kids who welcome caresses. If your child is undersensitive, on the other hand, he runs the risk of hurting others. He may hit when he means to tap or pat and shove when he means to touch. While he seems aggressive, he's really just trying to get and give affection in a way that feels comfortable to him.

Hugs Hurt

It's natural to feel upset when your child won't accept your hugs and shrinks from your touch. This is often interpreted as a sign of an attachment problem. But look at it in the larger context of your child's overall behavior. If your child seems to have goodwill toward you in general, and to enjoy your company and seek your attention and approval, but just doesn't like being touched or hugged, the problem may be one of tactile oversensitivity.

Why is my child comfortable giving hugs, but not getting them?
For a child who is overly sensitive to touch, tactile experiences that she instigates—that lack the element of surprise and can be controlled—are less threatening than ones over which she feels powerless. Try to respect her preferences in this.

That doesn't mean you should stop touching or hugging—your child needs to have those experiences. But show some understanding and ingenuity in the way you do it. Let your child know when he is going to be touched; let him see you before you touch. Pay attention to your child's sensory preferences and see if there's a part of his body that's less sensitive than others. One mother reports that her son resisted touch in general, but would allow her to hold the tip of his foot. So she started there, and eventually he became comfortable enough with touch for more normal cuddling and contact.

If your child hates being hugged, try letting her sit on your lap while watching television or reading a story, and get some of the same close contact going that way. She may prefer being hugged from the side, so that only her arms and back are touched, rather than from the front, where her whole body and face may get excessive tactile input. Most children with sensory sensitivity prefer deep pressure to light touch. Give your child a head's up by saying something like, "You know what I'd like to do now? I'd like to give you a big hug," and provide firm touch when hugging. Again, work within your child's comfort zones, and slowly try to expand them.

There's another way hugs can hurt: when your child hugs too hard. Children who don't feel pressure or pain may hug too hard, squeeze too tight, or add a pinch or a slap or a head-butt to an embrace. Try to avoid reacting to these modulation errors as if you are being attacked. Your child does not understand that what he is doing is inappropriate and uncomfortable to you. If possible, gently instruct that certain things hurt you, and try to take control of hugs by holding down arms or anticipating movements. Tell your child firmly, but without anger, when something is uncomfortable to you.

The Line-Up

Children with tactile processing problems may have particular trouble when forced to be in close proximity with classmates, as when walking single file. Your oversensitive child will feel even the natural jostling and bumping that comes with being in the middle of a line as acts of aggression, and she may respond aggressively. If your child is undersensitive, she may not feel when she's jostling too hard and be accused of hitting or pushing. Either way, it's worth asking your child's teacher to let her walk either at the front or the back of the line. This simple adjustment can prevent a lot of potential incidents.

One way your child's teacher can accommodate your child's need to be at the end of the line is to give him a job that automatically puts him at the back, like turning off the lights or closing the door. The teacher might also send him ahead on a real or manufactured errand, such as bringing a blank note to a cooperating teacher.

Head Cases

Hair combing, cutting, and washing can be intensely trying for children with tactile sensitivity. Your child isn't making it up when he screams, "You're hurting me!" when you barely touch him with the comb. The head is a particularly sensitive area for most people anyway, and it's so much more so when the sensations aren't being processed accurately. Use caution and sensitivity when handling your child's head or face, and seriously consider short haircuts that don't need much combing.

Fact

Dental work is a frequent trouble zone for kids who are sensitive to being touched around the head and face or to being held down. Make sure to share information about sensory integration with the dentist before the appointment. Having the child wear an x-ray bib during routine dental care provides deep touch pressure and is often calming for children.

Maybe your child isn't sensitive enough about his head and uses it as a blunt instrument, banging it against walls or doors or your face with little apparent feeling or concern. Discourage this behavior, but don't treat it as deliberate self-harm. He may honestly not know that's supposed to hurt.

Comfort Zones

Regardless of whether your child is over- or undersensitive to touch, your job as a parent will be to find out what is comfortable for her and work from there. Do not try to force things on your child that her nervous system can't handle, and never force your child to stop doing things that feel good to her. Your child is just trying to make sense of the world in the best way possible, and your understanding and gentle assistance will do more than treating everything like a conscious behavioral choice.

CHAPTER 9

The Visual Sense

When you worry about your child's vision, you may be concerned with near- and farsightedness. These problems with getting visual information into the brain are significant, but more to the point are the problems that occur when the nervous system has the information but mismanages it. Your child may overreact to the sight of something that seems nonthreatening to you; have trouble picking out important details from visual information; or be unable to place what he sees in the proper context without the help of information from other senses.

Seeing Is Believing

Chances are, vision is the sense you put the most value in. Vision adds a necessary dimension to the information received from every one of our senses. Unless your child has a severe vision impairment, seeing is how she learns about the world. Watching other people walk or eat or play with toys gives her a sense of how to do those things herself. Seeing the distance between her body and other objects helps her modulate movements. Vision is how children learn in school, from reading notes off a board to questions on a test to stories in a book. It's the one sense your child can easily turn on and off, and the one she trusts most to define her world. That makes any glitches in the system particularly troublesome.

Sight Unseen

Visual information is so compelling that it's easy to believe what you see and not put as much credit into information from the other senses, particularly those two senses rarely heard about, proprioceptive and vestibular. But the proprioceptive sense—your muscle and joint sense that lets you know what position your body is in—and the vestibular sense—the one that regulates balance and helps you tell up from down—are vitally important to successful visual processing and discrimination.

Fact

Though you experience reality as what you're looking at right now, your conscious mind is actually about a half-second behind. Your brain likes to put a little polish on your perceptions—filling in for missing information, making judgments on what's worth noticing—before you're fully aware of them. Your child's brain may not do that so efficiently.

To see successfully, your child needs at the very least to be able to keep her neck upright and unmoving, and to be able to turn her head whichever way she needs to look. The wobbly view she gets if she can't fine-tune those movements will impair her ability to use what visual information she receives. If your child needs to move a lot or make hard jerky movements to get any information about how her arms or legs or joints are positioned, she'll have trouble getting much of a detailed visual image through all that motion. Trying to process visual information without a smoothly working proprioceptive system is like shooting a movie with a handheld camera—the picture will be jumpy, sometimes nauseatingly so, and it may make quick switches and cuts that can be disorienting.

Feeling Topsy-Turvy

Also disorienting is any effort to make sense of what you see when you don't know which way is up. Poor proprioceptive and vestibular processing can get in the way of your child's ability to understand how high a slide is, how far away the ground is from the top of a teeter-totter, or how quickly cars are coming. Your child may seem excessively fearful, or essentially fearless, depending on how the messages from her joints and her center of gravity mesh with the messages from her eyes. If you find yourself saying, "Look! Can't you see it's safe?" or "Watch out! Can't you see it's dangerous?" to your child again and again, be aware that looking and watching may be the least of it. What he sees isn't worth believing if it's not the whole picture.

Children who have trouble with the proprioceptive sense aren't able to judge the distance between their bodies and the objects around them. If your child is walking into walls, hitting himself with doors, or walking too close to swing sets, it may not be a case of inattentiveness or poor vision, but of body awareness.

Lights and Colors

A certain amount of light is necessary for eyes to do their job, but different amounts of light may affect children differently. If your child is easily overstimulated by visual input, bright lights or moving lights may be excessively distracting. It may be difficult for him to concentrate in a room with a flickering overhead light or to calm down in a room that's overly bright. Dimmed lights may be calming and comforting for kids with sensory integration problems, and colored lights can also have a soothing effect. When you're looking into things that might be causing your child to be agitated or distracted, consider lighting as a potential problem.

Look out for glare as a possible distraction or discomfort for your child. Do windows let in too much light, and does that light hit your child in an uncomfortable way? Putting a shade on windows, or moving your child's desk to a spot where glare is not a factor, can lessen the problem your child has with too-bright light. If bright sunlight makes her squint, gives her headaches, or causes her eyes to water when she's outside, invest in a well-made pair of childproof sunglasses.

Colors can also be overstimulating for your child. Bright hues may be overwhelming if your child has trouble filtering out excess visual information, or motivating if your child needs a lot of input to get the message. You may find your child can fall asleep or calm himself more easily in a room with subdued colors and be more alert in a room that uses color to draw attention to important areas. Simple, bold contrasts between colors can be helpful in giving your child an idea of where things begin and end and what the distance is between them. Tune in to your child's color preferences and use them to help him maintain a good balance between over- and understimulation.

Essential

Natural light or regular light bulbs will be more comfortable for children with visual sensitivities than fluorescent lighting. While you may not have the ability to change the lights used in your child's school, let the teacher know that the lights may distract him. She may be able to turn the lights off if your child is acting up.

Too Busy, Too Boring

You may have noticed that certain rooms or certain environments make your child more overactive or stressed out than others. Take a look and see if you can find any consistency among these particular settings. Sometimes a room with too much visual stimulation can make it impossible for a child with visual processing problems to concentrate. Teachers often find that these children learn better in an uncluttered space.

It's important, though, not to remove all items of visual interest from the environment. Very young children in particular need some variety in order to learn to distinguish shapes, colors, movement, and interactions. Sensory deprivation can be as harmful as sensory overstimulation, and it is a particular concern for children who spend a long time in institutional settings, whether foreign orphanages or day care centers. Monitor your child's attention level to find the right balance between an environment that's too busy and one that's not busy enough.

The Forest and the Trees

Picking out the most important thing from a busy background pattern may be a problem for your child. He may pick out completely different details than the one you want him to find, or he may become so overwhelmed by all the detail that he can't distinguish anything at all. Games and puzzles that involve picking out a particular item from a large field of items—word search puzzles, "Where's Waldo"–style drawings, jigsaw puzzles—may be baffling to your child. Finding you in a crowded room of adults may be just as difficult.

This is an area in which you will want to give your child lots of supervision and guidance. Simplify as much as possible. Use color to highlight the one most important thing. Use your voice as a guide, or do things hand-over-hand with your child.

Who Made This Big Mess?

You'd expect children with problems processing visual information to keep their own environment neat. Yet your child's room might charitably be described as a disaster area. She may be telling the truth when she says she doesn't notice the mess or can't find a way to clean it up. If she doesn't see detail well or is unable to plan out a series of steps to complete an activity, she may not have much of a clue as to how to put things away.

Make things easier for your child, and yourself, by keeping a number of large storage baskets in your child's room and helping him to put toys in them every night. Talk him through the relatively uncomplicated task of putting one item at a time into one container. Help out to give him a model of what to do. Depending on your own personal tolerance for mess, you can help enough to get the job done, or you can let your child have a space that's less than tidy, but comfortable.

Attack of the Math Problems

If your child does well with math but balks at a sheet of math problems, take a good look at that page. Do the problems run together in tight rows and columns? It may be that the effect is visually overwhelming to your child, to the extent that she would rather be punished for missing homework than deal with a bewildering array of numbers. When problems are too close together, your child with visual processing problems may not be able to tell which numbers go with which problems, and she may make mistakes because she's adding or subtracting the wrong things.

Alert!

Math problems that involve borrowing or carrying over can add to the mess of a too-tight paper. Draw boxes above the problem to contain these little digits, or copy the problems to another sheet of paper with more space all around each problem. Watch as your child works to make sure he doesn't lose track.

To see if this might be what's going on with your child, cut a window out of a piece of paper, just big enough to let one problem show through, and place it over the first problem on the page. See if your child responds better with just one set of figures to work out at a time. You can also try putting a piece of paper under one row of problems so that she sees just those but not the rest of the worksheet. Folding the worksheet to expose just one row or column at a time is another option. Experiment until you find a combination that works for your child.

Standardized Confusion

Standardized tests, with their problems on one sheet and answer bubbles on another, can present a real challenge to children with visual perception problems. Picking the right bubble from a sea of little circles—selecting the right row to go with the problem, the right column to go with the answer—is a visual challenge.

Encourage your child to put a piece of paper under each row of bubbles as he goes along to make sure the line coordinates to the problem, and to take his time and match the letter answers to the proper bubble. Do some practice sessions at home before tests come up at school and see where your child is having problems.

There aren't a lot of accommodations allowed in standardized testing, but if your child has an IEP, she should be able to get extra time to complete the exam. Children with this accommodation are often brought to a different room than their classmates, with fewer students and a teacher who can provide small amounts of assistance.

Out of Shape

Math problems that involve matching shapes, identifying shapes from different perspectives, or fitting shapes together may also be challenging for your child with sensory integration problems. The discrimination needed to visualize a shape and to understand how those shapes change in appearance as they change position may be something your child will develop later than his peers. If your child doesn't integrate proprioceptive and vestibular information well with visual input, it can be very hard to understand things with multiple dimensions; things are just what they look like and nothing more.

Essential

Your child's self-esteem may be damaged by difficulties that are hard for her peers and herself to understand. Be her biggest cheerleader, and make sure she knows that her struggles are not her fault—and that problems with sensory reception, interpretation, and integration have nothing to do with intelligence.

Money is often a difficult concept, too, particularly if it is being taught with worksheets showing drawings of coins. There may not be enough visual detail for your child to distinguish drawings of each coin from the others, and he'll make mistakes based on misreading. Even actual coins can be hard to tell apart. Your child may require a lot of practice and a variety of different strategies to finally get it.

The more you can demonstrate these concepts for your child in ways that involve other senses, the more likely it will be that she will understand them. But the understanding may take a long time to really stick. Be patient and tolerant.

Overstimulating Reading

Just as lines and lines of math problems can run together for your child, lines and lines of words can be intimidating, too. The problem might not be as noticeable when your child is younger and books have bigger print, whiter pages, and larger spaces, but as she moves on in school and reading material gets more complex, she may very easily lose her way.

One solution is similar to that used for math worksheets. Use a bookmark or piece of paper to underline one line at a time. The store Really Good Stuff, online at *www.reallygoodstuff.com*, is a teacher supply store that offers bookmarks with clear yellow film along one edge to highlight a single line of text, and these may also be useful to improve visual processing. If necessary, a window can be cut out of an index card and used to highlight a few words at a time. Large type books might also be a good option to try.

Reading Aloud

For children who find the sight of words overwhelming, the sound of words is a useful alternative. Don't stop reading to your child once he's old enough to read for himself. You can try taking turns with your child, reading one page and letting him read the next, or alternating paragraphs. Use a bookmark or piece of paper to underline the lines of type as you read so that your child gets the connection between the written word and the heard one.

Try reading anything your child finds overstimulating or distracting into a tape recorder so she can have the extra dimension of auditory input to help her sort through it. This can be helpful with textbooks, reading books, class notes, and research material. You may be able to set your computer to read the words off of Web sites to guide your child through those busy and content-packed pages. It may also help your child to instruct her to read things out loud to herself when she's studying in private.

The Write Stuff

Words in print may not be the only problem for your child—printing words can be tough as well. Difficulty judging the distance between lines on the page can cause words and letters to bob around, while difficulty judging the distance between letters and words can make your child's writing a jumble. If your child can't see what's wrong but only hears people tell him again and again that he has to be neater, he's likely to feel frustrated and give up. Instead, try increasing the sensory input of the job by using paper with raised lines so your child can feel the pencil hitting a boundary. Paper with larger spaces between lines and thicker lines might help as well.

Professional catalogs with products for occupational therapists are good places to find writing tools for your child, like paper with lines that are raised, spread apart, or shaded to help your child see where to write. The following three offer products online:

- Therapro, at *www.theraproducts.com*
- Therapy Shoppe, at *www.therapyshoppe.com*
- Special Kids Zone, at *www.specialkidszone.com*

Consider allowing your child alternatives to writing by hand. A portable AlphaSmart computer is an accommodation that may be available to your child for taking notes in class. Some schools provide them for students, but you can also buy one direct from the manufacturer's Web site, at *www.alphasmart.com*. Learning to type is sometimes a good alternative to spending stressful time on printing and handwriting. A program like Read, Write & Type!, available online at *www.readwritetype.com*, will help your child pick up keyboard skills and also strengthen phonics awareness.

Avoiding Eye Contact

Adults expect eye contact from children. If your child won't give it, you probably assume she's not listening or is being disrespectful. You say, "Look at me!" when what you really want is for your child to listen, and you're likely to grab her chin and force eye contact if you don't get it. But for children with sensory integration problems involving the visual sense, looking into another person's eyes can be such an intense experience that they can't pay attention to anything else.

If what you want is your child's ears, don't worry so much about his eyes. You may have better luck saying "Listen to me" if that's indeed what you want to happen. Your child may be able to look at you or listen to you, but not both.

CHAPTER 10

The Auditory Sense

How is it possible that the same child who cowers in abject terror at the sound of a car alarm or a vacuum cleaner can completely ignore your voice when you're calling her to dinner? Your child may have trouble processing the sounds that come to her through her auditory, or hearing, sense—trouble identifying the source and urgency of a sound, trouble with the way the vibrations from sound make her feel, trouble picking out an important sound from a whole lot of noise.

Hearing Challenges

Next to vision, hearing is the sense most called upon by parents and teachers to educate, warn, and discipline. You expect your child to listen and understand when you help with homework, explain how to do something, or issue a command. Your child needs to understand language to make that happen and be able to pay attention. But on a very basic level, he needs to be able to correctly interpret the sound waves that come in through his ears. He needs to be able to pick your words out from other noise in the room. He needs to interpret differences in the pitch and volume of your voice to understand when you're angry or concerned. He needs to tune out distracting information from other senses. He needs to feel basic comfort with his body's position and balance to be able to even concentrate on auditory information. That's a lot of work.

Fact

Like the auditory sense, the vestibular sense starts in the ear—the inner ear, where three fluid-filled canals pass on messages to the brain about the body's position and the pull of gravity. They help you stand up straight, stay on your feet, and keep your balance.

Children with sensory integration disorder may not be able to do that work very efficiently. Your child may actually have trouble with processing information that comes in through the auditory sense, reacting in extreme ways to certain volumes, pitches, or vibrations of sound. Or her reactions to the things she hears may reflect problems with other sensory systems. An occupational therapist will probably address your child's sensory processing problems with activities that focus on the tactile, proprioceptive, and vestibular systems, since strengthening those areas often improves processing for the auditory system as well. Either way, though, understanding the problem your child may have with sound will help you judge behavioral reactions and make her more comfortable.

Too Loud, Too Soft

One of your first clues that your child has a sensory integration problem may be his reaction to loud noises. Maybe he screams and covers his ears when you vacuum. Maybe he's terrified beyond all comfort by the sound of an ambulance passing your house or a car alarm outside. Maybe his teacher reports that he behaved inappropriately during a fire drill or couldn't pay attention after that loud alarm went off. Maybe the sound of construction machinery, of jackhammers or big trucks backing up, seems not just distracting but painful to him.

Most kids are able to function when they hear a fire alarm, and they might run to the window in excitement when they hear an ambulance or police siren. An efficient auditory system filters out some of the noise so that it doesn't become overwhelming or painful. Reassuring information from the other senses—the sight of adults going about their business, the sound of a teacher giving instructions for a fire drill, the feeling that their bodies are moving normally, the lack of threatening smells or sights—modifies the alarming nature of the sound.

No Relief in Earshot

If your child is overly sensitive to auditory information, though, none of these comforts may be available to her. She may get the full blast of sound with no filtering, and her sensory system may not be able to process much else with all that input coming in. She may miss reassuring words or sights because her brain is too busy dealing with the sound, or she may have trouble processing the information from those other senses that would help tone down the auditory information.

For a child with sensory integration disorder, loud noises can cause a complete breakdown of the system and provoke a flight-or-fight response. Therapy and strategies to improve your child's sensory integration will gradually reduce his reactions to these scary sounds. But what do you do in the meantime, when you can't run the vacuum without a screaming tantrum?

Softening the Blow

One thing that helps is advance warning. For sounds that you know are coming, give your child some notice. Let her find a place far away from the noise, or put on headphones to provide some protection. Earplugs may also be an option, if the feel of them doesn't make her as uncomfortable as the noise. If your child's teacher can give you advance notice of planned fire drills, talk through them with your child and give her some ideas of what to do. If there's no way to keep her behavior from being a problem during fire drills and your schedule is flexible, ask if you can keep her home on days when one is planned. This won't be an issue forever—with the help of therapy and age, your child will eventually be able to tolerate the alarm. In the meantime, sometimes avoidance is best.

When avoidance is impossible, you can still help by giving your child some strong, physical input to offset the overwhelming auditory onslaught. A hard hug might help. Pushing down on your child's shoulders might give some strong comforting input to muscles and joints. Rocking might be comforting. When the noise stops, try talking right to your child to tell her that everything is all right. Just understanding that her reaction is normal for her and not a behavior problem will help limit the extent of the trauma from the loud sound.

Essential

During calmer times, talk to your child about what noises bother her and why. Share with her some sounds and other sensations that particularly bother you. If you can discuss the ways frightening sensory experiences make you both feel, it will make your child feel less different and give you some ideas for helping.

Hear No Evil

While some children with sensory integration disorder react with fright or pain to loud sounds, others seem to miss them entirely. If your child is undersensitive to auditory information, he may miss softer sounds just as you'd expect, but he'll also let loud sounds pass him by without notice. You may be amazed to see him working peacefully in a loud and distracting room, or to find that an alarm clock loud enough to wake him is an impossible dream. It's nice to not have a child who overreacts to every bell and whistle; the downside is that, just as your child can't hear noise made by others, he can't hear the noise he makes, either. He'll talk too loud, drum too hard, stomp too firmly, turn the volume all the way up, and have no idea why anybody would be bothered. Keep in mind, while deciding on a response to this behavior, that he thinks he's already being quiet.

Imperfect Pitch

It's not just the volume of sounds that can make them painful and frightening for some children with sensory integration disorder. Tones that are shrilly high or bone-rattlingly low can be just as distressing. This may become particularly apparent as children get old enough to want to go to rock concerts or school dances and are reduced to tears by the way the overloud bass tones make them feel. Going to the movies in a theater where the sound is loud and poorly balanced may also make your child feel fearful or nauseated for no apparent reason.

Sounds with very low or very high frequency are felt as much as they're heard, and they affect the vestibular system—which regulates your child's sense of balance and equilibrium—as much as the auditory system. A listening therapy approach that involves exposing children to carefully controlled sounds on the ends of the frequency spectrum in an effort to increase tolerance works to strengthen the processing and integration of information from the vestibular sense. Other forms of sensory integration therapy will also help improve your child's tolerance for high or low sounds.

Until your child's system is able to tolerate very high or low sounds, a pair of earplugs or headphones may be a good investment. Plugs designed for hunters, to protect their ears from the sharp sounds of gunfire, are available in sporting goods stores and should be helpful in filtering out the sorts of sounds that will distress your child.

Auditory Discrimination

Although loud, high, or low noises are a challenge for kids with sensory integration disorder, it's probably not something they have to deal with on a constant basis. Picking the important sounds out of a field of noise, however, is likely to be a problem that plagues them every day, throughout the day. And unlike reactions caused by bothersome noises, problems with auditory discrimination aren't traumatic and noticeable. While you can't ignore your child's screaming fit over a car alarm, you might easily ignore his inability to distinguish your voice above the din and accuse him of simply not listening.

Lost in the Shuffle

Far from not listening, a child with sensory integration disorder may be listening too much, or *to* too much. While most children can tune out extra noise, if your child is overly sensitive to information coming in through his auditory system, he may hear everything that's going on with equal volume and urgency. Speak to him in a room that already has a television going, a video game playing, a stereo blasting, another conversation or two on the side, and your voice may well get lost in the aural onslaught. Or your child may be so overwhelmed by the sound that he shuts down and refuses to deal with any auditory input at all. Either way, you're going to have to use something other than just verbal direction to get your child's attention and compliance.

How you get your child's attention will depend in part on what his other sensory integration issues are. Sometimes, tapping your child on the shoulder or back will let him know it's time to listen, but not if tactile sensitivity makes that seem a threat. And insisting on eye contact isn't an option if your visually sensitive child is bothered by it.

Auditory discrimination will also be a problem if your child is undersensitive to auditory information. She may not get enough details from her hearing sense to make out what is going on around her, or she may be too distracted by more urgent information coming in from other senses to care much about it. Deciphering language in an accurate way takes a great deal of auditory finesse, and if your child can't easily distinguish between the sound of different phonemes, following anything more than clear and simple commands may seem more trouble than it's worth, especially if there are other things going on that are easier to figure out.

Something Worth Listening To

If your child just experiences your voice as one of a competing jumble of noise, or a rumble amid the static of poorly processed sound, you're going to have to make an effort to rise above the rest. Try to get your child's attention before you speak—no yelling across a noisy room for this kid. Turn other sounds down if you can, put yourself in your child's field of vision if possible, touch your child or take him by the shoulders if tactile sensitivities don't make that a whole new problem, or devise a hand signal or other visual clue that tells your child it's time to listen. For the child with tactile sensitivity, firm pressure with an approach from the front rather than from the back, where the child can't see you, is often more acceptable.

Be sure to let your child's teacher know that your child will listen best in a room that doesn't have a lot of other auditory input going on. If a certain amount of other noise is unavoidable in the classroom, your child may benefit from having an aide who can keep her focused. You might also request that your child receive written versions of all information that is given orally in class. Most of all, the people who work with your child need to know that she is not ignoring them on purpose.

Watch Your Tone of Voice

The right tone of voice may help your child tune in to what you're saying and distinguish your words from the sounds around him. The wrong tone of voice may add to the load of stress that comes with too much information flooding the auditory sense. Tuning into the sounds that your child finds intriguing and the ones he finds stressful can help you communicate without confrontation.

Whispering, for example, is a surprisingly good way to get your child's attention. He'll have to stop and really listen to understand what you have to say. Other attention-grabbers include goofy motions, funny voices, and silly statements. Television and video games offer endless variety to your child; to compete, you may want to do the same.

Emotion in Motion

It may seem to you that the only way to get your child's attention is to get angry. The volume and pitch of your voice when you're mad may indeed raise a reaction. Whether it's the reaction you want, and whether you'll be able to respond appropriately, is another matter entirely. A child who has been ignoring you because the sound around her is overwhelming may be thrown completely into overload by the strong emotion in your voice. She may have no idea why you're so upset, since she hasn't been ignoring you on purpose, and feel attacked by your angry voice. You'll likely spend more time calming the both of you down than you would have if you'd kept your temper.

Make homework a "whatever works" situation. If your child is able to study effectively with the television on, allow that to continue as long as the work does. Although you might feel that you would be too distracted in that situation, your child may have a whole different way of processing; it may even make him more alert.

A child who hasn't responded because of undersensitivity to auditory information may be equally baffled by the sudden burst of anger being directed her way and will likely give you a good argument in return. To her mind, your reaction is surprising and all out of proportion; to your mind, her reaction may seem to be a whole lot of attitude. Nothing good can come of this particular interaction.

Good Boy!

If at all possible, try to keep emotion out of your voice. A good tone of voice for getting your child's attention might be the same one you'd use for your dog: sharp but not judgmental, commanding but not unkind. Keep the wording similar, too. The fewer words for your child to figure out, the better. Once you have your child's attention and have helped him tune out other information and tune in to you, you may be able to go into more detail. But for starters, follow the "Sit! Stay!" model.

Getting the Message Through

The most effective ways to get your child to listen to what you have to say need to happen before you even start to speak, or know you're going to. Changing the environment to make it easier for your child to listen is first and foremost among them. If you know that your child has trouble dealing with lots of different sounds at once, or picking out your important message from a lot of unimportant ones, then do everything you can to limit the amount of auditory overkill. Reduce the number of different sounds he has to deal with. If your child is easily overstimulated by noise, keep things quiet when he has to concentrate on what he hears or reads. If your child is understimulated by noise, on the other hand, some music playing while he studies may actually help him concentrate.

Giving your child lots of good input to his muscles and joints and his sense of balance and equilibrium will also most likely improve his ability to receive, interpret, and integrate auditory input. The proprioceptive and vestibular senses have an impact on all the others, and strengthening them will increase your child's feeling of well-being, decrease his need to concentrate on making his body feel comfortable, and integrate all the senses more effectively. You may find that your child can concentrate better after jumping on a trampoline, being wrapped tightly in a blanket, or having a good long session on a swing. He may even be able to listen better while he's doing those things, so try your "How was school?" conversation on a playground instead of in the car or around the dinner table.

As with every other sensory challenge, knowing how your child's sensory system works and providing coping strategies can make your child more willing to listen to you. Children with sensory integration problems often feel that no one understands the way their bodies work, and they have to follow their own instincts and interests over anyone else's. The more you can convince your child that you understand and have ways to help, the more you will make yours a voice to be heard.

CHAPTER 11

The Gustatory and Olfactory Senses

While you might not immediately realize that your child sees or feels or hears things differently than you do, you can probably come up with a handful of things off the top of your head that he loves or hates to eat or smell. What do you do if he won't eat anything but the blandest food? How do you handle it when he can't stand the way you smell? Your child with sensory integration disorder may have problems with these two senses that go over and above mere preferences.

Taste and Smell [illegible]er

It's hard to address eithe[illegible]ually, since they're so closely tied together. B[illegible]e taste buds and the olfactory nerves [illegible] in the environment and send message[illegible]ch interprets them as tastes and smells. Thos[illegible] only detect four different flavors: sour, bitter, salty, [illegible] the other rich rewards of flavorful foods—as much as three-[illegible]s of what we experience as "flavor"—are provided by the olfactory component.

It's not surprising that the sense of smell provides so much more input than the sense of taste, since the latter concentrates on just four variations and the former can detect some 400,000. As you've no doubt found if you've had a bad head cold, the loss of smell means the loss of most of what tastes good about food. You may

also have had the experience of smelling something so strongly you could taste it, too. The proximity of the nose and mouth and the fact that both taste and smell respond to chemicals in the environment cause a great deal of overlap.

Sense of "Cool" and "Sting"

Smell and taste aren't the only things that contribute to your experience of flavor. Another type of nerve that reacts to chemicals, called the common chemical sense, occupies the same territory as olfactory and gustatory nerve endings, and is also found in the membranes around the eyes. These nerves record sensations that aren't quite smell, aren't quite taste, but add to your perception of both. Think of the coolness you feel when smelling a menthol chest rub, the sting of sour lemon that makes you squint your eyes when it's on your tongue, or the heat of a super-spicy salsa.

Fact

Together, the sense of smell and taste plus the common chemical sense are called the chemical sensing system, or chemosensation. These make up the only senses that operate through interaction with chemical substances, as opposed to things like light waves, sound waves, or physical contact.

Taste and Memory

Chemosensation gives you your physical perception of flavor, but there's one more element that enters into your sensory enjoyment of food and odors: memory. When the brain interprets the input from the gustatory and olfactory nerves, it interprets them with a strong emphasis on past experiences of those sensations. Apple pie doesn't just smell good, it makes you feel the warmth and comfort of your mother's kitchen. These memories may not work on a conscious level, but they bring depth and emotion to otherwise straightforward chemical reactions.

That's one reason why you have to be so careful when dealing with your child's sensory problems with taste and smell. Fighting with your child over a food or an odor creates a stressful, scary memory that will be replayed every time that sensory information gets processed, leading to more battles. Whatever you may feel you need to do to get your child enough nourishment or to function in places that may have disturbing smells, think about what kind of memory you want to create.

Avoiding Sharp Sensations

As with touch and sound and sight, if your child is oversensitive to information from his sense of taste or smell, he will have big reactions to strong sensations. Food that is intensely flavorful may overwhelm his sensory system and make him feel upset or frightened. Strong smells may be impossible to ignore, and they may keep him from being able to concentrate on anything else.

Essential

Although you may assume that things you can see will be remembered most, memories associated with smell are actually the longest lasting. They also carry with them not just factual representations of events, but the emotions that went along with them. You may find that certain smells bring back more vivid memories of childhood than anything else.

If your child strongly resists going to a particular place or has a strong negative reaction to a particular person, consider whether smell might be a factor. A heavy air freshener or powerful perfume might make a place distracting and unpleasant for her overstimulated nose. Your child may resort to disruptive behavior in an effort to be removed from an environment that has strongly unpleasant smells.

Even good smells can be a problem if they cause your child to be distracted and to think of nothing else.

Cravings for Spicy and Sour

Most parents are familiar with kids who flatly refuse to eat anything unusual, strong-flavored, spicy, or slimy. But what if your child craves sharp tastes, drinks pickle juice from the jar, or sucks on slices of lemon? He also has sensory problems and may be unable to taste much of anything if it's not smacking him in the taste buds. A child who is undersensitive to information coming in from his gustatory sense may not stop at putting strong-flavored foods in his mouth. He's liable to put nonfood items in there, too, since he won't be stopped by unpleasant tastes that indicate inedibles.

Should I worry if my child likes to eat things like dirt, crayons, or paste?

The desire or craving to eat nonfood items is called *pica*. While it is not uncommon in young children, it can be dangerous if hazardous substances such as chips of lead paint are ingested, or if items are harmful to the teeth or digestive tract. Consult your pediatrician if your child does this regularly.

To some degree, having a child with an adventurous palate can be amusing. You marvel at the sophisticated, intense, adult things she enjoys. Sour candies, you may find, are good for keeping her alert while doing homework or sitting in church. Powerfully flavored cinnamon or peppermint candies might help her keep her fingers out of her mouth or distract from other bad habits. It may be unusual for a child to enjoy sauerkraut or Brussels sprouts or raw lemons, but most often there's no harm in it.

Early Warning

Oftentimes, it's true that being undersensitive to taste isn't actively harmful. But taste and smell are part of the body's warning system that something coming into the body might be dangerous, and disarming that system can have consequences. You know that the milk is bad because it tastes sour, and you stop drinking. The bitter taste of medication tells you right away that it's not candy. If your child doesn't receive those signals at all, or at a high enough level to sound an alarm, he's in danger of eating or drinking things that can make him sick.

Similarly, a working sense of smell protects you from all sorts of dangers. A child with an inadequate response to olfactory information may not smell smoke from a fire. She may not be put off by the strong smell of cleaning chemicals and think they're good to drink. She may enjoy sniffing strong odors like glue or paint thinner because they give such a strong jolt to her sense of smell, and become ill because of it. Like a smoke alarm without a battery, an underreacting "smeller" can't sense danger and can't warn your child of it.

Another distressing odor your child may not register enough to avoid is the smell of feces. Your little one may genuinely think that stuff in his diaper is okay to play with because the smell does not disturb him. Potty training may go at a slower pace if your child doesn't notice the odor of a soiled diaper and so isn't bothered by it. Flatulence and body odor may not register either, opening your child up to ridicule from friends and schoolmates.

A Sense of Caution

Since your child who is undersensitive to taste and smell can't reliably tell what's good to eat and smell and what's not, you'll have to be extra careful in not leaving things that could be hazardous within her reach. Carefully monitor the contents of your refrigerator and cupboards. If your child is old enough to understand, talk about things like expiration dates, prescription labels, and poison warnings that will provide a visual alert when other senses aren't up to the job.

Monitor your child's own odors, too, and stress the importance of personal hygiene. When your child's in diapers, there may not be much you can do. But an older child needs to know that, while the way his body smells may not bother him, it bothers other people, and soap and deodorant are not negotiable. This may seem silly to your child, and you may have to keep close track of soap usage. A strong-smelling shower gel, if he enjoys it, may be one way to interest your child in cleanliness. It will also give you a good olfactory clue that washing has taken place.

Fact

Unlike other nerve cells, new taste and smell receptors replace old and damaged ones. Nonetheless, your sense of smell and taste does tend to fade with age, becoming weaker in your sixties. Respiratory problems, smoking, and cancer treatments can also impair the effectiveness of these chemical sensors.

And finally, although it may be fun to see your child put away foods you'd never expect him to like, be protective of his digestion and gastric health. Just because he likes it doesn't mean it's good for him. Sharp, sour, and spicy foods are fine in moderation, but if your child's tucking in large amounts of the stuff, or seems not to know when to stop, check with your pediatrician to make sure it's not going to cause any problems. His underreaction to sensory information may extend to pain, and then you'll never know when he has a bellyache.

I'm Not Eating That!

It's a classic battle of the dinner table. In this corner, wearing an apron and a determined expression, is the parent who has lovingly prepared a meal, thought through the nutrients needed, balanced and planned, and cooked and served. And in this corner, wearing a face that could break glass, is the child who absolutely, positively, unwaveringly, will not eat it. This is the sort of test of wills that rarely ends well.

Next to toilet training, eating is one of the few areas of life over which your child truly has meaningful control. You can exert emotional pressure, you can threaten and bribe, you can force a spoon between hard-set lips and teeth, but it's pretty near impossible to make your child swallow or keep food down. This is a battle in which your child holds the most important cards.

Why They Fight

Your child's reasons may seem entirely good to him. If he is overly sensitive to tastes or smells, the food may be truly unpleasant, overpowering, or nauseating to him. If he is undersensitive to the same sensations, the food may seem unappetizingly bland or even upsettingly so—being unable to taste what you're eating can be an unsettling prospect. A poor sense of smell can also make food seem unappealing, flavorful in only one dimension instead of many.

Don't forget that tactile processing problems can also have an impact on your child's willingness to eat. Children who are oversensitive to touch may find foods to be hotter in temperature, chewier in consistency, drier, or more displeasing in texture than you might imagine. If your child is undersensitive to touch, there are foods he may have trouble eating neatly or quickly, and the memory of a difficult dining experience may ride along with the smell of the stuff to discourage future attempts. Problems handling a fork efficiently can make foods like rice or pasta seem like a bad bet to your child, and spooning soup or wiggly Jell-O can be similarly dangerous.

Eat It or Else?

As a parent, you do have the responsibility to make sure your child gets the nutrition he needs to be healthy. But there's a pretty wide variety of ways to make that happen, and chances are you can find one that suits your child's strong sensory needs. You may have wondered many times whether your child can't or whether she won't? Ask that question now about the ways in which you do or don't accommodate her sensory integration difficulties. Is it that you can't provide healthy meals that suit her sensitivities, or that you won't? If the answer's the latter, you're part of the problem, and you can be part of the solution.

Think of it as you would a food allergy: difficult, challenging, needing research and planning, but not a personal affront. If your child were allergic to dairy products, for example, you would have to work hard to get her enough calcium for her growing bones. You might wish it weren't so, but it wouldn't appear to you that your child was just doing it to throw her weight around. Approach your child's sensory integration needs in the same way. She didn't choose them, and you all have to live with them. Working together instead of at odds will make things run more smoothly.

The Compassionate Cook

That doesn't mean you have to be a short-order chef, making something different for your sense-impaired child at every turn. It does mean that you'll consider his preferences when planning meals for the whole family, just as you undoubtedly consider your own. When necessary, allow substitutions—let your child choose crunchy raw carrots instead of soft cooked ones, or vice versa. Try to involve your child in the shopping for and preparing of food. Whatever you can do to keep mealtime from becoming a battleground will eventually help your child eat more and try more.

If it helps, teach your child about nutrition and ask her what she would suggest for making sure she gets what she needs. Your child may be learning about this in school, too, and for some kids what the teacher says holds more weight. Regardless, share your concerns and work together to find some choices that will be acceptable to both of you. Understanding why you're insisting on certain foods may help your child find a way to compromise. It also gives her good practice in decision-making and informed choices that will suit her well as she gets older and has to be making dining choices for herself.

Scented Soaps and Shampoos

When your child flies into a fit over hair washing, it's likely a case of fear over being tipped backward due to bad processing of the vestibular, or balance, sense. But another possibility to consider is the product you're rubbing onto his wriggly head. Perfumed shampoos and other hair-care products are often overpoweringly scented. For a child who is overly sensitive to smell, the odor can be particularly overwhelming.

Essential

Unlike most other senses, the sense of smell doesn't turn off when you sleep. Because it's needed to warn you of dangers such as fire, this sense stays on the alert while you slumber. For children who are overly sensitive, that may mean that alarming smells can interfere with sleep.

An unscented or mildly scented product, such as baby shampoo, is one good alternative. At the very least, let your child smell a variety of products and choose one that he enjoys. Use the same caution with soaps and body wash, and as your child gets older, be aware of this potential problem with lotions, deodorants, and acne products. Don't forget about the hand soap you have by the sink that your child uses—if it's not acceptable to your child's sense of smell, those hands are likely to go unwashed.

As you're monitoring soaps and other products for their upsetting odor potential, be sure to include laundry detergent and fabric softener in your investigations. The way these laundry products make clothes, towels, and sheets smell can be a source of distress for your child. Unscented versions of these products should be available and may be a better choice. If you or a family member enjoys the scents and doesn't want to do without them, wash your child's clothing separately. It may seem like a lot of trouble, but it's not as much trouble as dealing with a child who won't wear a garment that smells unpleasant to her.

Cleaning products, room fresheners, laundry detergents, candles, carpet deodorizers—anything that has a strong scent may upset your sensitive child without his even knowing what's doing it. Your undersensitive child, on the other hand, may load up on scents without being aware that he has a cloud of smells surrounding him. Too much scented lotion, perfume, hair products, aftershave, or other items designed to smell nice in moderation may be a problem for your older child or teen. Provide some advice and guidance when he goes overboard.

Smoke and Other Environmental Hazards

Even a person with normal sensory integration can be bothered by the smell of cigarette smoke. It gets into every bit of clothing and hair and furniture and lingers long after the smoker has left the room. If you have a child who is sensitive to smells and you're a smoker, consider this one more good reason to quit. The odors may bother your child in ways she can't articulate, and the crabbiness that results is the side effect.

If your child is undersensitive to smell, you may have to alert her when dangerous odors are in the air. Steer her away from cigarette smoke or car exhaust, beware when cleaning with bleach or other products with noxious fumes, and help her know when a litter box needs changing or a room has some bad food hidden somewhere under the clutter. Just because your child doesn't notice these odors doesn't mean they can't be dangerous to her.

CHAPTER 12

The Vestibular Sense

Am I standing up or sitting down? Which way is down? Am I standing on my feet or on my head? These are questions the vestibular sense answers constantly, without bothering your conscious mind about it. Located in the inner ear, this system detects such important facts as balance, gravity, body position, and distance. When it's working, your child moves confidently around home and school and playground. When the vestibular sense is unreliable, however, every step, sway, and slip can leave your child convinced that he's falling off the face of the earth.

Keeping Your Balance

The "vestibule" in vestibular refers to the area of the inner ear where a trio of fluid-filled passageways resides: the semicircular canals, the utricle, and the saccule. As you move, lean, tilt, or spin, the fluid in those passageways flows over tiny hairs, sending signals to the brain about how your body is oriented. With that information, properly received and processed, your brain can make important determinations that make you sure and secure in your movements.

When you spin around, the liquid takes some time to settle down and give an accurate reading of your position—thus your dizziness and disorientation. Imagine feeling like that all the time, and you may begin to get an idea of what your child with vestibular processing problems is going through.

Balance is one of the most basic requirements for comfortable movement, activity, and thinking. It's the basis of developmental tasks like sitting, standing, and walking. Without good balance, things like throwing or catching or kicking a ball can become threatening endeavors. Standing on one foot or hopping or skipping are out of the question, as are games like jump rope or hopscotch. Poor equilibrium can cause nausea and headaches and at the very least make it difficult to concentrate on anything other than keeping your bearings.

Fact

Also in the inner ear is the cochlea, a snail-shell-shaped structure that is responsible for hearing. Like the semicircular canals, utricle, and saccule, the cochlea has tiny hairs that conduct sensations to the brain, but in this case they are interpreted as sounds. The auditory nerve carries information from the cochlea.

Dealing with a Spinning World

If your child is overly sensitive to information coming in through the vestibular sense, she may have a hard time making the world stand still. Slight changes in body position and angle feel like big swoops, and she'll need extra time to adjust. Big changes in position and angle, in turn, feel like a roller coaster loop. Your child with problems receiving, processing, or integrating vestibular information may resist any activity that involves even the slightest degree of precarious balance. Sometimes that will be obvious, as when she fights against going backward for a hair wash or becomes frightened in a dentist's chair. Sometimes it will show itself in clumsiness, an inability to judge distances, or a refusal to engage in simple tasks like playing on a jungle gym. And sometimes it may affect your child in less noticeable ways, like a quiet preference for safe and sedentary activities.

Children who are bad at sports and playground games are often stigmatized by both their playmates and the adults in their lives. Grown-ups may feel the child is not trying hard enough, is messing up on purpose, or is being lazy. You can be a powerful asset to your child just by believing that her problems with sports are not her fault.

"Safe" and "sedentary" aren't words you'll use much if your child is underresponsive to vestibular information. Unlike the child who feels every small movement as a big disruption, your child may need big movements to feel even a small amount of vestibular input. He'll swing higher, jump harder, sway wildly, rock vigorously, and sometimes even smack his body into people or things to get a good reading of where he is in relation to the ground and other objects.

Overinformed, Underinformed

If you're having trouble grasping the difference between getting too much information from the vestibular system and not enough, or understanding why either would be a problem, consider this comparison. Being oversensitive to vestibular input is like having a car with the most amazingly comprehensive and informative computer system imaginable. It tells you everything, including how fast you're going, how far and in what direction you're traveling, how hot or cold it is outside—anything you could possibly want to know and quite a bit you don't. And far more than just offering that information, it sets off lights and alarms and blizzards of additional information every time you turn the wheel or tap the accelerator. In and of itself, each piece of information is useful, and even the alerts may be helpful. But if there are too many, they become worse than useless—they make it impossible for you to absorb any information at all, or even to drive with the necessary concentration.

Being undersensitive to vestibular information, on the other hand, is like having an old clunker of a car in which nothing much works except the engine. You may be speeding without knowing it, careening around mountain roads or high bridges or roadside hazards with the eagerness that comes from not knowing what can happen. The only time you can be really sure of what's going on is when you go fast enough to make your teeth rattle, go over bumps hard enough to hit your head on the ceiling, or crash so hard your wheels come out from under you. As for the rest, what you don't know isn't going to slow you down much.

Playground Perils

The divide between information overload and information deficit is particularly easy to see at the playground. Watch your child as he plays. What sort of activities does he like? What does he avoid? Do you have to coax him to participate, or follow him around for fear he'll hurt himself? Does he quake at the site of the top of the slide or push other children away in his eagerness to dash to the top? Playgrounds are great places to observe your child's particular sensory strengths and weaknesses. In some cases, it can also be a good site for some fun, impromptu therapy.

Swinging and Spinning

Depending on your child's vestibular processing profile, hitting the swings at the playground may be a fearful experience or an absolutely joyous one. Many children who need strong vestibular input to feel at home in their bodies crave swinging, and they can do it for long periods of time with complete concentration. If this is your child, taking him out for a good swinging session will be a great way to calm him before a potentially trying activity or help him unwind after one.

Other children, however, may find swinging intensely stressful. They may be terrified by being tipped backward as they swing upward or forward as they swing back down. Your child may constantly feel that she's falling or being hurtled to the ground in a hurtful way. An occupational therapist may work with your child to gently introduce swinging on a flat platform or inner tube. Since there's rarely a reason why your child has to swing, other than your feeling that it's just something a kid's supposed to do, don't push it if it upsets your child.

If you have something important to talk to your child about, try doing it during or after a strenuous session that involves lots of good hard vestibular input. He may not seem to be paying attention to you, but he will receive and retain the information much better if his balance and movement needs are being met.

The same holds true for playground merry-go-rounds, those flat round platforms that can be pushed until they're spinning quickly. That dizzying experience may feel great for some kids, scary for others. If your child falls into the latter category, don't assume that making her face her fear and try it, again and again, will solve the problem. Occupational therapy with a sensory integration approach that targets vestibular-proprioceptive input may help the problem and make the motion more tolerable. All forcing the activity will do is make your child miserable, embarrass her in front of her playmates, and convince her that she needs to manage all her sensory needs because you cannot be trusted. No little ride is worth that.

Ups and Downs

A child who overreacts to information from his vestibular system may react to your invitation to climb to the top of a slide as though you'd asked him to step out of the window of a skyscraper and slide down the side. Heights seem higher to him, ladders more precarious, and slides full of more swoops and whoops than his sensitive system can stand. He may resist all efforts to get him to the top, or, once there and faced with such a scary drop, he may remain frozen. What seems silly and harmless to you feels hazardous and harmful to him. Pushing, pulling, and threatening is only likely to raise his stress level and make him hang on harder.

Essential

If your child likes spinning, try buying a spinning disk he can sit on, spin on, and get some of that good sensation at home any time he needs it. You may be able to find one at your local toy store, or you can order a Dizzy Disc from an occupational therapy catalog like Sensory Comfort (online at *www.sensorycomfort.com*).

No such fear is felt by the child with an underreactive vestibular system. He'll be the kid standing up on the top of the slide, flying down head first, or hanging off the side. With his vestibular system giving out no particular information about how high, how far, and how fast he's going, jumping around ten feet up isn't much different than jumping around on the ground. Whooshing down the slide gives his system a nice feeling of gravity that he doesn't often get. Landing hard, on his feet or on his hands, gives a nice earthbound jolt.

You'll note similar reactions—fearfulness or fearlessness—on any playground equipment that involves heights. Your oversensitive child may resist crawling to the top of the jungle gym, hanging from ladder bars, or soaring to the top of the teeter-totter. She may find a safe activity like a sandbox or a low platform with a steering wheel or games and stick to that. Your undersensitive child will use the top bar on the jungle gym as a balance beam, hang upside-down from the bars, and work the teeter-totter so hard she thumps other kids off of it. She may get such a rush from those activities that she resists leaving and begs for more.

Instant Therapy

Giving the vestibular system lots of strong information may help it work better and learn more. For your oversensitive child, try to find small, nonthreatening ways to expand his comfort with movement. Hold him on the swing, or put him in one for a smaller child that has a seat belt. Find a park with a low slide and hold him all the way up and down. Hold his hand or shoulders while he walks on a balance beam. Without forcing your child to do anything he's uncomfortable with, try to slowly expand that comfort zone.

Bending Over Backward

Just as some kids fear the feeling of tipping backward on a swing, they may panic at being bent backward in other settings—during hair washing, for example. When your child screams and fusses over having her hair wet or rinsed, it may be hard to know what the problem is: hatred of water? slimy shampoo? perfumed shampoo smell? cleanliness? Depending on your child's particular sensory sensitivities, it could be any of these things. Or it may just seem like pure obstinacy, a tantrum without reason. But it may feel to your child, when you bend her over backward, that she is losing all connection with the ground. The fact that her eyes are looking the opposite direction than her body is going keeps visual information from being available to counter the vestibular panic, and the fact that the ears are underwater adds auditory oddness to it. All in all, it's an unsettling experience for your child.

It's also one that's easily avoided. If your child hates being tipped in this way, there's no need to fight it. Consider ways to let him stay upright. Pour buckets of water over his head to wet and rinse; use a shower spray nozzle; or have your child shower instead of taking a bath. Looking for a compromise respects your child's preferences and can save a lot of tantrums. If your child is going to get his hair cut at a salon that normally washes the hair first, be sure to wash it at home before going and ask the stylist to skip that step.

Other backward maneuvers may not be so easily avoided. If your child needs to be tipped back for a dental or eye exam, be sure to let the doctor know that it may be distressing. Giving your child a demonstration of how the chair tips back before she's actually in it is one way to lessen the fright factor. Leaning back slowly and with a lot of talking and support is another. You may even be able to sit in the chair with your child and hold onto her during the ordeal. The most important thing is to respect your child's discomfort, help her understand what causes it, and let her know that you're looking for ways to ease it.

Don't Sweep Me Off My Feet!

In addition to going backward, losing contact with the ground can also be a feared or favored experience for children who have problems with the vestibular sense. For the overly sensitive child, being picked up, swung up onto shoulders, or thrown over a shoulder can cause all those dials and meters to go into overdrive. The actions change the center of gravity, which causes new information to stream in. Your child may feel the motion to be much more extreme than it seems to you. If you're taking your child's screams as just for fun, or thinking it's silly for him to burst into tears when you're just playing, consider what sort of chaos may be going on in his sensory system.

Fact

Motions that involve many changes of direction at once will likely be more upsetting than a simple upward or downward movement. If you need to pick your sensitive child up, do it carefully. Describe what you're doing, have her look at you so her head doesn't turn, and try not to twist or fling.

If your child doesn't get enough information from the vestibular system, all she may scream when you pick her up high is "Again! Again!" With no particular indication of lack of balance or direction or orientation, being picked up is free to be fun. It's being put back down that's the problem—she may like the action so much that she never wants it to stop. A trampoline can be a good way to give your child that sort of input without giving you a part-time job providing it, but be sure to get one that's small and safe. A one-person version with a handle for holding on to might help, or an inflatable trampoline with sides may be a fit for a smaller child. Keep in mind, though, that while trampolines can be fantastic tools for children with vestibular or proprioceptive problems or needs, they can also be dangerous. Be aware that homeowners' insurance policies often expressly forbid large backyard trampolines. If you do choose to get a big trampoline, make sure there's a net around it, only one child jumps at a time, and children are closely supervised.

Gravitational Insecurity

Gravitational insecurity is a profound mistrust of gravity and its ability to keep your child firmly anchored to the ground. It's like what you feel when you momentarily lose your balance, times ten and without end. If your child's vestibular system is giving him unreliable or hard to process information about where the pull of gravity is coming from and how it's keeping him upright, he will likely take very few risks with getting very far away from the ground.

This can cause problems in all sorts of areas. Your child may be in a constant state of low-level panic, which means that small things can become big problems. She may be afraid to go down stairs, clinging to the railing for dear life. Hopping aboard an escalator may be an impossible task. Walking a balance beam an inch off the ground will get the same response as if it were a mile high.

Parents naturally want their children to face their fears and overcome them, but in the case of a child with gravitational insecurity or other sensory processing problems, this often backfires into bigger fears and bigger tantrums and less control. Follow your child's lead. Unless there is a compelling reason, don't force things that will make him uncomfortable. There's rarely a situation that doesn't offer alternatives.

What should I do if my child freezes on an escalator?
Three possibilities: Pick your child up and carry her down; hold her hand and count together, to take your child's mind off the anxiety-producing activity; or skip the escalator completely and take the stairs instead.

Note that even a child who is understimulated by vestibular information and who usually plays the daredevil can have gravitational insecurity in some instances. Things that require balance while standing up may be more likely to trigger this than those that involve sitting down—she may be fine sitting on a swing or a slide, for instance, but scared standing on an escalator or a balance beam. Observe your child, and look for things that get extreme reactions. Use this information to help your child feel more comfortable and avoid unnecessary discomfort.

Judging—and Misjudging—Distances

In the familiar children's party game Pin the Tail on the Donkey, kids are blindfolded and spun around, then sent out to find a specific location on which to stick the tail. The combination of dizziness and lack of vision makes for a lot of humorous trips and turns, and usually a completely inaccurate estimation of where the proper spot on the donkey might be. Children with sensory integration disorder may always be operating in blindfolded and dizzy mode.

To understand the distance between your body and other objects, you have to have a good idea about where your body is and also a good idea of where the object is. Those can both be problems for kids with sensory integration disorder. Trouble receiving information or integrating information from the visual sense can distort ideas about items in the environment, and problems with the vestibular sense can do the same for the body's own position. That may result in a child who's excessively cautious, moving about the way you might if you were walking through a pitch-dark room. Or it may result in a child who just crashes his way through everything, bumping and ricocheting like a ball in a pinball machine.

Fact

Next time your child has trouble with an activity, break it down into small steps and examine each one. You may be surprised to note how often one of those little steps involves balance, controlled movement, or judging of distances. Your child may balk at something that's not obvious to you but is terribly obvious to him.

Telling your child to stop being such a scaredy-cat or stop being so clumsy won't help. Occupational therapy with a sensory integration approach will, as will being understanding and watching out for your child's weaknesses. Expect problems with things like catching a baseball, throwing a dart, kicking a soccer ball, or tagging someone out. If your child's a bull in a china shop, keep breakable things where he won't break them and they won't injure him. If your child is fearful of heights and distances, make sure there are good sturdy rails on stairways and choose the elevator instead of the escalator. Don't hesitate to do things that make your child more comfortable—chances are that you make similar choices for yourself every day. Strike a balance that enables your child to grow in confidence and coordination.

Chapter 13

The Proprioceptive Sense

When your foot falls asleep, it's hard to feel just exactly where it is, and it commands your attention. You need to move it, stamp it, and stamp it again to clear that strange tingly feeling. If you walk before the tingling clears, you may feel clumsy, or you may walk on it tentatively. If you're somewhere you can't give that foot a good stamping, the desire to stamp is probably all you'll be able to think about. If your child has sensory integration disorder, this may be what he feels like much of the time.

Muscles and Joints, Reporting In

The word "proprioceptive" comes from the Latin *proprius*, or "own," plus receptive. However he reacts to information coming in from the outside world, you expect your child to be receptive to the signals that are contained in and coming from his own body—the location of his limbs, the position of his joints, the speed and force with which his muscles are moving. They're the most basic of impressions, the ones that define your own body, where it begins and ends and how it moves. Yet for children with sensory integration disorder, even this fundamental information can become fuzzy. Proprioception becomes poor reception.

Just as tactile information comes through the skin, auditory information through the ears, visual information through the eyes, vestibular information through the inner ear, gustatory information through the taste buds, and olfactory information through the nose, proprioceptive information comes through receptors in the muscles, joints, and bones. Much of the information never makes it to conscious thought. You don't often think about how your arms and legs are placed and what's moving where and when. You're likely to notice it only when something changes—when different shoes make your feet feel heavier, an awkward position gives you a cramp, a sudden bout of claustrophobia makes you feel that you must move at once. You may also notice it when you lose it—when your arm becomes numb from sleeping on it, or illness or medication gives you a feeling of disconnection from your body. Either way, it's an unsettling feeling.

Unsettled is exactly the way your child feels if she is not getting good information from her proprioceptive sense. Those feelings you experience only intermittently—of compulsion to stamp a tingling foot, move about when you're claustrophobic, or adjust your limbs when you're cramped—are feelings your child may live with every day. If her proprioceptive system is overreactive, she may have to concentrate constantly on sensations that are meant to hum softly in the background of her body's activity. And if she's underreactive, she may have to engage in wild movement just to learn anything at all about where her body is and what it's doing.

Fact

Unlike other senses, where behavior for kids who are underreactive tends to be desperately sensory-seeking and those who are overreactive are just as desperately sensory-defensive, children who have problems with proprioceptive input may react much the same way, with a lot of hard movement.

Your child doesn't understand why he's doing all this. He just knows he needs to do it to make himself comfortable. That process may not look comfortable to you. It may involve hitting his head, throwing his body against things, rocking back and forth, or moving in unusual ways. But before rushing in to stop it, see what effect the activity has on your child. If he winds up calmer afterward, there may be a method to his seemingly mad behavior.

Jumping and Flapping

Jumping—really hard, high-impact jumping, with maximum concentration and the whole body thrown into it—is a common activity for kids with proprioceptive difficulties. It serves a number of purposes. It gives a jolt to the joints that can jump-start balky receptors and send some much-needed information to the brain. It can flood a brain that is underreactive to such information with enough input to make an impression. It can give some good convincing contact with the ground to let your child know where his body ends and the sidewalk begins. And it throws in some strong vestibular input for good measure. Of course, all your child knows is that it feels good, calms him down, and helps him feel more organized.

Flapping may accompany jumping, or the action may be a little proprioceptive party all by itself. Flapping of the arms or hands gives the shoulders and elbows and wrists the same sort of joint-jolt that jumping does for the hips and knees and ankles. Together with jumping, it gives the whole body a lift. Children with autism spectrum disorders are especially prone to flapping, often at times of distress, but any child with sensory integration disorder and issues involving the proprioceptive sense may do it when in need of sensory input, calming, or control.

Feet on the Ground

Should you make your child stop jumping? It sometimes seems that if you don't, you might lose control. It can be maddening to watch your child jump, jump, jump, slamming his body into the ground with such concentration and intensity. Your child may jump while watching television or listening to music, or just at random times. "Cut that out!" you want to cry.

Resist the urge. You may be able to get your child to stop the physical activity, but he will still feel uncomfortable and fidgety, and he may resort to even more disruptive movements to ricochet himself back into a comfort zone. As your child goes along with occupational therapy with a sensory integration approach, and you supplement that with at-home therapy and a sensory diet, his need to jump may lessen. You can always suggest that he jump on a trampoline or with a jump rope when he needs that input, if it makes you more comfortable. But your child's comfort is the primary concern here, and letting him jump in place when he needs to may be the best way, in the short run, to achieve that.

A doctor or teacher may refer to your child's flapping and other odd habits as *stimming*—a word used to describe the self-stimulating movements of people with autism—and insist that it must be eliminated through behavior modification. Don't be persuaded. Stimming may be a stress-relieving activity that does not hurt your child, and it may be helpful.

Flipping over Flapping

Flapping is often troubling to parents and professionals. Whereas jumping can be reframed as a useful activity, flapping seems to serve no purpose at all. It looks weird, and your child may be teased for doing it. This behavior may disturb you more deeply than others because it seems so indicative of serious neurological impairment. It may also seem to agitate your child rather than calm him.

But as with jumping, if you can keep an open mind on this, you may learn a lot about your child's needs and compensations. Is it the flapping that's agitating her, or is she doing it to calm herself because she's agitated already? Can you use the flapping as a signal that something doesn't feel right to her? Instead of specifically telling her to stop flapping, can you apply other comforting strategies to try to give her some good feeling from her proprioceptive sense? Whether this makes the flapping go away or just makes your child feel less stressed, it will be a bigger help than merely ordering the behavior stopped.

Hitting and Pushing

Jumping and flapping may be annoying to watch and may make your child look somewhat unhinged, but at least nobody gets hurt. The same can't be said for two other activities that are common for kids who have problems with the proprioceptive sense—hitting and pushing. Both give your child the same sort of joint jolt as jumping and flapping, but woe to the innocent bystander who happens to be on the receiving end of that much-needed movement.

Although it doesn't make the blow hurt any less, your child probably doesn't really mean to hit and hurt. Along with a need for hard input to his joints, he likely has little understanding of how hard or how fast he's moving that hand. He also is most likely a bad judge of the distance between what he's pushing with and the thing that he's pushing, so a touch becomes a nudge, a nudge becomes a push, and a push becomes a hit. Your child may be as surprised as the injured party that any damage has been done; he may, in fact, refuse to admit any connection between his movement and the bruise on somebody's arm. Since he didn't intend it, how can there be a connection?

If your child's tactile sense is such that he doesn't feel pain, hitting and being hit may not feel bad to him—and so he may lack an awareness that it could feel bad to someone else. Letting him know, over and over again, and in as a calm a way as you can muster, that hitting hurts may eventually help him understand.

Unfortunately, although striking a blow can have genuine therapeutic usefulness for your child, it's not something you can just let go the way you can jumping or flapping. No amount of proprioceptive benefit makes it okay to hurt another child, or just as likely, you. This is another good reason to remind your child's teacher that your child should always be at the front of a line of children or a little ways behind, so that push doesn't come to shove. If he seems to have trouble keeping his hands to himself at home, a punching bag may be a useful therapeutic item to have around. You can also try pushing your hands against his hands to give him some of the same input.

Biting and Butting

More troubling still may be the way your child bites or head-butts when she needs some strong proprioceptive input. It's hard to consider such pain-inducing activities as anything but acts of aggression, but you may have noticed that your child doesn't seem to act very aggressive about them. You may be holding your child on your lap when she casually bites your hand or butts her head backward into your nose. She may not seem angry when she does it, although the person on the receiving end will surely be angry afterward.

There can be many reasons for this sort of behavior in children, but if your child has sensory integration disorder and you've noticed other proprioception-related behaviors, you might want to try looking at this in the same light. Biting and butting also give good input to the joints, although in this case it's the jaw and the neck and the shoulders that receive the most impact. This again is behavior that may be explained by sensory integration theory but not condoned by it. You have to find alternatives for your child, since these behaviors truly are unacceptable. If you can see things from his point of view, however, you'll want to coach alternatives without blaming your child for behavior that to him is just a matter of comfort.

Many children get their bite cravings satisfied with a piece of plastic tubing that they can chew on whenever they need to. Some parents use surgical tubing from a medical supply store for their children's chewable necklaces. You can also employ cheaper and easier-to-find aquarium tubing from a pet store. If your child likes, knot some beads into the tubing to make the necklace a little more festive, but be sure your child cannot chew through the tubing and get the beads out.

Chewy foods and candies may also be a good substitute for biting. For head-butting, there are few good alternative choices, but you may find that by addressing proprioceptive needs in other areas, the desire for this particular bit of input will subside. If not, try pushing down on your child's shoulders when she seems to need this sort of input.

Running into Walls

Sensory-seeking behaviors like hitting and pushing, biting and butting are unacceptable because your child might hurt somebody else. Running into walls, on the other hand, is unacceptable because your child might hurt herself. She may enjoy crashing because, once again, it gives some good strong input to her muscles and joints. Or she may crash because she just can't get the hang of where her body ends and blunt objects like walls and tables and corners begin. If her vestibular sense is weak, she'll be particularly poorly equipped to judge distances before things come crashing in on her. And if her tactile sense is weak, she won't be feeling any pain when she bops into that corner again and again and again.

A lack of understanding of distances plus a lack of fear of bumping or being bumped can cause problems in areas other than walls. One mother recalls the way her son used to walk into the car's rearview mirror every time he passed the vehicle. Your child may bop his head more than you'd expect, on doors, doorframes, bunk beds, furniture, and other things that seem easily evaded but are nevertheless in the way. You'll certainly want to keep an eye on your child when he walks by a swing set on which other children are swinging—he may not keep a safe distance and wind up getting kicked in the head.

Rocking and Rolling

Like children who have problems with the vestibular sense—and vestibular and proprioceptive problems often go hand in hand—children who don't get good information from their muscles and joints may enjoy rocking hard, whether forward and back or side to side when sitting or standing, or side to side when lying down. Your child may need to do some hard rocking in bed, throwing his body from side to side, sometimes even ricocheting off a wall if there's one beside his mattress, before he can calm himself to sleep.

Essential

For your child with proprioceptive issues, you can buy a weighted blanket from an occupational therapy catalog, or you can contact a business like DreamCatcher Weighted Blankets (*www.weighted blanket.net*) to get one made. If you want to see if it works before investing, take a heavy afghan or blanket and fold it in half or in quarters to concentrate the weight.

Rocking is another one of those behaviors that disturbs parents but serves a need for the child. If she will allow you to find substitutes for the rocking, such as sitting in a rocking chair with her before bed, giving her a lot of hard exercise in the evening, or putting a heavy blanket on her to give her some good input as she lies still, that's great—go ahead and do that. If not, you may be wise to put aside your personal qualms and let your child rock. Make her stop, and you'll both pay the price for sleeplessness the next day.

Fingers and Thumbs

One final proprioceptive crutch that baffles and annoys parents while giving a child great comfort is thumb- or finger-sucking. You can't beat those digits for some quick, powerful sensory input. Sucking gives a lot of tactile input to the mouth, and providing a lot of proprioceptive tugging at the joints of the fingers and hands. It is an activity that can be intensely calming, comforting, and organizing to a child with sensory integration disorder.

Again, as with all the activities your child seeks out to bolster proprioceptive input, you're really going to want to take a good look at the pros and cons of stopping sucking. Damage to your child's teeth is a good reason to make your child stop, but you can't necessarily assume that's happening. Keep in close consultation with your child's dentist so you'll know as soon as there really is a problem, and then don't spend a lot of energy and worry anticipating one. The opinions and attitudes of others may seem a compelling reason to remove the thumb or fingers—school playmates can be cruel about the habit, and so can grandmothers—but if your child doesn't feel the social pressure personally, you may want to stop feeling it on his behalf.

Fact

Try things like chewing gum or lollipops to give your child the same sensory input she gets from sucking on her thumb or fingers, and it may work—while the gum or candy is in her mouth. But unless you're providing a constant supply, your child will probably revert back to those always-convenient fingers.

In the end, finger- and thumb-sucking is a lot like smoking cigarettes. It's an activity that bears a social stigma and a potential for bodily harm, but it is so highly calming to the individual that he may decide to put up with all the trouble rather than give it up. If you're determined to make your child stop, be aware that it will carry about the same degree of difficulty as a smoker giving up cigarettes. It's not likely that your child will be able to just stop through a desire to please you or sheer force of will. Especially if the decision is not his, there will need to be lots of support and alternatives and distractions offered to help him make it through. Try to start with one short period of the day being thumb-free, or one room in the house. A little at a time is best—at least until somebody invents a thumb-sucking patch.

Too Hard or Too Light

Any activity that involves modulation of movement—a careful calibration of the amount of force or speed needed to accomplish a task—will be difficult for a child with sensory integration problems around the proprioceptive sense. Whether your child is not getting enough information to know effortlessly where her body parts are and how to move them, or whether she is getting so much information that she can't find the pieces she needs, there are going to be problems with pencils and erasers and spoons and forks and glasses. Your child will have to learn how to manage these things, but the more you can understand what a struggle that is, the better you will be able to help her.

You probably process proprioceptive information smoothly enough that the proper pressure for writing clearly or lifting a glass just comes naturally to you. But think about how you feel when a pen's ink doesn't flow smoothly. You might write with it so hard that you leave grooves in the paper, with no luck. You may rap the pen hard against the paper, trying to get the ink flowing. You may try holding the pen at a variety of different angles in the hope that something will get the ink going. This may be similar to your child's experience with writing—the feeling that whatever you do, nothing can make the writing come out right.

Similarly, when you watch your child struggle with a fork, think about an experience you might have had with chopsticks. It takes a careful modulation of just the right pressure, and a quick sure movement from plate to lips, to use those utensils properly. Your child may have the same problem with a fork. Drive the tines into a piece of meat too lightly, and it won't stay; drive them too hard, and the meat may scoot across the plate or right off the edge. It's no wonder that fingers seem the more reasonable alternative.

The best thing you can do for your child is to understand that his problem is legitimate and not just a matter of laziness or sloppiness. The second is to see just where and how he's having problems and give him tools that can help. A child who writes too softly may do better with a gel pen in which the ink flows without much pressure. A child who writes too hard may break fewer pencil points if you give him a pencil that's only partly sharpened. A short pencil may give a better, surer hold than a longer one. A soft eraser will be less likely to tear paper when used strenuously than a harder one. Plastic forks and spoons may be easier for your child to manipulate, or you may want to play with different weights and grips to find a good fit. Food that everyone eats with their fingers—like hot dogs or chicken nuggets, raw carrots or corn on the cob—may be a good thing to work into meals as much as possible. Occupational therapy with a sensory integration approach will eventually enable your child to need these accommodations less, but while he needs them more, try to give them to him.

Remember, too, that the more stress your child is under—the more she is blamed for the things her sensory integration profile will not allow her to do smoothly and accurately—the less able she is going to be to exert any sort of control. Forcing her to rewrite and rewrite, or to use a fork or go hungry, will not get you the sort of increase in skill level you may be hoping for. Don't do that to your child, and don't let relatives or teachers do it, either. Sometimes the biggest hurdle all children with sensory integration disorder have to deal with is not the difficulty with how their brains process information, but the condemnation of those who do not understand how their brains work.

CHAPTER 14

Motor Planning

Think about how much information needs to come together to drink a glass of juice. See the cup on the table. Move the hand to grasp it. Grasp it hard enough to pick it up, but not too hard to tip it. Lift it at the right speed. Tip it to drink. Feel the heaviness to know how full it is. If any information is missing, juice is going to wind up on the floor. If that's a common occurrence at your house, consider whether motor planning could be a problem for your child.

It Only Looks Easy

"Motor" in this case refers to the movement of the muscles, and "motor planning" means the ability to visualize how to do something and correctly sequence the movements needed to do it. Even the smallest movement can be a motor-planning challenge if your child has trouble judging distances and force. When you string a couple of simple movements together into a complex movement—drinking juice, say—the degree of difficulty soars. And when you string a number of complex movements together into a more involved request—"Go to the refrigerator, get out the carton of juice, open the carton, pour yourself some juice, and drink it up for me, okay?"—you might as well be asking your child with sensory integration disorder to assemble a rocket ship and fly to the moon.

Fact

Another word for motor planning is *praxis*, which is Greek for "action" or "doing." Therapists may refer to praxis or dyspraxia (impairment in praxis) on evaluations, and many of the tests used to determine whether a child has problems that could be helped by occupational therapy have the word praxis in their names, including the Sensory Integration and Praxis Tests (SIPT).

While motor planning isn't specifically a sensory activity, good and accurate motor planning calls on information from the senses. If your child isn't processing those well, her brain doesn't build up an internal image of the body. This is needed to give good information to her muscles about where they are and what they should do. Without accurate sensory information, motor planning can't proceed with the sort of smoothness and effortlessness most of us take for granted. For this reason, many children with sensory integration disorder also have trouble with motor planning and sequencing. They get the steps in the wrong order. They forget the steps. They do things backwards or too hard or too gently, and everything falls apart. Then they get in trouble for not complying with a "simple request."

You may have to accept that what seems easy and clear-cut to you may not look that way to your child. When your child balks at an activity for no apparent reason, stop and think about what that activity entails. Are you asking your child to do something he truly can't figure out how to do? Is he starting but getting lost and frustrated quickly? Or is he too puzzled to even try? Kids have a hard time understanding their problems and explaining them. Sometimes, misbehavior is the best communication they can offer.

Imagine how stressed you would be if someone demanded you do something you couldn't even begin to figure out how to do. What would you want from that person? More specific instructions? Less pressure? More understanding for your lack of ability? More appreciation of the effort you do make? Offer these things to your child. She does have to learn how to do these things, but you can't assume that she will be able to do them quickly, easily, and with as much grace as other children her age. Being your child's advocate means anticipating problems and being the person with the solutions.

Every Activity Has Steps

Virtually everything you ask or expect your child to do has multiple steps. And most likely, each of those steps has multiple steps. And even those may have multiple steps. Show your child what the whole activity looks like so she understands the goal, and then break it down. Think on the micro level when asking your child to do something or showing her how it's done. Be particularly sensitive to these mini steps when an activity involves an area in which you know her sensory system is over- or underreactive. But since sensory areas intertwine, it can be hard to anticipate exactly what's going to be problematic. Take things one tiny piece at a time.

Alert!

Problems with motor planning can result in major motor-skill delays for your child. Children who can't figure out how to do something will avoid that activity, whether it's making a bed, buttoning a shirt, cutting with scissors, or riding a bicycle.

Think not just of actual movements, but of the things that need to inform the movements. This is the level at which things often fall apart for kids with sensory integration disorder. Consider, for example, the many factors that go into the seemingly innocent task of buttoning a button. To slide that small object through that only slightly larger hole, your child must do the following things, drawing on the following information:

Action	Requires	Potential Problems
Understand the command	Auditory attention; auditory processing	Child's attention is caught by something else and command is missed; child has trouble making a transition from current activity to new activity
Put her hand where the button is	Proprioceptive, tactile, and vestibular information about the position of the hand and the body	Child can't find button if she can't see it; requires additional input to make up for poor tactile and proprioceptive processing
Put her other hand where the buttonhole is	Same as above, but with the added complication of the hole being the lack of an item rather than an item, and being on a different piece of fabric than the button	Same as above; child may need to see it or have her hand guided to it to find it
Grab the button with her fingers	Tactile sensitivity to feel the actual button; proprioceptive sensitivity to hold it just tight enough and stay steady	Grab it too hard, it slips away; grab it too lightly, it slips from grasp or can't be manipulated; the concentration required may get in the way of being able to concentrate on the rest of the activity
Grab the buttonhole with the fingers of her other hand	Same as above, plus ability to do different things with different hands	Put finger through hole and button won't fit; child may need to see hole in order to grab it properly; grabbing something that isn't there may be a little abstract

Action	Requires	Potential Problems
Position the buttonhole over the button	Lots of tactile and proprioceptive information, since the two pieces of fabric are moving in opposite directions and must be moved with accuracy and precision	Moving two sides too much or not enough; putting too much space between them; inability to coordinate activity of two sides of the body
While stretching the buttonhole over the button, push the button through	Proprioceptive information to move things the right direction with the right force; tactile information to feel when the button is going through properly	Inability to calibrate movements with the accuracy needed to get the button through the hole; child may need to see what she's doing, and even a mirror image may make things too confusingly backwards
Now, do the same thing six or eight more times	Sufficient motor planning abilities to recall the sequence of movements; same good information over again from the senses; no distractions	Tears; screams; cries

It may seem silly to break things down so excruciatingly. Popping a button through a hole is one quick gesture; what's the big deal? But to your child, it may seem like a momentous task. His brain does not give him the same information your brain gives you. Just as a quick trip to the store seems like nothing unless you have a map that shows everything backward, an odometer that gives you bad information on how far you've gone, and a gas gauge that reads full when the tank is empty, a lack of good reliable information can turn a simple task into an endless journey.

Your child won't always get so lost. She may be able to do okay with motor planning for a short while and then lose her way. She may have the patience to work with things when she's not stressed and fall apart when she is. There may be problems of distractions at certain times and places that aren't present elsewhere.

Mapping It Out

Instead of just telling your child to do something, walk him through all the steps it will take to get there. If he has trouble understanding multiple steps at one time, you may have to follow along and prompt each step. For activities that need to be done on a regular basis, draw up a little map or plan of action to help your child follow along by himself.

For example, instead of just saying, "Make your bed," walk your child through the steps. Take the pillow off the bed. Straighten out the fitted sheet. Spread the top sheet over the bed. Tuck it in. Pull up the bedspread. Straighten it over the sides. Smooth out the wrinkles. Put the pillow on. The smaller the steps, the easier it will be for your child to do them. With digital cameras more common than ever, you may want to take pictures of each of the steps, print them, and put them on the wall so your child can see the sequence.

Fact

Do2Learn, a Web site that offers educational resources for people with special needs, has a variety of pictures to print out and use to make schedules—strips of steps needed to complete a task or activity. You can find an overview with links to the pictures and how to use them at *www.dotolearn.com.*

In *Steps to Independence: Teaching Everyday Skills to Children with Special Needs*, Bruce L. Baker and Alan J. Brightman suggest breaking a task down into steps and then teaching them backward (an approach called backward chaining). Make the bed yourself up to the last step, and then let your child do the last step. When he's mastered it, let him do the last two steps, and so on. This way, your child always ends with an experience of success.

One technique that can be very helpful in getting your child to remember steps, follow steps, sequence steps, and successfully complete steps is to put them into visual form using picture prompts. That form will have to be clean and easy to follow, or else visual perception problems may interfere. And for a child who has trouble with the visual sense, talking the steps through or doing them along with your child may in the end be the best choice. But picture prompts can give a child a feeling of independence and empowerment as she follows the pictures, does what they show, and successfully completes an activity.

Depending on how well your child is able to follow visual cues, you may want to add a tactile element to the plan. Have your child remove a picture card from a chart and slip it into an envelope. As she finishes that step, move a peg or magnet along as she completes each additional step, or put a sticker next to each completed component of the task. Be sure to give her lots of encouragement and positive reinforcement when she is able to do even one of these things for herself. It may not be a big deal to you, but it's a big deal to her.

Getting from A to B

Sometimes your child's biggest challenge when starting a new activity is stopping the old one. Problems with transitions are often nothing but a bad motor planning problem. Stopping what you are doing isn't a simple ceasing of movement. It may, in fact, involve a burst of coordinated movement—getting up from the floor, or getting down from a chair. It may involve disengaging from a rewarding and pleasant sensory experience—getting off the swing or turning off the iPod. It may involve finding the way out of a story, if your child is engaged in pretend play, or finding the way out of an interaction, if your child is engaged in conversation. All of these things can be significant challenges in themselves for your child with sensory integration disorder. And that makes stopping one of the hardest things about starting.

Be sure to allow your child enough time to move from one activity to the next. While many behavior experts (including, most likely, your mom) suggest giving a child a count of three to stop what he's doing and do what you say, your child may need longer than that to process your message, plan his way out of what he's doing, and figure out how to start what you want. Try a count of ten instead, and let your child know that if he needs more time he should ask. However much time you give him to make a successful transition will be far less than the time wasted in tantrums and time-outs.

Failure and Frustration

It would be so much easier if your child could just say, "You know, I'd like to do what you're asking me to, but my motor planning abilities are so weak that I just can't figure out how to do it. Perhaps you could give me a little help?" But that would require a degree of self-awareness that most children with sensory integration disorder don't have. Your child doesn't know why she can't button that button; she just knows that it's hard and frustrating.

She may flat-out refuse to do it or ignore requests in the hope that they will just go away. If your child seems generally compliant but has certain activities she ignores, avoids, or resists having to do, look to see if there might be a motor planning component that's serving as a roadblock. Patiently talking or guiding her through it, structuring the activity so that it's easier for her, or finding an alternative activity will be far more effective than yelling and nagging in these situations.

Diversionary Tactics

In addition to avoiding you or ignoring you or refusing to do what you say, a child who can't figure out how to plan the activity you want him to do may try to divert your attention. Maybe he'll throw a tantrum and hope that at the end you will have forgotten what you wanted him to do. Maybe he'll try to start a conversation on something entirely unrelated. Maybe he'll insist that another activity needs to be done first. These efforts to delay the inevitable may be frustrating to you, but they're signs of frustration on his part, too—and a fairly clever attempt to circumvent a dreaded action.

Essential

Resistance for no good reason in a child with sensory integration disorder may be a sign that there's a sensory side to the story. Your first reaction may be frustration and anger, but you'll be your child's best friend if you can step back and see where the problem might be.

In response, you might try a diversionary tactic of your own. Doing or saying something silly might get her attention. Offering a small reward for starting an activity might do it, too. A chart with picture prompts can be an exciting thing for a child to work with, and that might motivate her to overcome her reluctance and do the job. Sometimes, just having your time and attention as you guide her through an activity will be diversion enough to get her over her fears and reluctance and on to the task at hand.

Show, Don't Tell

Whenever you're trying to get your child with sensory integration disorder to do something, remember that he may have legitimate difficulty translating your words into action. Although he seems to be ignoring you, or giving up too quickly, or getting angry over nothing, the root of the problem may be an inability to visualize what needs to be done and to give his muscles the information they need to do it. Anything you can do to show your child what you expect and how to make it happen will improve the situation.

Whether you do that showing with words, pictures, hand-on-hand guidance, or doing the activity for your child to imitate will largely depend on her particular strengths and weaknesses. Try a few possibilities and see what works best for her and for you. You may have to use different techniques for different activities. But your child should respond to the increased assistance and understanding and show a willingness to do things she might have resisted before.

Chapter 15

Low Muscle Tone

It's easy to confuse muscle tone with muscle strength or muscle bulk, something you can improve with weight lifting, running, and regular workouts. Muscle tone refers to the level of tautness or looseness in a muscle and its ability to hold joints in place—something that is sorely lacking in many children with sensory integration disorder. This kind of muscle tone can't be improved by working out and bulking up. Sometimes it improves with time and therapy, but in the meantime, it makes kids extra floppy.

Limp As a Dishrag

Low muscle tone, or *hypotonia*, is often a sign of central nervous system or muscle damage. It is linked to a number of hereditary, neurological, or muscular disorders, including the following:

- Achondroplasia
- Aicardi syndrome
- Canavan disease
- Cerebellar ataxia
- Congenital hypothyroidism
- Down syndrome
- Encephalitis
- Fetal alcohol spectrum disorder
- Guillain-Barre syndrome
- Hypervitaminosis D

- Infant botulism
- Kernicterus
- Klinefelter syndrome
- Krabbe disease
- Marfan's syndrome
- Meningitis
- Menkes syndrome
- Metachromatic leukodystrophy
- Methylmalonic acidemia
- Muscular dystrophy
- Myasthenia gravis
- Myotonic dystrophy
- Poliomyelitis
- Prader-Willi syndrome
- Rickets
- Riley-Day syndrome
- Sepsis
- Spinal muscular atrophy type 1
- Tay-Sachs disease
- Trisomy 13
- Vaccine reaction

Some of these disorders can be quite serious, and when researching low muscle tone you may be panicked to think that your child may have one of them. In many cases, though, a child will have low muscle tone for no apparent reason. Low muscle tone in children with disorders of sensory integration is not as severe as in children with conditions such as Down syndrome, and the mechanism may be different. Rather than a sign of a serious disorder, it may just be the result of mild, unspecified brain damage or dysfunction or your child's unique neurological and muscular profile. At any rate, low muscle tone is rarely the only sign of a serious disorder and is instead just one of the factors involved in it. In and of itself, low muscle tone is not a reason to panic, although it will offer some challenges as you care for and raise your child.

The term "congenital hypotonia" indicates that the lack of muscle tone has been present since birth. You may have first noticed it when your baby seemed particularly floppy. You probably found it impossible to pick her up under her arms—she slipped right through. She may have been unable to hold her head or arms up while lying on her stomach and was probably slow to sit, crawl, or stand.

Fact

"Benign congenital hypotonia" is another term you may hear for low muscle tone. This is sometimes used to describe hypotonia in cases where there is no serious underlying disorder found and the low muscle tone does not seem to be causing severe problems. It may not seem benign to your child or your family, but in medical terms, it is.

Sensory integration disorder and hypotonia are both often caused by probable neurological inefficiency, but there are other connections between them. Since children with low muscle tone have trouble holding their joints in position, the information from their proprioceptive system—which reports in on how the joints are situated—is weak. In turn, inefficient information from the vestibular and proprioceptive senses may not give muscles the information they need to do their job, causing low response and insufficient work from them. Sensory integration disorder can, for some children, be the cause of mild hypotonia, and for other children, hypotonia can be a factor in sensory integration disorder. Many of the behaviors described in children with low muscle tone are similar to those that will be familiar to parents of children with sensory integration disorder. In both cases, understanding of unavoidable behaviors will go a long way toward helping you help your child.

Lying Low

Is your child's favorite position face down on the ground? Does he tend to flop instead of sit? When sitting on the ground with a group of kids, does he often lean against someone sitting next to him or actually find a way to lie down? Your child isn't being lazy or rude. It may just be really difficult to sit upright. The effort it might take for you, say, to stand on one foot might be the same effort it costs your child to sit upright with no support, as when seated on the floor. How long could you hold that position without help? It should be no surprise that your child will quickly find some support for his floppy frame, be it a nearby shoulder, a piece of furniture, or the floor.

It may bother you to see your child always tossed about on the ground, but if you're someplace where it's really not a problem, don't make it a problem. Clothes and body parts can be washed, and in most places lying on the floor doesn't have to be a major breach of protocol. If you're someplace where it's truly not allowed, make sure your child has something to lean on or provide support. That might be a chair with arms, some pillows, a table, or two adults sitting on either side. If there's a possibility of lying your child down on a church pew or a ballpark bench, allow for that option, too.

Essential

Beanbag chairs can be a great compromise when you don't want your child on the floor and she can't sit up straight for a long period. Allow your child to lie face down across the beanbag if she wants. Another good option might be a big free-form dog bed, or a special rug or mat just for your child.

W Is for Weak Joints

If your child isn't spread out on the floor, you may notice her sitting in a "W" position, with her bottom on the floor and her legs bent backward at the knee. Try it yourself, and you're likely to end up in some serious pain. But since your child's muscles don't hold her joints together all that tightly, she may be able to sit this way comfortably, or without even knowing it's a problem.

While most children pass through the "W" position while playing, your child with low muscle tone may prefer it, because it offers a lot of stability for a floppy torso. Your child's bent-back legs serve as nice supports to keep him from flopping from side to side. Unfortunately, they also keep him from bending from side to side to reach and play with toys, or from rotating his trunk easily. It may place limits on his playing and slow his development in motor tasks. W-sitting results in the stretching of some muscles that make balancing muscles on both sides of a joint more difficult. The stretching of these muscles may make the child more prone to injury. You don't have to outright forbid this sort of sitting, but you can get him to try other positions. One possibility may be having him sit on your lap and supporting him with your hands as he leans to reach his playthings. An adjustable chair called the Trip Trap can provide good support to your child's trunk and feet.

Food for Thought

Although low tone in the muscles that control sitting, standing, walking, and holding may be the most obvious, don't forget that low muscle tone can extend into places like the mouth, too. Kids with hypotonia may have trouble chewing certain foods, swallowing, and keeping their mouths closed when they eat, and they may have problems avoiding drooling. They may also have trouble making speech sounds accurately. Just as their torso or arms or legs may be floppy, their tongue may be floppy, too.

Low muscle tone can even affect your child's ability to master the skill of potty training. It may be hard for him to control his bladder, or to sit comfortably on the toilet, or to deal with zippers and snaps. He may decide that avoiding the whole thing is easier than dealing with so many difficult activities at once, some of which may seem out of his control. Don't assume that failure to control this function is always a power play. It's worth looking at all of your child's problems with a mind toward muscle-tone weakness and to mention it to doctors any time there's an illness or injury.

Spaghetti Legs

Most parents have experienced spaghetti legs—the way your child, when he does not wish to be moved, will make his body limp and his legs like wet pasta. Kids with low muscle tone are pretty close to spaghetti legs in the normal course of events, so they're particularly adept at this maneuver. When your child is fatigued or reluctant, expect to have to carry or drag him. An umbrella stroller is a good thing to have around for emergencies until your child is too big to fit in it.

Your child may not understand why he has such a hard time with standing. He may just know that it makes him tired or uncomfortable or antsy. And he may respond with bad behavior just to get out of having to do it. Sitting in the time-out chair may be preferable to standing anywhere else, and going to his room to flop on the bed may be more desirable still. Terrible behavior at a shopping mall can be a reaction to all the sounds and lights and sensations, but it could also have something to do with the labor of walking from one end of the place to the other. It could be all of these things rolled together. But you can be sure that if you tell your child with sensory integration disorder to "Stop that or we'll leave right now," you're all but asking your child to misbehave. Leaving right now is just what he wants to do—to get to a nice supportive car seat, maybe, or anywhere he can stop walking.

Games that involve standing still or controlling motion may be particularly hard for your child. He will be the one sitting down in the outfield in the middle of a baseball game. Kicking can be a problem, along with any skill that involves holding the joints in a particular position, including anything from catching to throwing to shooting a basket.

Playground activities like hopscotch or jump rope may require more physical coordination and control than your child can muster. If she prefers to be flopped somewhere with a book, it may not just be because she loves reading and hates sports. Her body may be telling her that this is the safest way to be.

Modulating Movement

When you're working with wobbly equipment, one of the best and maybe only ways to stay upright is speed. Like a bicycle that needs to keep moving to remain on its wheels, a child with low muscle tone has to move it or lose it. If your child seems to be always in motion, consider whether it might be the only alternative to falling to the ground in a heap.

Keeping your child safe when he's running on all cylinders can be a challenge. Childproof your home as much as possible with soft padding on corners. Put gates on stairs and other areas that could cause a fall, and keep your eyes on that child at all times. He may find ways to get hurt you could never anticipate.

The problem with headlong movement without true control or support is that it tends to be a little heedless. Movements are big and fast and propelled by compulsion, which makes modulation—the sort of careful adjustments that make movements efficient and accurate—pretty much impossible. Kids with low muscle tone who use movement to keep their bodies together tend to crash into things, put things down too hard, touch things too roughly, and move things too quickly. The sort of balance and control required for careful work isn't available to them.

There are things you can do to help, but yelling "Slow down!" isn't one of them. Be a hands-on helper. Provide physical support. Use hands on shoulders to guide a child, work hand-over-hand to do things that require modulation, and put covers on cups so that abrupt movements won't cause spills. Adjust your expectations to allow for your child's particular needs, and the not-always-wise strategies she's come up with to meet them.

Comfortable Listening

Lying on the floor while doing homework isn't necessarily a sign of laziness or sloppy work habits. In fact, it might be the best way for your child to work and concentrate. A prone position, besides being more comfortable for your child, may be the one that allows her to pay the most attention. It seems so unlikely that the kid who's rolling around on the floor there could possibly be listening. But you may find that she'll pop up and answer a question even after seemingly spending story time in dreamland.

The attention problem may come for your child when he's forced to sit upright. For a child with low muscle tone, this takes an enormous amount of concentration. Think, again, of how much concentration you would have to use to stay standing on one foot without support. How well would you be able to listen to what someone was saying to you? In situations where you need your child's attention, letting him lie down may be your best bet.

Getting a Grip

Dropping things seems like carelessness. Letting a cup tip appears to be a deliberate way to make a mess. But if your child has low muscle tone, it's possible that she really can't hold a tight grip on a cup or glass. Holding a cup securely means tightening the joints into place around the vessel, and that's something your child may have trouble doing. Similarly, holding a fork in a straight and secure way that facilitates neat eating, or a spoon in just the position needed to get soup from bowl to mouth, may be enormously challenging. Pencils, too, may be impossible to grip with sufficient force to write legibly. You may notice your child holding a pencil awkwardly, or so lightly that the letters stretch like bits of feather across the page.

There are things you can use to help your child hold things tighter. Pencil grips may give him a better handle on writing utensils. Forks and spoons with special handles are available that may make holding those items less trying. Cups with lids can prevent spills due to a loose grip, but keeping the glass on the table and letting the child drink with a straw may be a better strategy. Most of all, it helps to know—and let your child know you know—that your child is not just dropping and spilling due to neglect or carelessness. She really does have trouble getting a grip.

Essential

For items to help children get a good hold on objects, turn to occupational therapy catalogs. Online, try these two for these fine-motor tools: the Therapy Shoppe, at *www.therapyshoppe.com*, and Therapro, at *www.theraproducts.com*.

A Lifelong Challenge

Low muscle tone may improve, or the skills your child finds to compensate for it may become more refined, but it most likely won't go away. As your child grows, new challenges may arise. Growth spurts may be particularly difficult, as your child has to learn all over again how to move his body and keep it together and avoid bumping into things. The transition most kids go through as their bodies change will be particularly difficult for your child, who gets so few strong signals about his body's position and direction.

School can also be a real problem. Your child's teacher may complain that she always has her head down on her desk, or that she leans against the wall while walking in the hallways, or that she spills her lunch tray. You will need to explain to the educators and administrators who work with your child that her looseness is not by choice and that she will need help and understanding to navigate school without incident. As you learn more about your child's unique strengths and weaknesses, you may be able to suggest strategies that will solve problems in a socially acceptable way. Your child's occupational therapist, whether school-based or private, should be able to help you out with this as well.

Fact

Low muscle tone has no impact on intelligence, but it may be a factor in apparent learning disabilities or school problems because the child has trouble with writing, sitting, or performing physical tasks. If your child balks at work you're sure he can do, it may be a problem with the mechanics of showing what he knows.

Low muscle tone by itself, if not part of a more serious disorder, should not significantly impair your child's opportunities in life. An awareness of why certain things are difficult will help your child understand that he's not lazy or bad or incompetent but just has muscles that work a little differently. As vestibular and proprioceptive problems are addressed by occupational therapy with a sensory integration approach, it may be easier for your child to coordinate and fine-tune his movements, but flopping may always be a fallback position. Making sure he has a comfortable place to do it, and understanding why he must, will be a parent's best move.

CHAPTER 16

Hypersensitivity and Hyposensitivity

It's one of the key contradictions of sensory integration disorder that kids can be too sensitive, not sensitive enough, or both at once. That's the kind of thing that raises eyebrows when you tell someone about this new diagnosis, and that makes it sound like such a catch-all it can't possibly be legitimate. But when the basic apparatus for processing sensation is out of whack, it's not surprising that problems occur all along a spectrum.

When a Little Is Too Much

A thermostat that's broken will leave a house cold in the winter, hot in the summer. A broken clock can make you late or early. Broken sensory integration can leave a child wildly unable to process properly, making much of a little, a little of much, and not much sense of anything.

You might think that having a heightened sensitivity to a certain kind of information would make your child smarter, more creative, more capable, and more able to react quickly and effectively. That's the way it worked with Superman and the Six Million Dollar Man, anyway. You've heard of people who lose the use of one sense, like sight or hearing, and get heightened use of other senses, and that seems like a good thing, too. So why is your child's extreme sensitivity in certain areas a hindrance instead of a help?

The problem is that the increased sensitivity does

not bring your child an improved quality of information, just an improved quantity. It's like turning up a radio. To a point, it helps you to hear better, but once you pass that point the volume becomes distracting and even painful. Adding additional sound well past the point at which you can process it does not improve your ability to hear and enjoy it, it diminishes that ability—and also makes it impossible for you to concentrate on anything else. This is the experience your child has with any sensory input to which she is hyperreactive.

The challenge of sensory integration disorder is that the sort of sensory overload one might expect from these intense experiences happens just as frequently with much less obvious ones. Even a small amount of sensory stimuli comes in with the sound turned way up. Both a little bit and a lot seem like far too much. This makes things particularly hard on your child, as well as hard on those who are trying to help her.

When Too Much Is Not Enough

As with oversensitivity, undersensitivity can also sound like a good deal. The ability to screen out excess input is one we value, and being especially adept at it should, theoretically, allow a child to focus only on things that are vitally important. You may admire the kind of hyperfocus that inspires inventors to invent, actors to put on stirring displays of make-believe, writers to create worlds out of words, all the while shutting out whatever deflects them from that goal. For the children with sensory integration disorder whom we've called underreactive, undersensitive, hyporeactive, or hyposensitive, however, even things that are or should be of compelling interest get screened out. That makes paying focused attention harder, not easier.

Think again of that radio, the one that was turned up so loud you couldn't think of anything else. But this time, imagine that the radio is faint and clouded with static, and to get any music at all you have to spend every second fiddling with the controls, turning the antenna every which way, and straining to get any useful content. It's a frustrating and unproductive process, and it takes all the attention and ingenuity you have. Maybe sometimes you just give up. Other times, when there's news you need to hear or a program you really want to catch, you stand on your head with that antenna to try to make that signal come in. This is the experience your child has with any sensory input to which he is hyporeactive.

Faulty sensory integration isn't a problem with the senses themselves so much as with the neurological wiring that gets the information to the brain and processes it there. Your child may be tested as having perfect hearing and vision but still have sensory integration problems with the auditory and visual senses.

It's a cruel irony that much of the behavior that bothers you in your hyporeactive child is in fact his desperate attempt to pay attention. He is fiddling with every control in his body, moving around looking for better "reception," making heroic attempts to turn the static and faint input into information that his brain and his body can use. All that running, jumping, bumping, pushing, rocking, swaying, and singing may be his equivalent of dancing around with an antenna, trying to find that one spot that will make the reception clear.

Swinging Between Extremes

Just when you get your child figured out in one area, another one comes along that completely shakes your faith. Your child screams when she hears sirens, vacuums, and alarms. She's hypersensitive. Got it! But then, how come she craves spicy and salty foods? Or loves to swing as high and hard as you can push her? Or smacks into walls and feels no pain? Doesn't that mean she's hyposensitive? Isn't that inconsistent? Surely someone who's sensitive is sensitive, and someone who's not is not, and there is no in-between.

With sensory integration disorder, there is no such assurance. Children with difficulty in sensory integration often have difficulty staying in the mid-range. A child can be hypersensitive in some areas, hyposensitive in others, and have no problem at all in others. In fact, since a breakdown in the senses' ability to work together is the basis of sensory integration disorder, too much information in one area can cause another area to be drowned out, providing too little information. Think again about that radio. Whether the station is coming in clearly or not, there can be things that influence your ability to enjoy it. Maybe the car next to you has its stereo turned up so loud that you can't hear your own. Maybe you drive by a construction site with jackhammers blasting. Maybe your children are talking so loud or arguing so ferociously that you can't concentrate on anything else. Or maybe you're so busy listening to the radio that you completely miss your exit.

Fact

You may hear the term "emotional lability" used to describe your child. This refers to emotions that come on strong and then change unpredictably. It may make your child appear unstable or manipulative, but as you learn more about her sensory integration struggles, you will realize that she may be reacting to unpredictable changes in her sensory processing abilities.

Too much input in one area can cause not enough in another, and concentrating on getting more input in one area can cause input from another to be lost. The key to understanding sensory integration disorder is to focus on the fact that your child has trouble receiving, interpreting, combining, responding to, and executing a response to sensory input—not so much on what input is affected and what the response is. Occupational therapy with a sensory integration approach, combined with your follow-through at home, will help your child have fewer over- and underreactions and struggle with fewer sensations. Until that happens, problems can occur in any area, to any degree.

Both at Once: An Apparent Contradiction

Problems can also occur to different degrees in one area. Your child may hate it when you touch him even lightly, but he may then rock so hard in his bed that he bangs his head against the wall. He may recoil from strong-tasting foods, yet put strange and inedible things in his mouth. He may hate being tipped back for a shampoo, but love to pump himself higher and higher on a swing set. Such inconsistencies can be hard for parents to follow, but they're common for children with sensory integration disorder. Again, it's not so much a matter of what sense and which way, but an apparatus that just doesn't work well at all.

Your child may try so hard to jump-start a system that's not giving her enough input that she boomerangs it right into too much input. Or she may shrink from excessive input so effectively that she finds herself understimulated and uncomfortable. Children with sensory integration disorder may swing back and forth like this, uncomfortable with a sensation one moment, dying for it the next. Hard as it is for you to keep up, it's harder for your child.

Essential

Your child may be more comfortable with things that he does than with things that are done to him. He may feel powerless and panicky when you tip him backwards in the bathtub for a hair wash, but powerful and confident when he's pushing himself on the swings. As much as possible, give him power over the sensations he experiences.

What It Takes to Stay Alert

Imagine yourself in a meeting. You want to stay alert, or at least look alert. But your attention wanders. The room is warm. The voices drone. How do you keep your mind focused? Maybe you drink a cup of coffee. Maybe you play with the top of your pen, or use it to doodle quietly. There are hundreds of ways in which people move and fidget and twitch to maintain a reasonable level of alertness. And that's just what children with sensory integration problems do. The only difference is that they tend to do it bigger, louder, and with less recognition of whether someone will think they're disruptive.

It may be impossible for your child to sit still and be quiet at once. To control her words, she may have to move around a bit. And to control her actions, she may have to do some self-talk, coaching herself to stillness. Some sort of fidget toy may provide necessary movement, just as music through headphones creates some discrete sound.

These behaviors, though extreme and disruptive, don't necessarily mean your child is ignoring, tuning out, or otherwise not taking care of business. He may be doing the very best he can to get his inefficient sensory system to stay alert.

If your child seems to be able to answer questions, summarize what she's heard, and otherwise indicate that attention has been paid despite a great deal of excess motion and busyness, consider that the very purpose of the motion and busyness has been to pay attention. Try not to insist that your child sit still and be quiet—if she somehow succeeds at doing that, she'll probably fall asleep. Instead, work with your child to find less disruptive ways to maintain alertness, or decide not to let her current ways bother you.

Finding the Comfort Zone

The child who swings between extremes has trouble finding the comfort zone—the area in which her body is comfortable, efficient, and alert. Her efforts to reach that zone may send her careening from understimulation to overstimulation; distract her so much that she's unable to regulate other areas or pay good attention; or prove impossible if she's stuck on one end or the other. The ability to correctly attune the sensory system so it gets just enough of everything is called sensory modulation, and in children with sensory integration disorder it is woefully lacking.

It may be useful to think of sensory modulation in terms of the climate control system of a house. Some houses have thermostats that constantly keep the temperature within a comfort zone, turning on the air conditioner when the weather gets warm, cuing up the heat when the weather gets cold, keeping things balanced. When the temperature sneaks outside of the comfort zone, it's quickly brought right.

Different houses may have different comfort zones—what seems like a good temperature to you may seem cold or unbearably warm to your neighbor—but the person who has set the thermostat doesn't have to do much more than that to keep things within an acceptable range and doesn't have to think much about the whole process.

Making Adjustments

Some houses, though, don't have thermostats. Maybe they have window air-conditioning units and space heaters. It's still possible to keep things within a comfort zone with these tools, but it's a little more work. More effort has to be put into the fine-tuning. Things can get out of hand more quickly.

Then, too, if these tools are working too well, they can actually reverse the problem. An air conditioner on full blast can make a room too cold. A person sitting right next to a heater may get too warm. Still, with a little effort, a comfort zone can be maintained more often than not.

Then there are houses where windows and the fireplace are the only sources of climate control available. Staying within a comfort zone can be very difficult in those environments, with constant monitoring and adjusting needed, and even those efforts are limited and often inadequate.

In some extreme circumstances, a comfort zone is unattainable. A power outage, an area with extreme weather, windows that won't open, or a lack of useable fuel can all make a reasonable range of climatic comfort a pipe dream.

All efforts must be focused on basic survival, never mind comfort, and there is always a certain degree of physical or environmental danger involved. Any attempt to get in the way of these survival measures will be met with severe resistance. Energy must be zealously conserved, or used only in the pursuit of coolness or warmth.

Love Your Thermostat

When it comes to sensory integration, most of us have reliable thermostats. You may swing into the discomfort range now and then, but get back in line so easily you hardly notice the effort. Some people have to work a little harder at it, making frequent adjustments and accommodations that are noticeable but not a nuisance, while others find it a nuisance but attend to it anyway. But children with sensory integration disorder are often like those powerless, fuel-less houses in which survival is the only goal and measures that would be unthinkable for most are the only options available.

If only you could install a reliable thermostat in your child. Sadly, it's not that easy. Things may never be that simple or that regular for him. But you can shoot for window units and space heaters, or even windows that slide open easily and big cords of wood by the fireplace. Any move toward a more reasonably regulated comfort zone will be an improvement. Even finding the comfort zone is sometimes a very large achievement for parents and kids alike.

CHAPTER 17

Sensory Integration and Behavior

Is sensory integration disorder just a massive rationalization for bad behavior? Sometimes it may seem that way to others, if not to you. You know that traditional discipline will not work if your child's behavior is driven by a need to feel comfortable in her body, but not everything a child with sensory integration disorder does is going to be motivated by that. Your child is still a child, and she will still test limits and bend rules. How can you tell the difference between can't and won't?

Behavior Analysis

One way to start out is with an informal behavior analysis. For a couple of weeks, keep a record of every time your child has a behavioral flare-up. Jot down the time of day, what preceded the event both right before and earlier in the day, what consequence, if any (negative or positive), followed the event, and any sensory factors that might have been present. Look particularly for things that you know to be a problem for your child—sounds, smells, body positions, physical movements, fabrics, people standing too close, and so on.

After two weeks or so, review all your notes and look for patterns. Does your child tend to misbehave in particular places? At certain times? Before or after certain activities? If your child tends to misbehave at some times and not others, and the times can be linked to his sensory integration problems, that's a good sign that

sensory integration techniques will be more helpful in addressing the behavior than traditional discipline. In fact, traditional discipline may make matters worse, adding to your child's stress, confusion, and feelings of abandonment and misunderstanding. On the other hand, if there seems to be no pattern and no explanation for your child's behavior, and he seems to be showing some willfulness and manipulation, then you may be better off using other measures to address it.

Keep in mind that the event that throws your child off his sensory balance may occur well before the misbehavior. Coping with something difficult in the morning may leave your child no resources to deal with frustration in the afternoon.

Changing the Environment

A maxim to remember when dealing with your child with sensory integration disorder is, "When you can't change the child, change the environment." This means that if your child has trouble with something, you can change things around so that she never has to deal with it in the first place. This takes forethought and ingenuity on your part, but it pays off beautifully in a less-stressed child and a more relaxed parent.

Once you've done your behavior analysis and identified patterns that link your child's misbehavior to his sensory integration difficulties, think about what you could do to avoid those patterns. Think about the things around your house that cause your child the most stress. Identify sights or smells or activities that regularly spur a breakdown. Then consider how you might change things to accommodate your child's needs.

My child has tantrums over things one day and tolerates them the next. Does that mean it's not really a sensory integration issue?
No. Your child's overall level of stress on any given day may make her more or less tolerant of sensory integration problems. Then, too, some kids swing from overreactive to underreactive within the same sensory area, so something that bothers your child one day may not even be noticed on another.

Instead of constantly reminding your child not to play with small breakable items because he's too rough with them, move the items out of reach. Instead of yelling at him for hopping up from the table in the middle of homework, let him sit on a big inflatable exercise ball while working so that he gets the movement his body needs. Instead of criticizing him for not using his fork, find things that he can be allowed to eat with his fingers. Quietly changing the environment can save you from nagging and your child from failing.

Tantrum or Sensory Overload?

Armed with the information you've gleaned from behavior analysis, and the ideas you've developed for changing the environment, look at one of the major mix-ups of bad behavior versus bad sensory information: the tantrum. When your child loses it—cries, screams, refuses to move, bangs her head, kicks her feet—is she being a brat or expressing sensory distress? When all of your own buttons are being pushed, it can be hard to tell. But step back, giving yourself a little time-out if necessary, and ask these questions:

1. Does my child seem to be in control of her behavior?
2. Will my child negotiate?
3. What's in this for my child?

4. Have we fought this fight before?
5. Does my child show remorse?

A child who is throwing a tantrum for effect may look like he's giving a performance. A child who is throwing a tantrum due to sensory defensiveness will look like he's fighting for his life. The less control your child seems to have over his out-of-control behavior, the more likely it's related to sensory integration.

A child who is willfully misbehaving may be interested in negotiating to see what he can get away with before giving in. A child who is suffering from sensory overload will most likely be unable to think that clearly. All he can think of is getting out of or away from whatever is bothering him, and it's an all-or-nothing proposition. If there's any negotiating to be done with a child who's acting out of sensory seeking or sensory defensiveness, it will have to be done before the fact.

With a willfully misbehaving child, you can usually understand the point of the tantrum. She wants something, wants to do something, or wants to get out of doing something. Whether you agree or disagree, you can generally see where she's coming from. When a child with a sensory integration problem has a tantrum, however, it can often be very hard to see what set her off. Behavior analysis may clue you in, but even then, the trigger may be so far from the blast as to make cause-and-effect confusing.

Purposeful misbehavior may be driven by the wants and desires of the moment. Your child wants the toy you've said no to, the cookie you've put out of reach, or the television show you've turned off, and he is willing to throw a fit to get it. A child whose misbehavior is related to sensory integration disorder will overreact to the same things over and over—loud places, head washes, scratchy clothes.

Any child is likely to want to get back into your good graces with an "I'm sorry," and in some cases, it may even be genuine. But a child whose tantrum has been triggered by sensory integration disorder may be devastated to know she has upset you. It seems as though she was possessed, and she is heartbroken to see the damage done by the person using her body. This can be one of the most confusing things about children with sensory integration problems—that they seem to be so sweet and eager to please and yet can be so resistant.

Distraction or Sensory Seeking?

Another common difficulty for parents of children with sensory integration disorder is telling the difference between distractibility and sensory-seeking behavior. Is your child really ignoring you, or is he just preoccupied with finding the sensory input he needs to feel safe, comfortable, and alert? Ask yourself these questions:

1. Does my child's activity fit his sensory profile?
2. Does my child know what's going on?
3. What's my child getting out of this?
4. Is there a pattern here?
5. What happens when I make my child stop and pay attention?

A child who's distracted or deliberately not paying attention may be attracted to whatever's interesting, eye-catching, or close at hand. A child whose lack of attention has its roots in sensory integration will be engaging in specific and familiar activities aimed at jump-starting his system. When your child with proprioceptive or vestibular problems is jumping, swaying, or rolling, you can be pretty sure he's doing it so he can pay attention, not to avoid doing so.

When your child is distracted or is paying attention to something other than you, the words you say and things you do will pass her right on by. If you ask a question, she'll be stumped even if it's within her ability. When your child is engaging in sensory-seeking behaviors to address sensory integration problems, however, you may be surprised to find that she's been following your words all along. Ask a question, and she may stop her wandering, turn and answer you, then go back to it.

If your child is deliberately doing everything but paying attention to you, or even if he's just following his attention wherever it wanders, you will likely see some purpose in the activity, some reasonable area of interest taking its turn. If your child is responding to the needs of his sensory system, he may do things that seem nonsensical, like making loud noises, spinning around, or banging his head or body against hard objects.

Another sensory integration problem that may look like distractibility is auditory overload. If your child is overly sensitive to what comes in through her ears, every sound may register the same: the television, the dog's collar jingling, a sibling's phone conversation, a videogame soundtrack, and your voice calling her.

If your child is more likely to be distracted by certain things—television, music, books, friends, activities—that may not be a sensory-integration-driven behavior. If she's more likely to be distracted at certain times—when she's expected to sit still, when she's expected to be quiet, when she's tired or stressed or has had many demands placed on her—it's more likely that sensory integration problems may be driving the behavior.

When you force a distracted child to pay attention, you get attention. Whether you do it by making yourself the most interesting thing in the room, or making threats, or holding the child's head in your hands, forcing attention gets attention. But with a sensory-seeking child, forcing attention often gets you just the opposite. Many children with sensory integration problems need to move to pay attention; if you force them to be still, they may get sleepy and listless. Even if you force stillness and quiet, you can't force attention.

Disobedience or Poor Motor Planning?

You give your child seemingly simple instructions, then check back to find that he's done something else entirely, or done only part of what you've asked. Is he deliberately defying you, or is this a sign of poor motor-planning abilities? Even a request like "Go downstairs to the kitchen, get me a roll of paper towels from under the sink, and bring it back up to me" can be too complex for a child for whom just getting down the stairs is a pretty complicated task. If you're not sure whether your child's disobedience is willful or motor-planning related, ask yourself these questions:

1. Does he seem to want to cooperate?
2. Does he respond to one-step commands?
3. Does talking help?
4. Do pictures help?
5. Is the request unreasonable?

The child who is ignoring you or deliberately disobeying will probably serve up a little attitude along with the lack of action. If your child is really unable to sequence the steps you've requested due to sensory integration problems, he may seem confused, frustrated, or genuinely surprised that he hasn't pleased you.

Ask your child with sensory integration disorder to do a truly simple command, one with just one step that's completely within her abilities. Most likely, she will do it happily. If you see an escalation in "disobedience" as the request becomes more complex, that's a good sign that it's sensory integration-motivated, not deliberate.

Fact

Multi-step commands can confound children with sensory integration disorder. In addition to the motor-planning challenge, they may get distracted by a noise and forget the instructions, get stuck on one part and endlessly repeat it, or perform some ritual to stay alert and lose track of where they were. If you must give a multi-step command, give it one step at a time.

Try to talk your child through the task. If the behavior is due to motor-planning weakness, this may help your child do what you want and do it cheerfully. If the behavior is due to bad attitude, you'll just be accused of nagging.

Illustrations showing each step of an activity that your child can refer to when needed may help your child with motor-planning problems get with the program and stay with it. She may be enthusiastic about the way these pictures help her do things by herself, like a big kid. On the other hand, if your child is disobeying for other reasons, she may find a picture plan to be unbearably babyish.

Think hard about your child's particular sensory profile, muscle tone, motor-planning abilities, and coordination. Then look again at what you've asked your child to do. Does your request require holding something while going down stairs? Using an appropriate degree of force to open or move an object? Finding something in a cluttered environment? Hearing a buzzer or bell? Manipulating items like bedsheets or shoelaces in a specific and organized way? Although your request may have seemed reasonable when you made it, there may be something about it, even one small step or part of a step, that is not within your child's ability. If you're sure it's neither impossible nor too complex a request, then you can assume disobedience. (But be very sure.)

Giving Children Choices

Analyzing and interpreting behavior, striving for fairness, making adjustments based on your child's strengths and weaknesses—these may be seen as signs of parenting weakness by those who have never parented a child with special needs. Don't let others make you doubt yourself. You do not have to apologize for being a caring, involved, perceptive parent. You do not have to feel guilty for being the best parent for your child. These are things to be proud of. Blind obedience in the face of tyranny is not, in the end, a useful gift to give your child. The ability to make good decisions based on realistic expectations is.

It's not wrong to give your child choices. Few adults would be happy in a world without them. You may hear that arranging things so that your child will be successful is harmful because in "the real world," he won't have anyone to do that for him. But that's simply not true. He'll have himself. You will teach him what works for him, and what doesn't, and he will use that information to make good choices that can keep him safe and happy and in sensory balance. Forcing him to do things that make him uncomfortable or punishing him when his sensory integration problems force him to depart from the norm teaches him only that nobody understands and he must defend himself more staunchly. That leads only to more misbehavior, not to healthy functioning.

Essential

If you can't solve the mystery of a behavioral challenge by your child, but your gut tells you it's sensory integration related, trust your instinct. Your child needs to trust that you understand how she feels and that you will help her. Betraying that trust is more damaging than letting her get away with something now and then.

To the untrained eye, sensory integration problems seem invisible. But your eye is trained. You know your child, you're attuned to her sensory needs, and you can see the difference between standard misbehavior and the sort of sensory defensiveness, sensory seeking, and disorganization that comes with a diagnosis of sensory integration disorder. Go ahead and discipline your child when the behavior is in her control; kids need limits, and they need to know you know when they've been breached. They also need to know that they won't be blamed for things that aren't in their control. Your mercy and understanding in that area will be rewarded with a more trusting, less stressed-out, more in-control child. The choice is yours.

Chapter 18

Sensory Integration at Home

Your child's sensory integration disorder may show itself in spectacular fashion when it impacts behavior and becomes a disciplinary challenge. But it's always a factor in your child's life, manifested in dozens or hundreds of small ways all through the day. Understanding how your child's entire outlook on the world is affected by the inefficient way her brain processes information from her senses can help you ensure more relaxed days, quieter nights, a happier child, and a calmer household.

Self-Care Challenges

All parents look forward to that time when their kids will be able to take care of themselves: put on their clothes in the morning; use the toilet; eat neatly; tie their shoes. If your child has sensory integration disorder, you may have to wait a little longer. These areas of self-care require a degree of motor planning and sensory organization that your child simply may not have at an age-appropriate level. Lectures and punishment will not change that, but understanding and assistance can make life much less stressful for all.

Dressing

Getting dressed is a common trouble spot for kids with sensory integration disorder. If you're not getting good information from your sense of touch, it can be hard to button a shirt. If you have a poor concept of

where your body begins and ends, or where exactly your limbs are, working your way into a shirt or tights can be extra challenging. Shoe tying is a motor-planning nightmare, calling on a variety of abilities that may not be up to the job.

If your child consistently resists dressing herself—telling you she will and then doing anything but—it may be a sign that her sensory processing problems are getting in the way. Helping with dressing, whether physically or by talking through each step, will work better than shaming and blaming. Try Velcro-fastened shoes instead of lace-ups, and eliminate any fasteners that your child has trouble with. If you feel skills like tying and buttoning are important for your child to learn, focus on these activities during a less busy and stressful time of day.

Fact

A Dressing Cube like the one offered by Therapro (*www.theraproducts.com*) is a good way to work on dressing skills in a fun atmosphere. The cube has a different fastener on each side, so your child can practice tying, fastening Velcro, buttoning, zipping, and buckling. You may find a similar device in a toy store, or you can make one yourself.

Eating

Dining with a child who has motor-planning problems, a poor awareness of where his body begins and ends, low muscle tone, and a need to move to stay alert can be a distressing experience. You, your child, the table, and the floor may wind up with more of the meal than your child's stomach. It's important to realize that your child may not be deliberately making a mess of things but honestly has trouble with the sensory challenges involved.

Eating with a fork might be particularly challenging for your child. He must know where his hand is and where his mouth is, which is no small feat. Sometimes the fork has to be turned to spear food and sometimes turned to scoop it, making it a double motor-planning challenge. When it's working as a scoop, it must be turned at just the right angle so as not to lose the food on it. It's no wonder that kids try to turn fork foods into finger foods. Spoons have their own challenges, turning one way for stirring and another way for scooping, holding different amounts depending on their sizes and depths. Knives may require too much coordination to even contemplate.

Be sympathetic to your child's mealtime struggles. Try for foods that will be easy to maneuver with a poorly held fork. Put lids on cups if spilling is a problem, and use a straw if sipping's hard. Take your child's sensory-based food preferences into account. And, if necessary, cover the table and floor with plastic and let the vegetables fall where they may.

Washing Up

You've sent your child to wash her face and hands once, twice, and still she comes back with ketchup on her mouth or jelly on her cheeks. Is she deliberately trying to be a slob? Probably not. Remember that some kids with sensory integration problems can't feel things on their skin, and they may be less likely to see minor differences such as a little smudge of red by the lips. If you don't want to clean your child up, at least accompany her to the sink and provide some guidance for where the mess is and whether it's taken care of.

Tying Shoes

It's a major goal of early childhood to be able to tie one's own shoes, but think about whether this is a reasonable or necessary goal for your child. It is a blessing for children with sensory differences that Velcro shoes and pull-ons are now widely available and somewhat fashionable. Take advantage of this ever-so-helpful trend and give your child a break. Shoe-tying is a complicated motor-planning task that depends on tactile sensitivity to feel where the laces are going; visual acuity to be able to see the ins and outs of the loops; vestibular sensitivity to be able to do it while balancing on one side of the body; and motor sequencing to get the steps and the order correct. It's a tall order, and one you can give short shrift.

Potty Training Problems

Many potty training techniques are focused on the discomfort a child feels in a wet diaper. But children who don't process tactile sensations well may be oblivious to this. The moisture and the cold may not register, and if the child's pain threshold is high, neither will the rashes that accompany it. While your child may want to comply with your wishes and be motivated to win big kid underwear or special privileges, she may genuinely not realize when she has an accident.

Alert!

Just because your child doesn't feel when his diaper's wet doesn't mean his genitals are without sensation. Your child may rely on masturbating when he needs strong input to his underreactive tactile sense. You may not feel comfortable allowing your son or daughter to engage in this activity, but be aware that it may be a legitimate sensory-seeking behavior.

Compounding the problem is the fact that your child also may not feel the urge to use the toilet until it becomes urgent. Sensations from the bowel and the bladder have to be processed just like any other, and they may go astray just as well. If the sensations aren't strong enough to interrupt your child from play, they certainly won't be strong enough to awaken him from sleep. So again, toilet readiness may be hard to discern and hard to achieve.

If you believe that sensory integration is interfering with your child's ability to potty train, your best strategy may be to wait. Your child may improve in her ability to recognize the necessary signals, or she may grow in the maturity needed to see the importance of doing so. Although you may encounter pressure from teachers or family members to push your child through this transition, hang in there until your child is ready. The negative attention and frustration and anger that goes with unsuccessful potty training struggles will be bad for your child and bad for you.

Maybe you're determined to get your child using the toilet because of deadlines imposed by preschools or day cares. This can make it hard to wait for your child to be ready, but waiting is important. Consider looking around for a child-care provider that will allow your child to continue wearing diapers if that's what's right for her. Special education preschool through your school district should allow this, but even private facilities may bend the rules for children with special needs. Ask around.

The Appeal of Routines

Most people like routines. It's good to know what to expect. You make plans based on predictable patterns of activity, and that organization makes you feel comfortable and in control. Breaking routine from time to time can be fun and exciting, but only because the routine itself is comforting and stable.

For children with sensory integration disorder, however, any variation of routine can be terrifying. Since your child can't count on being able to process new experiences with any degree of accuracy, she may try hard to avoid them. It's tough enough, oftentimes, to cope with the challenges of the sensory input that needs processing on a routine day. Your child may develop elaborate strategies for negotiating those difficult passages. Changing plans cause those strategies—and usually your child—to fall apart.

It would be nice if life was always predictable, and we could always ensure our children that each day would be exactly like the one before, easy to plan for and navigate through. Unfortunately, there will always be changes—planned ones like vacations or appointments, unplanned ones like accidents or natural disasters. Try as much as possible, though, to keep things predictable for your child. Don't change routine without a reason. When you have to change things, talk to your child about it ahead of time and try to help him develop new strategies to take it on. Make respecting the routine a routine.

Fact

A stable routine is a necessity for most children with neurological impairments, including autism, Asperger syndrome, and fetal alcohol spectrum disorder. It may be to your child's benefit to attend school in a classroom that is very structured and predictable, whether that means a self-contained class or the choice of a particular teacher known for her consistency.

It may help your child to put a schedule for the day up on the wall, with words for older children, pictures for younger ones. Go over it in the morning or the previous night before bed. This will provide a good opportunity to talk through trouble spots and reassure your child that her concerns are being taken seriously. Remember, your child often feels that she is the only one who knows what it's like to be her, and she therefore has all the responsibility for making things tolerable. Take some of that responsibility away, and you may have a less-stressed, better-controlled child.

Realistic Expectations

It's natural to have expectations for your child. You want him to be able to make his way comfortably in the world, to behave appropriately, to make friends, to play with pleasure and ability, and to learn efficiently. Those are understandable hopes, and you don't have to abandon them entirely. But if you are expecting your child to do things that he truly is not able to do, on a neurological level and at this time, that can be a little cruel. Realistic expectations are not the same as no expectations or reduced expectations. They're just expectations that set your child up for success instead of failure. And what parent wouldn't want to do that?

Your job as a parent—and it's an important one—is to accurately assess your child's ability and set your expectations accordingly. Just as you wouldn't expect your five year old to be able to do things your ten year old does, don't expect your youngster with developmental delays to be able to do things at the same level as her peers. If you know your child has trouble with motor planning, don't expect her to be able to clean up her own room without help; give her small tasks one at a time and all the assistance she needs. If you know your child can't distinguish individual sounds in a roomful of noise, don't keep calling to her and getting angry. Instead, walk over to her, tap her on the shoulder, and then expect her to listen. You know your child better than anybody. If even you can't accommodate her, how can she ever trust that anyone else will?

Essential

If your child is old enough, talk to her about how much she may be able to do or for how long. The more you can make her aware of her particular needs and sensitivities, the more she will one day be able to understand her own limits and set appropriate tasks for herself.

Knowing your child's limits and respecting them isn't just a kindness to her, but to you and to anybody who's within earshot when she melts down or blows up. When you force a child who hates noise to go to a mall, or expect your child with low muscle tone to endure a long walk, or ask your child with vestibular dysfunction to sit through a long family dinner without moving, or put a bunch of foods your child finds hard to smell and swallow on the table at once, you are as good as asking your child to have a temper tantrum. The fault does not lie with your child. The fault lies with you, for knowingly exceeding the limits. As they say in traffic court, ignorance of the law is no excuse.

A smart use of your knowledge of your child's limits, on the other hand, can leave both you and your child with a feeling of success and empowerment. Figure out how long your child can keep it together at the mall, and plan to leave ten minutes before that. Congratulate him on doing such a great job of self-control. Take your child on short chatty walks, and let him know how well he's doing. Give your child little jobs to do during mealtimes to give him an excuse to move. Introduce one very small portion of one difficult-to-deal-with food and give your child lots of enthusiastic positive feedback for trying it. Work within your child's limits, and you'll be able to congratulate yourself, too, for a situation well handled.

Sibling Conflict

It's one thing for you to understand your child's sensory integration problems, but getting your other children to extend appropriate understanding and sympathy is another. Depending on the age of your child's siblings, you may be able to give them a little bit of an explanation as to why their brother does those strange, annoying things. But any special treatment you give him to compensate for his sensory challenges is liable to meet with cries of "No fair!" from the others.

You'll be doing your children a service to teach them now that fair doesn't mean equal treatment for each person. It involves each person getting exactly what is appropriate for her. Talk about some ways in which your other children "get" things that your child with sensory integration disorder does not. Does the sibling participate in more activities? Have more friends? Have an easier time in school? It's not fair that your child has this disorder, it just is. "Fair" means she gets what she needs to be safe and happy and comfortable, and your other children get that, too.

Playing to Strengths

You'll need to make accommodations for your child's weaknesses, respect his limits, and plan for success by changing the environment, but no child is all weaknesses. Every child has strengths in some area, and those need to be applauded and supported as much as the weaknesses need to be compensated for. Make sure your child has plenty of opportunity to participate in something he's good at and enjoys.

Fact

A Mind at a Time, by Dr. Mel Levine, can help you identify areas in which your child is particularly strong. He identifies eight systems: attention control, memory, language, spatial ordering, sequential ordering, motor, higher thinking, and social thinking. Though your child may have significant gaps in some of these systems, there may be strengths in others that can compensate.

Those positive areas can help the child with sensory integration disorder in a number of ways. If your child has an activity she enjoys and is good at, you can use it as a reward to help her get through more difficult activities. You may also be able to substitute areas of strength for areas of weakness—allowing an artistic child to make your picture schedules for the day instead of making a bed or setting a table, for example. Giving children extra work in an area of strength can make them feel better about the tough stuff you have to help them avoid. Everyone wants to feel competent and useful. Being competent and useful as a parent means finding a way for your child to feel that way, too.

CHAPTER 19

Sensory Integration at School

When your child is in your home, you can exert a lot of control over his environment. You can arrange things so that they'll work best for his particular sensory integration needs, and you can give him some understanding when his behavior shows the strain of dealing with the world. But what happens when you send your child to school? Classrooms are often particularly difficult places for children with sensory integration disorder.

The Classroom

If you wanted to design a place that would be as uncomfortable as possible for a child with sensory integration disorder, you couldn't do much better than some contemporary classrooms. Many are so cluttered, with assignments on the wall and writing on the board and piles of books and papers all around, that even people without any problems with visual perception and organization may find it difficult to concentrate. An increasing emphasis on standardized tests means your child has to spend longer hours sitting at a desk, with less time for physical education or recess or less restrictive subject matter. Overcrowded classrooms have made teachers less able to allow students to move or make noise or learn in individualized ways. And if you can't behave, you lose recess—the sort of break kids with proprioceptive or vestibular problems most crave.

Alert!

If your child needs movement to be calm and comfortable, stress to your child's teacher that the one thing she should not do to discipline your child is take away recess. Withdrawing recess will almost surely make his behavior worse. Suggest some alternatives if you can, and give the teacher some information on sensory integration disorder to back it up.

Although there are many obvious distractions and discomforts in the classroom, the things that upset your child with sensory integration disorder may be less apparent. The slight flickering or buzzing of fluorescent lights may disturb her. The sound of cars going by a window, a squeaking seat, or a classmate's scratching pencil may grate. Smells from a lunchroom or the odor of the teacher's perfume may distract or irritate. The fact that your child is confined to one place for most of the day, with no ability to make adjustments that might make her feel more comfortable, will tend to magnify these problems.

De-Clutter, De-Stress

While you may not be able to do much about your child's classroom environment, it may be worthwhile to try. Let the administration know that your child will do best in an uncluttered classroom with a lot of structure and predictable routine, and in some cases you may be able to get your child assigned to a teacher who is well-suited to his needs. You might also request that your child be seated far away or facing away from distractions such as windows and doorways. Sitting close to the teacher may be helpful for your child if it keeps him from being distracted by other visual information, harmful if the teacher's tone of voice or personal style is a distraction in itself.

Make sure that your child's school supplies don't provide a distracting source of clutter in and of themselves. Go through your child's backpack each night and remove unnecessary material. Have a clearly marked place in a folder or binder for your child to store her homework so that it's easy to find the next day. Make sure the homework is there when she leaves for school in the morning. Get a single binder to hold all subjects, or color-coded folders and spiral notebooks, or whatever system seems to work best for your child. If organization is a problem for your child, go ahead and help do the organizing for her as much as you can. As she gets older and less distracted by sensory integration problems, you can teach her the techniques that work best for her.

Back to School Night is often a good time to get a useful impression of your child's classroom and teacher and pinpoint some areas that may be problematic. Follow that up with a meeting with the teacher to suggest some simple changes that might make it easier for your child to succeed in the classroom.

Dress for Success

Make sure that you're not adding to your child's classroom stress with the clothes and accessories you're sending with him. Comfort is more important than fashion when it comes to clothing. If he's most at ease in sweats, don't sweat it. Stay away from scratchy fabrics and high collars if those things are a problem. On the other hand, if your child struggles with the proprioceptive sense and likes to bite or chew on his shirt collars, a tight crewneck might be a good choice, since it's harder to bite on. Or choose a button-down shirt; chewing doesn't show as much on buttoned collars as it does on rounded ones.

Choose shoes with care, too. If shoe-tying's a problem, pick a cool pair of slip-ons or Velcro-fastened sneakers, or replace regular shoelaces with the curly, stretchy variety that don't need to be tied.

You should be able to find curly elastic shoelaces in shoe stores like Payless, but they can also be ordered from Life Solutions

Plus (online at *www.lifesolutionsplus.com*) or Therapro (*www.theraproducts.com*). The laces come in a variety of colors and patterns. If the teacher complains that your child is slipping his shoes off in class, try a pair that won't slip off easily, like high-tops or boots.

Sitting Still

Sitting still is the downfall of many children with sensory integration disorder. It may be physically impossible for them if they have low muscle tone. It may be excruciatingly uncomfortable for them if their proprioceptive systems demand movement to feel alert and in control. Yet school is a place where sitting still is expected, and there are consequences for movement. This puts the child in a position between getting in trouble with the teacher and getting in trouble with her body.

Suggest to your child's teacher that your child be given as much chance as possible to move. Ask the teacher to send your child on errands if he gets fidgety, or pick up things in the classroom, or pass out papers. Another tool that can be useful is a rubber cushion on the child's seat that automatically provides a certain amount of movement without the child actually needing to initiate it. Fidget toys like a squeeze ball or small stuffed animal can also help burn off some of the movement your child needs.

Web sites with occupational therapy products are good places to shop for classroom aides like a cushion to sit on or toys to fidget with. Southpaw Enterprises (*www.southpawenterprises.com*) has rubber cushions that let children move a little while sitting, as well as a selection of fidget toys.

If your child's feet don't touch the ground while she's sitting at her desk, she may have a hard time keeping them still and supporting her body in an appropriate way. Ask the teacher if you can send in a heavy box or block that's the right size to go under your child's feet and give her a natural seating position. This may increase her sitting comfort significantly and allow her to get some proprioceptive input in her feet and ankles.

Another possible desk difficulty is one-piece desk-chair combos that can rock, tilt, or fall over entirely if too many books are piled atop them. If your child has poor motor planning, getting in and out of these contraptions without disruption can be a challenge, and if proprioception is a problem, it may be hard for him to resist moving or rocking the desk. While you may not be successful, it's worth requesting a separate chair and desk for your child. The increase in comfort and stability might be significant enough to make the teacher glad you pushed for it.

Paying Attention

Nothing gets a child with sensory integration disorder tagged with an ADHD label than an inability to pay attention in class. To teachers, this seems clear cut: If a child is daydreaming, fidgeting, talking to himself, or doing poorly on tests, she's not paying attention. If a child is unable to answer a question when asked, find a spot on a page to read, or locate information in an open-book exam, she's not paying attention. If a child complains about noise, light, smells, or uncomfortable seating positions, that child is not paying attention.

But as you've learned, children with sensory integration disorder can want very much to pay attention and try very hard to do so. Whether they need to move to do it, or whether they are thwarted by their body's inability to process the information from their senses, they need help and understanding, not judgment. Teachers can only make things worse by laying on punishment and raising stress.

Now Hear This

Giving the teacher her undivided attention may be hard for a child who has sensory integration problems with the auditory sense.

It may be difficult for her to distinguish the teacher's voice over other sounds in the classroom. Anxiety over sudden sharp sounds like fire alarms may preoccupy her, and loud noises from outside can be distracting. Unpleasant sounds like the squeaking of chalk on a chalkboard or chair legs on a tile floor may cause her to tune out, missing the teacher's talk along the way.

Difficulty with the visual sense can also keep your child from being as attentive as he wants to be. The many jumbled sights of a cluttered classroom will vie for his attention. If he has trouble organizing visual information, it can be hard to follow along in a textbook, all the more so when the book in question is full of illustrations and captions. Picking out the block of writing on a blackboard that the teacher is referring to can also be a challenge. While the teacher may assume a child has lost his place due to inattentiveness, he may really be struggling to find the right place out of so very many possible places.

Additional Difficulties

When your child with proprioceptive and vestibular problems just has to move in order to pay attention, the situation is especially tricky. If the teacher insists that your child stop moving, she might as well insist that he stop paying attention this instant. Your child may ignore the directive and get in trouble, or he may zone out into a sleepy state that's movement-free but learning-free, too. Either way, he's not getting what he needs from the classroom, the teacher, or the lesson.

Tactile sensitivities can make your child seem inattentive, too. A hard chair, a cramped desk, a seatmate who bumps into him, a teacher or aide who gives pats on the head or back—any of these can be so distracting to your child that she literally cannot concentrate on anything else. A school uniform that denies your child the right to wear what's comfortable and calming to her may also take its toll. The teacher will likely not spot any of these things as a potential distraction and will assume that your child is purposely goofing around.

Writing Right

You also know when writing is a trial for your child. Problems with muscle tone and motor planning can turn writing a simple sentence or completing a worksheet into a Herculean task. Teachers who are sticklers for penmanship may make things worse by forcing your child to repeat the writing over and over again, with severely diminishing returns. But even if the teacher doesn't add to the stress load by disciplining your child for writing problems, the problems alone will be stressful enough.

You'll want to talk with your child's teacher to make sure he understands that your child has good reason to have such writing trouble. Make sure, too, to arm your child with good tools that will make writing as easy as possible. Thick pencils may be easier to hold onto than thinner ones, shorter pencils easier to manipulate than longer ones. Pencil grips may make grasping a pencil more comfortable and secure for your child. Pencil grips are soft rubber tubes that fit over the lower end of a pencil and give your child a fatter, less slippery surface to grab onto. They're generally formed in such a way as to make your child's fingers naturally fall into the proper position. OT Ideas (online at *www.otideas.com*) has a wide variety of colors and styles, including a sampler pack that can help you find just the right fit for your child.

Essential

When your child brings home her textbooks, sit down and look through them with her. If they're visually busy and hard to follow, talk with her a little about the elements on the page and help her identify some features that can show her the way through. Chapter subheads are often useful for pinpointing information, as are summaries in the margins.

If writing at school is a problem for your child, doing homework is likely to bring all that unhappiness home. Homework can be of great value to your child, and it can also help you get a good first-hand look at what his academic strengths and weaknesses are. Too often, though, homework turns into an endless battle—hours of forcing your child to write, struggling to produce blotchy torn-up papers. Don't fall into this trap with your child. Confer with the teacher and see if you can get permission to adjust homework when needed. Perhaps your child can write the spelling words once or twice instead of five times and spell them out loud to you. Maybe you can transcribe long written answers for him or let him use a word processor.

Ideally, the goal of homework is to reinforce material learned in class and let the teacher know whether the students have mastered it enough to do it independently. Only for penmanship is the goal of homework good penmanship. Reducing the writing burden may give your child a much better chance to show what he knows. With luck, you'll have a teacher who understands that.

Working with Teachers

Some teachers are a dream to work with. They're eager to collaborate with parents and learn what they can about each of their students. You can give them material and know it will be read, processed, and utilized. A free and open exchange between parent and teacher in situations such as this is an exciting process, and it's one that can help you, too, learn how best to help your child.

Some teachers, alas, are nightmares. Maybe they're set in their ways after years of teaching and aren't about to buy into any newfangled theories. Maybe they're overwhelmed with the demands of teaching children with multiple disabilities. Maybe they're new to teaching and insecure and feel the only way to get respect is to act like they know everything. Since sensory integration disorder isn't a universally accepted diagnosis, such teachers may refuse to consider it as a reason for your child's struggles. They may have very firm impressions about your child's laziness—and your gullibility.

Most teachers, in truth, are somewhere in between. They may want to cooperate with you, but they're overworked, overstressed, and undersupported. Giving your child the accommodations she needs may take time, study, and administrative support that the teacher just doesn't have. It's easier to do things the way they've always been done, and few of us make a big effort of finding the hardest way to do things in our own jobs.

Making the Job Easier

Your job, then, in dealing with in-between teachers, is to convince them that doing things your way will in fact make their jobs easier, not harder. Certainly it's no easy feat to deal with an uncomfortable, fidgety, inattentive, easily upset, overreacting or underreacting child every day. Techniques that will allow your child to learn and participate in appropriate ways will most likely help other children in the classroom, too.

Try hard, then, to present your child's accommodations to the teacher as strategies you are offering to make working with your child less difficult, not things you're demanding. You may, ultimately, have to demand them. But for starters, if what you're requesting is that the teacher be more understanding of your child, it doesn't hurt to be more understanding of the teacher.

Promoting Understanding

Be sure to offer the same information you give the classroom teacher to all the other professionals your child works with at school. You might expect the teacher to do this, and you might be right in expecting that this will happen, but don't take it for granted. You're always safer to offer the information yourself. Include copies for any classroom aides, the gym teacher, the music teacher, the principal, the school nurse, even the cafeteria workers if smells and flavors are a source of distress.

The best possible situation for your child is for everyone at the school to understand his needs. One staff person shouting at him in the hallway as he jumps or bumps or does whatever he needs to do to be comfortable can set your child up for a bad day. If you have any skill at public speaking, you might even offer to do a little workshop on sensory integration for the staff. Most likely, once they know more about sensory integration disorder, they'll be able to identify more children in the school who can benefit from the information.

Fact

Answers to Questions Teachers Ask About Sensory Integration, by Carol Stock Kranowitz, Stacy Szklut, and others, is a good resource for helping education professionals understand your child's special needs. It's available in book and audio form from Sensory Resources (online at *www.sensoryresources.com*).

When the Teacher Won't Cooperate

There may be times when you just can't get your child's teacher to listen to your concerns, and you may fear that she will give your child an even harder time if you push. If your child has other special needs sufficient to qualify for an individualized education plan (IEP), you can have the accommodations he requires for sensory integration problems written into that document. These are legally binding, and the teacher will not have the option to ignore them. If she does, you will have recourse to the child study team, the district's department of special education, the state special education authorities, and even the courts if it comes to that. (It's unlikely that it will.) Most sensory integration accommodations are reasonable and similar to those that might be requested for any child with developmental delays.

If your child doesn't qualify for an IEP, your options may be more limited. You can ask the school occupational therapist to talk to the teacher. You can talk to the principal and request whatever support the teacher will need to be able to accommodate your child. You can request another teacher (do a little research first to see which teacher in your child's grade would be the best choice). You can request frequent conferences to offer new ideas or suggestions; it is possible that the teacher will eventually go along just to shut you up. But in the end, it may be that you will just have to help your child hold on through a bad year and hope for better luck next time. Provide your child with plenty of extra support and understanding to make up for what she's not getting in school.

Chapter 20

Sensory Integration at Play

Play is a big part of occupational therapy using a sensory integration approach and of the therapy you do with your child at home. But playing with other children in an unstructured and unsupervised setting represents a whole different degree of difficulty for your child. You will want to anticipate the areas in which your child's sensory needs may get in the way of safe and enjoyable play with other children and be ready to provide or suggest solutions that keep the fun going for everyone.

Swing Set Showdown

If your child has problems with the vestibular or proprioceptive sense, a playground can be like one big therapy room—or like a chamber of horrors. Either way, the work you do with your child on the playground, or the work your occupational therapist does on playground-like therapy equipment, will be particularly meaningful. Being sensitive to your child's needs and making sure she gets lots of good hard input from the swing and the slide—or lots of gentle, well-modulated, closely supervised exposure to balance beams and teeter-totters—will make you a true playground pal, and you may find that a trip to the park is a highlight of your times with your child.

When there are other children on the playground, though, things can get tricky. Your child who is under-reactive to information from his vestibular sense may derive great benefit from hard swinging, but that doesn't give him the right to monopolize the swing set when other children are waiting for a turn. He may have a deep need for the calming and organizing vestibular input he gets from swooping down the slide, but that doesn't mean he can push other children off the ladder in an attempt to get back up. Takings turns and sharing equipment are cardinal rules of playground behavior, and they mesh poorly with the sort of determined need that some children with sensory integration disorder bring with them on their playground visits. Similarly, a child who freezes in legitimate terror in mid-play—blocking the slide until someone can talk her down or clinging to jungle gym bars for dear life—is also going to be an unpopular playmate.

Different Strokes

Chances are, your child is operating at a far more primal level during playground activities than his peers. For most children, the playground is a social activity. They want to do what other kids are doing, see who can swing higher or jump off the swing farther, and compete for the most daring jungle gym maneuver or sliding-down position. They may work together in a sandbox or take turns pushing the merry-go-round. The presence of others motivates them to develop their own play skills.

Essential

Disrespect from peers may be hurtful to your child, but it's generally not enough to change behavior that is driven by sensory seeking or avoidance. Making a big deal of what other kids will think is, therefore, an ineffective way of getting your child to change her behavior, and raising her anxiety level will likely only make the behavior worse.

For your child with sensory integration disorder, on the other hand, the playground is more about internals than externals. She's more interested in the way her body feels than in what her peers are doing. She's driven by cravings for physical activities, not by competition or collaboration. When something floods her overreactive sensory system, she doesn't care if she looks like a wimp or a scaredy-cat, she just wants to protect herself from the threat.

This may make your child's behavior baffling to kids who enjoy swinging but don't need it, who want the admiration that comes with sliding in a daredevil way but don't crave the vestibular input, and who are motivated to appear brave and never fearful. When your child won't cooperate and won't collaborate and won't play by the social rules, other children simply will not know what to make of him. They'll call him a bully or a baby without ever understanding that no amount of social disapproval is going to change his intense need.

Encouraging Etiquette

As a parent, you don't want your child to be known as either a bully or a baby, but you may feel as powerless to deflect your child's primal needs as she is. Changing the environment is one way to address the problem—go to the park only when there are few other children there, or invest in a swing set and slide for your backyard. You can also try monitoring your child closely throughout your playground time, stepping in to distract and remove her when she's causing a problem. Instead of swinging, she might agree to push another child on the swings, thereby getting some nice proprioceptive input to her arms. Distracting her with another desired game or activity may head off some bullying or babyish behavior. That activity doesn't necessarily have to be a playground activity—the best strategy may be to know when to get your child out of there.

If you feel strongly that your child needs to learn to socialize with other children, or that other children need to learn to accommodate differences among their playmates, there are a few things you can do to prepare your child for a smoother playground time:

- **Give your child lots of good input**—maybe on a trampoline, a punching bag, or a game of wrestling—before going to the playground. This may make his needs less intense.

- **Talk your child through the experience.** Prepare him verbally for the fact that he will need to share and take turns, and arrange a signal you can give him when it's time to do so.
- **Work out some alternatives.** Strategize "What would you do if . . ." scenarios, and help him make a plan for handling transitions.
- **Bring a fidget toy** he can keep tucked in his pocket to play with while waiting in line.
- **Set a specific period of time you will spend at the playground**, and let him know that you will give him warnings when time is getting close.
- **Establish a signal he can give you if he's feeling overwhelmed or out of control**, and you'll come up with an acceptable excuse to leave at once.

You may not be able to implement some of these effectively with a younger child, but as your child gets older, techniques like these will help you work together to manage her sensory needs without managing to make her look foolish.

You Touch Me, I Hit You

Not sharing a swing or a slide is bad enough, but your child with sensory integration disorder may well strike out at any kid who so much as taps him on the shoulder. Whether he's overreacting to tactile information and interpreting light touch as aggression, or just wanting some proprioceptive input in his wrists and arms and pushing someone to get it, hitting and pushing are never okay. Helping your child control that behavior during unstructured, rough-and-tumble play, though, isn't so easy.

Since you can't always anticipate when your child will touch or be touched, you may not be able to intervene on her behalf quickly enough to prevent the action, although you can certainly intervene when adults want to punish your child for her unintentional responses. You can remove her quickly from activities in which she seems to be unable to keep control of her hitting and pushing, and you can try to structure activities with children so that your child is less likely to be put in a position of jostling or being jostled.

The school is complaining that my child is aggressive at recess. How can I help?

If your child has an IEP, put the strategies you've found successful in it so that aides or teachers will carry them out. If not, talk to your child's teacher and any playground aides and advise them on why your child acts as he does and what they might do about it.

What may work better, though, especially as your child gets older, is to help him understand why he acts that way, and why people react to him the way they do. If your child can understand that what feels like a hit to him may just be a touch, and that if he responds aggressively others are going to be surprised and defensive, it may help him control his anger. If he can understand that the pushing he does to make himself feel better feels bad to his friends, it may help him find alternatives. None of this is going to matter when your child is running on pure reaction, but giving him lots of good sensory input before group activities may put that point off a bit.

Motor Planning and Sports

Sports can be a great outlet for kids with sensory integration problems. Running, jumping, hitting, tackling, wrestling, and throwing can all give good input to the proprioceptive and vestibular senses and bring about euphoric feelings of power and control. If only sports play were just about those things. Unfortunately, the coordination, organization, physical control, and motor planning required to play those games well and compete as part of a team may elude your child with sensory integration disorder. Even when the individual components of the game aren't a problem—and quite often, they are—putting them all together without reliable sensory information can be impossible.

Fact

Adapted physical education is individualized to the needs of children with delayed gross motor skills. It is worth asking about if motor problems are making gym a dangerous and depressing place for your child. You can find more information on adapted physical education online, at *www.pecentral.org.*

Consider, for example, the motor-planning challenges of kickball. Your child has to organize her body sufficiently to complete the involved task of getting her body and foot to where the ball is going to be and kicking it with sufficient force to move it out into the field. This involves almost all of the sensory systems in a unified effort, and the movement can be quite complicated and require an enormous amount of attention. But then, when that task is complete, your child can't stand and enjoy the feeling of success. She has to turn toward a base and run to it, again involving most sensory systems in an effort to run in the right direction at the appropriate speed without bumping into anybody and without running too far.

Children with motor planning and other sensory problems may be able to complete one half of the job and not the other, but both are needed to participate in games and avoid social stigma. These problems, together with other sensory challenges that make your child look weird to his peers, can turn recess and gym class into times of real despair. Don't make the mistake of assuming that your child could play better if he tried harder or wanted it more or feared humiliation or practiced harder. Indeed, practice will help your child, but only if you can break down the activity into its smallest components and allow him to practice in a way that will be meaningful to him.

That can be hard to do when the games are being played at school. The gym teacher may not be able to give your child the kind of attention and special instruction she needs, and in fact may not want to. If the teacher is at all sympathetic, ask to be kept informed of what sports are being done at school so you can work with your child at home. You may also be able to get the school occupational or physical therapist involved, either attending classes with your child and fine-tuning the instruction, or coordinating with the teacher so that the skills can be worked on in therapy, or you may be able to hire a high school student to practice some of the skills with your child.

Playing by No One Else's Rules

Given the difficulty your child may have with the games children play, he might quite understandably decide to either play alone or to organize elaborate games that fit into his particular comfort zones and strengths. Or he may bring his own set of strategies to his peers' games and be accused of cheating. He may try to keep things in his sensory comfort zone by being bossy and controlling, or he may withdraw from the whole complicated process of dealing with other children and go into a fantasy game of his own.

Your child's play skills may be delayed by motor planning problems, and he may still be in a phase of parallel play—when kids do their own thing when playing together—while his peers have moved on to more collaborative games. If he has problems processing auditory information, he may have trouble following the sometimes involved rules that other kids spell out for playing their games. If it's visual information he has trouble with, some board games may be difficult to follow. All these factors may make your child feel that doing things other people's way is too unrewarding to bother with.

A Different Playtime Drummer

Kids gravitate to the sort of play that best suits their developmental and sensory abilities. Even children without problems severe enough to be identified as sensory integration disorder prefer certain types of activity to others. Generally boys prefer rambunctious play and girls prefer play that is more oriented to social role-playing, but you most likely know girls who are tomboys and boys who prefer creative play. Other children may not react as strongly to play that's outside their preferences as your child does, but given a choice, they'll pick what suits them. Give your child the freedom to do that as well.

Plan for success when your child has friends over. Talk to your child about what he might like to do and what he doesn't want to do. If he has toys he does not want to share, put them away so there will be no conflicts. Settling these things in advance ensures a peaceful play date.

You can still help your child socialize by creating opportunities for play with one or two other children. Children without sensory integration problems may be more able and willing to adjust their play styles to your child's than she will be able to adjust to theirs. Creating small group situations, planning activities that all the children will enjoy, and supervising play so that your child can comfortably participate will help your child have some positive experiences of friendship and socialization. As playing with others becomes less stressful and her sensory abilities improve with therapy, your child may be able to branch out and play more collaboratively.

Teach Your Children Well

On the other hand, if your child seems to want to play like other kids but just can't figure out how, practicing with her may be a good solution. Play board games with her to teach things like taking turns, the right direction to move around a board, moving her piece without knocking over the others, accepting setbacks with grace, rolling dice, and all those other mechanics of game playing that you probably take for granted. Play card games to help your child practice holding cards without dropping them or pulling too many out at a time. Muscle tone, motor planning, tactile, and visual difficulties can all make game playing a much more involved process for your child than you realize. Therapy will help, but explaining and practicing the immediate skills involved will be necessary, too.

You may also need to practice games like hide-and-seek, jump rope, and hopscotch with your child. He may not understand the rules of playing house or other social role-playing activities that other kids enjoy. It may be hard for him to adapt to other kids' ideas and scenarios when he's carefully planned out his own. Playing these games with your child—with sensitivity to his needs and difficulties, but an understanding of what other children will be expecting of him—can gently lead him to a greater understanding of how to interact with others and the ability to do so. If nothing else, he'll enjoy having your undivided attention.

Fact

You can purchase special card-holders to make it easier for your child to handle a hand of cards. Many retailers offer a round plastic disk to insert cards into, making them easier to hold onto. Innovative versions can also be ordered from Einstein Design (online at *www.cardholda.com*) or Life with Ease (*www.lifewithease.com*).

Computers and Video Games

Computers and video games get a bad rap. Parents are told to limit the amount of time their children spend with them and to encourage kids to get out and do other things. But when those other things are difficult for or threatening to your child, and if they present a social difficulty, video and computer games can be very good things indeed. You should still closely monitor your child's activity, and make sure that he is playing games that are appropriate to his age and developmental level. But this can be an area in which some children with sensory integration disorder can find social success that eludes them in more traditional childhood activities. If your child can't hit a ball or run fast, but he knows all about the latest games and can play them with friends, he may be able to find his social niche there. At the least, it gives him something age-appropriate to do during play dates.

Pay attention to the rating system on games and watch your child as he plays. Some increase motor skills and coordination, and others are fun and provide an experience of success. Other games, though, even some with family friendly ratings, may be visually or auditorially overstimulating for your child. If a game spurs out of control behavior, pull the plug.

These games have another advantage: If your child enjoys them, they can be a powerful incentive to get her to do things she doesn't enjoy. Allow your child a Game Boy break for finishing a difficult homework task; allow video game minutes for dressing quickly in the morning; give computer time as a reward for eating neatly or making the bed. You may also find that the games can be a fun activity for you and your child to do together. Let your child teach you how to play—she may enjoy that turn of the tables as much as she does the game.

Social Insecurity

There's no getting around the fact that sensory integration disorder can cause social problems for your child. Whether other kids see him as aggressive, immature, or disruptive, his inability to play within the parameters set by his peers may cause him to be cast out by them. This is sometimes more painful for the parent than for the child. Try to follow his lead—if he seems to be upset about the way other children treat him, work with him to improve his abilities and find ways to play more successfully. If he's happy, try to be at peace with that, too; he may be able to find his own way and his own understanding playmates.

Parents have to walk a fine line here between being part of the solution and part of the problem. You want to do what you can to facilitate successful play for your child, but you don't want to go around making apologies for her. You want to put her in situations where she can be successful, but you don't want her to fail and fail again until you find the right combination. Don't force things. The very best you can offer your child is constant, nonjudgmental understanding.

CHAPTER 21

Sensory Integration in the Community

The fear of public meltdown may make you reluctant to take your child out into the community. At home, her environment can be carefully controlled, but outside, in the wide world, it's harder to make sure that her sensory systems get appropriate input. Rather than sheltering your child, try to make a certain amount of public activity part of her routine. The more she's exposed to it—in well-regulated, well-modulated doses, with a backup plan in place—the more she will be able to integrate it into her supply of sensory experiences.

At the Grocery Store

The supermarket may not seem like a very spectacular place to you, but to your child it is a hodgepodge of bright lights, squeaky cart wheels, and alternating aisles of cold and warm. Visual overstimulation can be caused by colored boxes and bags, and auditory overstimulation can result from music and crying children in passing carts. Your child may fuss and squirm and beg to leave, or he may want to touch every single thing in the place. He may plunge his hands in the ice around the seafood counter or shrink from the smell of detergents in the cleanser aisle. Though no more than a weekly chore for you, grocery shopping is a full-body sensory experience for a child with sensory integration disorder.

If you were able to give your undivided attention

to helping your child process all the sights and sounds and smells and sensations around her, that might be a good thing. But the fact that you have a different agenda in that overstimulating space makes shopping a likely source of stress for both you and your child. You can't keep a constant eye on your child when you're trying to fill a grocery list. And you can't take an overwhelmed child home when you've got a full cart to pay for.

Divide and Conquer

Perhaps the best solution to the grocery shopping dilemma is to have more than one adult available when you do it. If you have a spouse, family member, or trusted friend who can either watch your child while you run out to shop or come with you to the supermarket and engage your child while you check your list, things will go much more smoothly and be much more satisfactory and successful for all of you. If a meltdown occurs anyway, an extra adult can make a quick exit to the car with a child who has suddenly hit the limits of endurance or control.

Essential

An extra authority figure is your best accessory in almost any situation involving outings with a child with sensory integration disorder. If you don't have a spouse or a friend who can help, this may be a good job for a young teen who isn't ready for the responsibility of supervising children alone but can do so with minimal assistance.

Siblings may also be able to help out. While you might not want to leave your child in the care of a brother or sister while you traipse around the store, try dispatching children to retrieve items while you keep an eye on your child with sensory integration disorder. Working together can become a fun family activity, and your sensory-challenged child may be distracted by keeping track of the items as they come, or working with you to pick out certain things. The trip will also go quicker if you divide the list up.

The Power of Distraction

Supermarkets are distracting places, but your child may need even more distraction to get through a shopping trip without acting up or melting down. Bring along some toys or rewards your child likes, and use them to get him through tense or overwhelming moments. A pocketful of hard candies, doled out one by one, may get you through your store time. If your child likes playing with keys, that will be something good and calming for him to focus on. A project of counting how many items are in the cart or on the list can be a quick impromptu distraction. You might want to keep a package of stickers on hand for incentives, too.

No distraction can work forever, though, and the best strategy may be to plan your shopping trips very carefully, know exactly what you want, and get in and out of there as quickly as possible. If you have items you need to really take your time to concentrate on and pick out, try to schedule some child-free supermarket time. In the end, it's not fair to subject a child with sensory integration disorder to endless waits in a place where he will be uncomfortable and unsuccessful. A little organization can save a lot of embarrassment.

At the Shopping Mall

Malls can also be terribly overstimulating for children with sensory integration problems. The noise of shoppers and piped-in music, the flashing of store signs and overhead lights, the smells of food court cooking and perfume counters, the vestibular challenge of riding an escalator, the long tiring walks from one end of the mall to the other—all can combine to overload the circuits in a child who gets overwhelmed by even small combinations of sensations.

So should you never go to the mall? As with grocery shopping and so many things you do with your child, anything's possible with the proper planning. If you must take your child to the mall, go with a specific plan and a shortened time frame. Go in, do what you need to do, and get out. Ideally, you should have another adult with you who can whisk your child out of there if necessary. Try to shop at times when crowds are at a minimum and when your child's tolerance is at a maximum.

No Mall Marathons

Remember those endless afternoons you used to spend wandering from shop to shop, then back from shop to shop again as you zeroed in on the object of your desire? Forget about them. Or, at least, forget about doing that with your child along. Instead of marathon sessions in which you load up on every possible purchase or consider and reconsider before making a decision, think in terms of mall sprints. Pick one or two stores to visit. Make sure they're child-friendly stores, or have someone along who can watch your child while you zoom in. Do your business, and get out. Give your child lots of praise for good behavior. Give yourself some, too.

If you know just what you're shopping for, and it doesn't require trying anything on or comparing prices at different stores, call ahead of time. Make sure the store you're visiting has the item in question, and ask them to hold it for you. Many stores also allow you to reserve an item for pick-up through their Web site and even pay for it beforehand.

Do you resent the sort of changes accommodating your child makes to your shopping schedule? That's understandable, but consider that your child probably resents being dragged along. When you bring your child to a place where you know he will be uncomfortable and where there is a good chance that he will have an unpleasant experience, the burden is on you to manage things for maximum comfort. As your child matures and his sensory integration problems improve through therapy, you may be able to lengthen your mall visits and even enjoy them. But if going to the mall makes your child overwhelmed, it's your job as a parent to protect him. With planning, you can do that and still make your purchases.

Timing Is Everything

Foremost in planning is picking a time when the mall won't be packed. Forego big sale days, or leave your child home with a spouse, friend, or sitter. Do not subject a child who will already find the mall overwhelming to the craziness of jostling customers and endless lines.

Try visiting the mall first thing in the morning or just before closing (which has the added advantage of ensuring that you won't stay beyond your deadline). Keep in mind, too, what time of day or after what activities your child is most able to handle stressful situations. Right after school may be a bad idea, if she's already used up all of her control. Right after some good calming activity might be a better time. You know your child best; use that knowledge.

If your child enjoys being at the mall but gets easily overstimulated by it, bring him there sometimes just to hang out, without any need to shop or chase around. Many malls have playground areas, and stopping by with your child, playing for a while, and going home can help acclimate him to the place and get him used to it in a more sensory-friendly way. Maybe your mall opens early, before the shops do, to allow mall walkers to get exercise. Strolling around with your child during this time, when the sensory stimulation is so much lower, can also make the mall a less threatening place. The overwhelming sensory input will always be there when you come back later to shop, but at least your child will not enter the building with a sensory system on high alert.

At Worship Services

Taking a child who can't sit still or stay quiet to a place where those two skills are specifically demanded can seem like an overwhelming challenge to a parent. How can you honor your child's sensory disabilities without disturbing other worshipers? Some churches offer "cry rooms" in the back where you can isolate yourself and your noisy disruptive child from the rest of the congregation, but when those rooms fill up with crying babies and wandering toddlers, it may set your child off even more than the silence of the sanctuary.

There may never be a perfect solution, but being prepared is a good first step. If your child has small, quiet toys or items that are comforting to him, bring them along. An iPod or portable music player might provide some calming auditory stimulation, and even a Game Boy (with headphones or the mute button on) might not be too ridiculous a helper to bring. While you may get some disapproving looks from other worshipers, it may be worth it to bring an electronic device to a worship service if it buys everyone some peace. Set your goal not at a complete and spiritually enlightening experience for your child, but at being comfortable in a place of worship.

Pew Position

If your child has low muscle tone, remember that sitting upright without support will be a problem for him. Put an adult or older sibling on either side of him so that he has something to lean against, or, if there's enough room in the pew, let him lie down. It's not even a bad idea to let your child fall asleep. Pretty much anything you do is going to arouse the attention and sometimes indignation of the people around you, but it's better to do things to keep your child quiet than to be unable to do so.

Your child may be unable to stay pew-bound, so be prepared to take her for walks every so often. Try offering these as rewards for short periods of controlled behavior. Consider setting a short time as a goal for any given week, and take your child outside or to the car at that time, while she is still being successful. That goal can expand as your child is more able to control her needs for noise and movement. The important thing is that she sees your house of worship as a welcoming, nonthreatening place—and that won't happen if you're whispering threats between clenched teeth.

Essential

Wondering what rules or accommodations your faith or denomination has on record for worshipers with disabilities? A good place to check is Faithability, Religion and Disability Resources at *www.faithability.org*. In addition to information on "Faith Group Specific Sites," you'll find articles, ministries, and organizations that deal with religion and disabilities.

Spiritual Guidance

It may be hard for you to really participate in a worship service when you're so busy managing your child. You may also feel so defensive at the looks and imagined judgments of your fellow worshipers that you leave the service feeling full of resentment. Talk to your pastor, rabbi, or other spiritual guide about the problems you're having. If lack of acceptance of your child and his needs is really a problem for your fellow worshipers, that may be something that needs to be addressed by someone in charge. If you're taking things too hard or judging yourself too harshly, you'll want to address that, too.

Be sure to let the people in charge of religious education or preparing children for milestones in their faith know about your child's special needs, just as you would your child's teacher at school. Your child may need extra assistance or an expanded timetable to meet those goals, but there should be an effort made to include him. If this can't be done at your particular house of worship, see if there might be another in your area that has a program specifically for children with special needs. Don't assume your child is automatically excluded from these special moments or that he will simply rise to the occasion without assistance.

In the Car

Driving is hardly something you can avoid if it offends your child's sensory sensibilities. Even getting to therapy probably involves some car time, not to mention getting to school. Children with sensory integration disorder may have a hard time tolerating the tactile pressure of a seat belt, the auditory onslaught of a rumbling engine, the olfactory offense of car exhaust, the vestibular challenge of stops and starts and bumpy motion. The car may always be a trouble spot for your child, but with a little thought and planning, you can drive without driving him crazy.

Seat Belt Struggles

Your child with sensory integration disorder may have a valid complaint about the seat belt. If she is oversensitive to information from the tactile sense, the feeling of the belt against her lap or rubbing her neck and shoulder can be hard to tolerate. If she has low muscle tone, she may wind up flopping sideways against a shoulder belt in a way that's particularly uncomfortable. Pulling the belt out far enough and getting it clamped right can involve complicated motor planning. Your child has good reason to whine. No matter—use of a seat belt is not negotiable.

Fact

Car seats are available for children with special needs over the 100-pound limit. Two Web sites that sell them are Adaptivemall.com (*www.adaptivemall.com*) and Sammons Preston (*www.sammonspreston.com*).

One potential way to help is to keep your child in some sort of car seat for as long as possible. Booster seats are now available for older children that provide similar support and containment as what used to be called baby seats. These are good until children weigh up to 100 pounds. If your child has outgrown a car seat but still feels the seat belt at an uncomfortable shoulder angle, you can purchase devices that adjust the angle of the belt, or seats that lift your child a little higher so that the belt angle is correct. Take your child's comfort seriously. Your rides will be more peaceful, and by addressing his discomfort, you'll also find and fix anything that is not fitting him correctly. Even if the uncomfortable belt is positioned correctly for safety, if it's uncomfortable he may move it or take it off in ways that will compromise his protection.

"Mom, He's Touching Me!"

Keeping kids in car seats until they absolutely outgrow them may also help with the jostling that seems inevitable when siblings share the back seat. Whether your child with sensory integration disorder is doing the pushing—attempting to get some calming proprioceptive feedback, or flopping against seatmates due to low muscle tone—or protesting against it due to tactile sensitivity, a peaceful ride may look like an impossible dream. Car seats or the sort of individual seats with arms that come in some minivans may help solve the problem.

Stuck with regular bench seats in the back of your car and no booster seats to block contact? There are a few other tricks you can try. If there's a spare seat in the middle, put a big pillow, stuffed animal, or empty car seat there to split two warring children. Invest in a car DVD player to distract at least your non–sensory-sensitive child from fussing and fighting. Letting your child listen to an iPod or other portable music device may give some aid and comfort. Putting an older child in the front seat, even if it means an adult has to sit in back, is another possible remedy, though if your car has airbags, you'll want to make sure your child is old enough to sit there safely.

At the Doctor's Office

The pediatrician is where you're supposed to go for solutions, but often you wind up finding more problems. A long wait in a crowded waiting room, another in a cold examining room, anticipation of pain from shots, and other indignities of an office visit can make your child with sensory integration disorder seem more out of control than usual.

Waiting Room Worries

Doctors' waiting rooms vary in their appreciation of the fact that young children will be passing time in them. Some have a toy or two scattered about. Some have a television. There might be a fun-looking chair or a rocking horse. But few have anything that will provide much comfort for your child with sensory integration disorder. (Indeed, any doctor who put a trampoline in his waiting room would probably be accused of trying to drum up business.)

The burden of occupying your child during a long spell in the waiting room will therefore fall to you. Bring supplies. If your child is occupied by a Game Boy or soothed by a portable music player, have those items ready. A portable DVD player may also be good for passing time. Fidget toys should always come with you on trips away from home. Hard candies or gum may give some good gustatory or proprioceptive input. Fill up a backpack with necessary supplies, and err on the side of toting too much.

The Doctor Will See You . . . Soon

Of course, once you leave the waiting room for the examining room, there's still no assurance that you'll be seeing the doctor right away. Often, you'll sit with your child—perhaps your unclothed child—in a cold and sterile room for many more minutes. Your child may feel anxious about the possibility of shots, tests, touch, and uncomfortable examinations, and waiting in the presence of tools and tables and not much else will only increase that. You'll want to have enough toys and books and other distractions along with you to get through this time, too.

This is also a good opportunity for some soothing, calming contact. If it comforts your child to have you push down on her shoulders or against her hands, make a little game of that now. If she enjoys a foot massage, rub those tootsies. For some kids, tickling can be helpful and fun. Even rocking, if that's your child's most reliable source of comfort, can be okay.

To avoid waiting as much as possible, try getting your doctor's first appointment in the morning. There's less likelihood he'll be running late, and you may be able to get right in. It's not foolproof—doctors are sometimes late to work, and an epidemic of colds may fill the waiting room—but it's probably your best chance at a quick visit.

With Family and Friends

Your close family and friends should be your child's greatest supporters, understanding his special needs, accommodating his fears and preferences, and supporting you in your efforts to help. Unfortunately, that is often not the case. Get-togethers with family and friends can be some of the most stressful times you and your child will experience. It's hard to say who will behave the worst—your loved ones, providing unwanted advice and criticism, or your child, responding to the tension by bringing out all his worst and most disruptive behaviors.

As you've learned when dealing with your child, you can't control another person's behavior, but you can control your reaction to it. This is not easy with family members, with whom you have been building up behavioral routines for a lifetime. You will naturally tend to fall into old patterns. Keep in mind, though, that your child responds to your stress as well as her own. If you are upset, it will decrease her ability to feel safe and in control. Your child needs all your concentration and attention. Don't spare much for people who have nothing useful to say to you.

Avoid family members who push your buttons if you can. Enlist sympathetic allies to help you keep your child happy and in control. Focus on doing things that he enjoys. If you're always on the floor playing games with kids, or running around the yard with them, you'll be less available for cutting comments. You'll feel better, and your child will, too.

Don't Apologize for Being a Good Parent

It's easy for others to sit in judgment of your parenting abilities. You probably do it to other parents. But it hurts when the people you love and trust don't understand the important things you're doing for your child. You may not be able to explain sensory integration theory in a way that convinces them, but you can make sure that nobody disciplines your child in an inappropriate way, and convey your confidence in what you're doing. While others may not get it, you know, and your child knows, that what you are doing comes from a deep understanding of your child's needs, and a growing skill at meeting them. That makes you a good parent, and you don't have to apologize to anybody for that.

Make sure, though, that the person giving your child the most grief at gatherings isn't you. Maybe you feel compelled to look like the parent everybody expects you to be—a strong disciplinarian who brooks no disrespect, perhaps, or a neatnik whose children are perfectly turned out. That's not who your child needs you to be. You know the best way to parent her, and that doesn't stop when somebody's watching. Be proud of your ability to be a knowledgeable, therapeutic parent to your child.

CHAPTER 22

Sensory Integration at All Ages

Many books on sensory integration deal most intensively with preschool-age children, since this is the age at which problems may really start to show and cause the child and parents the most trouble. But sensory integration has complications and special management needs at all ages. Here are some trouble spots and strategies.

Babies

If children who are old enough to talk have trouble expressing their sensory needs in any way other than behavior, how much more difficult is it for infants to make their discomforts and preferences known? The earliest months of life are meant to be a time of learning for children, as they begin to notice things in their environment and bond to the people who love them. But for babies with sensory integration problems, the world may seem like a threatening, even terrifying place, and touch meant to soothe and comfort may feel like an attack. Babies who cry all the time for no apparent reason and who refuse to be comforted may be left alone more—further decreasing the range of experiences they are exposed to and further setting back development.

Special Concerns

Consider the areas in which sensory integration can cause complications for an older child, and see if any of those might be factors for your baby. Does she seem upset by bright light? Do certain blankets or outfits cause her more distress than others? Is she overreactive to sounds or underreactive? Is there any sort of touch she tolerates? Does being picked up or put down in a particular way cause distress or relieve it? How does she respond to rocking, swinging, and riding in a car? If you can find some narrow margin of comfort, start there and work outward. Introduce new experiences while your baby is in that comfort zone.

Well-meaning friends and family members may tell you that some babies are just fussy, and you shouldn't make much of it. Your baby is fussy, due to sensory integration problems. If you can pinpoint those problems and bring her some comfort, you will make it easier for her to grow and develop and for you to get some peace.

Alternatively, an infant with sensory integration challenges may be underresponsive—quiet and "good," but not interested in relating. Rather than crying and fussing constantly, this child may seem perfectly happy with his own company, lost in thought, rocking himself and possibly banging against the crib. If your baby is understimulated in this way, you'll need to work hard to get him to make a connection against considerable resistance. Try activities that give him a lot of input—swinging, rocking, or flying through the air. Unlike the baby who is easily overstimulated and needs to be kept in a comfort zone, understimulated infants may need big gestures, loud noises, and bright colors to get them out of their comfort zones.

Missing Milestones

While it may seem that they're not so terribly busy, children in their first year or so of life have an enormous amount of work to do.

Developmental tasks for this period often focus on responding to the environment, something children with sensory integration problems will have trouble doing. Your baby also may not be laying the groundwork necessary for essential skills that come later.

The Auditory Sense

Children who have trouble with information from the auditory sense may be unable to achieve such infancy milestones as these:

- Reacting appropriately to loud noises
- Responding with pleasure to noises like bells or whistles
- Being comforted by lullabies or soothing speech
- Enjoying surprise games like "peek-a-boo"
- Finding the source of sound

The Visual Sense

Children who have trouble with information from the visual sense may be unable to achieve such infancy milestones as these:

- Differentiating between people
- Reacting appropriately to bright lights and colors
- Imitating or tolerating movements
- Making eye contact

The Tactile Sense

Children who have trouble with information from the tactile sense may be unable to achieve such infancy milestones as these:

- Manipulating simple toys
- Feeding properly
- Being comforted by touch
- Investigating things with hands and mouth

The Proprioceptive Sense

Children who have trouble with information from the proprioceptive sense may be unable to achieve such infancy milestones as these:

- Playing with toes
- Manipulating simple toys
- Grasping objects
- Trying different body positions

The Vestibular Sense

Children who have trouble with information from the vestibular sense may be unable to achieve such infancy milestones as these:

- Sitting up
- Lifting head
- Copying movement

Low Muscle Tone

Children who have low muscle tone may be unable to achieve such infancy milestones as these:

- Sitting up
- Lifting head
- Kicking feet
- Maintaining a steady position

Toddlers

The toddler years are when things really start happening for most children. They're moving and investigating their environment in creative and often infuriating ways. All of this may leave your child with sensory integration disorder behind in the dust. He may experience the world at an infant's level well past the point at which his peers have moved on. He may have trouble with the complex layering of motor skills involved in grasping and moving objects and decide it's not worth the effort. He may be overwhelmed with the sensory challenges of balance and speed and modulation. It's a challenging time for you as a parent, too.

Special Concerns

In addition to the questions and observations made about babies in the previous section, consider how your child is dealing with the unique challenges of this time in her life. It's easy to see how problems with muscle tone, motor planning, proprioception, and the vestibular sense would get in the way of learning how to walk. See if you can pinpoint the specific things that are impeding her burgeoning mobility. Does she feel more sturdy and comfortable crawling, or does she dislike the tactile sensations of rug and floor beneath her hands and knees? Is she afraid of losing her balance when she stands, or does she make up for the lack of balance by launching herself with speed? Is she able to stand without moving? Often children with low muscle tone move right from crawling to walking with no standing in between.

Fact

A good book with lots of information on working on language with young children is *Teach Me How to Say It Right*, by Dorothy P. Dougherty. It can help your child with language processing and acquisition, and it gives specific examples of games and exercises to do with your child and what to say to model good language.

Sensory integration problems can also get in the way of your child's attempts to communicate. If your child seems to be uninterested in speaking or unable to connect, note whether sensory issues could be involved. Are there particular tones of voice that he finds upsetting? Is he more attentive in quiet rooms than busy ones? Does he have trouble telling similar sounds apart? Is it hard for him to associate sounds and words with objects? You will need to tune in to your child's sensory needs and sensitivities to help him tune in to the world.

Missing Milestones

Toddlers with sensory integration problems may still be working on milestones from their baby years, and they may miss additional milestones during these active and developing toddler years. In addition to walking and talking, there may be some delays in social and fine-motor development, too.

The Auditory Sense

Children who have trouble with information from the auditory sense may be unable to achieve such toddler developmental tasks as these:

- Following spoken instructions
- Paying attention when read to
- Imitating spoken words
- Answering questions

The Visual Sense

Children who have trouble with information from the visual sense may be unable to achieve such toddler milestones as these:

- Sorting items by shape or color
- Seeing similarities between real objects and pictures in a book
- Copying shapes
- Finding hidden objects

The Tactile Sense

Children who have trouble with information from the tactile sense may be unable to achieve such toddler milestones as these:

- Turning book pages
- Sorting shapes by touch
- Showing and receiving affection
- Being comfortable with other children

The Proprioceptive Sense

Children who have trouble with information from the proprioceptive sense may be unable to achieve such toddler milestones as these:

- Building block towers
- Kicking a ball
- Holding a pencil and using an appropriate amount of force for writing
- Moving body parts purposefully

The Vestibular Sense

Children who have trouble with information from the vestibular sense may be unable to achieve such toddler milestones as these:

- Descending stairs
- Bending over
- Standing on tiptoe
- Walking without support

Low Muscle Tone

Children who have low muscle tone may be unable to achieve such toddler milestones as these:

- Standing and walking
- Maintaining a seated position in a chair
- Carrying toys
- Holding and controlling a pencil

Preschoolers

There was a time, probably when you were young, when preschoolers mostly focused on things like learning colors and playing house and finger painting. Even that stuff might be a problem for your child with sensory integration disorder—you need a smoothly working visual sense to notice color distinctions, good motor planning to do pretend play, and no tactile sensitivity to enjoy that goopy finger paint—but things are much more complicated than that now. More and more, preschoolers are expected to do academic tasks that might at one time have been the job of kindergarteners or first-graders. For children who have delays in movement, auditory and visual perception, and tactile discrimination, that can fill the preschool years with frustration.

Special Concerns

Since many children with sensory integration disorder have developmental delays stemming from missed milestones in infancy and the toddler years, you'll want to still consider the points raised in those sections. But additional concerns will probably spring up with the increase in social and academic expectations. If you have your child enrolled in preschool, you may start hearing about him jostling other children, moving excessively, being underattentive, having behavioral outbursts, fighting transitions, and generally not being with the preschool program. If your child's sensory integration problems have delayed toilet training, you'll likely hear about that, too.

Keeping your child out of preschool and working intently on sensory integration therapy and at-home sensory diet activities (as described in Chapter 6) is one option. On the plus side, you may be able to provide her with a more predictable, less threatening environment in which to work on her delays and weaknesses. On the minus side, your child will still have a difficult transition to make into the world of school and children, and having her make it at the kindergarten level may put her behind in school readiness skills on top of everything else. If you can find a preschool that is willing to accommodate her special needs and work with you on appropriate behavior management, it might be worth having your child there at least a few days a week.

Depending on the degree of your child's special needs, special education preschool through your school district might be an ideal choice. Usually available to three and four year olds, it can include speech, occupational, and physical therapy along with a curriculum tailored to children with delays and challenges. Contact your school district's special education office for information or to request an evaluation.

Missing Milestones

Preschoolers with sensory integration problems may still be working on milestones from previous years, and they may miss additional milestones during these learning-packed preschool years. Social and self-control challenges will be added to those involved with walking and talking.

The Auditory Sense

Children who have trouble with information from the auditory sense may be unable to achieve such preschool milestones as these:

- Having a conversation
- Identifying words that rhyme
- Knowing 2,000 words
- Singing and playing with words

The Visual Sense

Children who have trouble with information from the visual sense may be unable to achieve such preschool milestones as these:

- Sorting items into categories

- Counting objects
- Identifying similarities and differences
- Adapting to new environments

The Tactile Sense

Children who have trouble with information from the tactile sense may be unable to achieve such preschool milestones as these:

- Dressing self
- Playing dress-up
- Playing interactively with other children (which could apply to all senses)
- Enjoying new experiences (which could apply to all senses)

The Proprioceptive Sense

Children who have trouble with information from the proprioceptive sense may be unable to achieve such preschool milestones as these:

- Understanding spatial concepts
- Following complex commands
- Drawing a body with all body parts
- Kicking a ball with appropriate force

The Vestibular Sense

Children who have trouble with information from the vestibular sense may be unable to achieve such preschool milestones as these:

- Standing on one foot
- Hopping
- Skipping
- Moving forward and backward

Low Muscle Tone

Children who have low muscle tone may be unable to achieve such preschool milestones as these:

- Holding fork and knife
- Drawing shapes and letters
- Potty training

School Age

When your child reaches school age, you lose a significant amount of control over his environment and his routine. Kindergarten may still be half day, but many school districts are putting even these young ones on a full day schedule. At least from first grade on, your child may be spending as many waking hours in a classroom as in your home. If you've been working for years on sensory integration therapy and a sensory diet, he's probably more in control of himself and more able to adjust to change. But the degree of change involved in switching to a full school day, full of academic and behavioral expectations, may be more than he can handle.

Special Concerns

As days get longer, recess gets shorter, class work gets harder, homework gets heavier, and tolerance for unusual behavior lessens, your child's stress level may soar, making her even less able to face the sensory challenges of school. The complaints you may have received from preschool teachers will be all the more distressing coming from elementary school teachers and administrators. Your child may begin to develop a record of disciplinary problems, and she may struggle academically due to her trouble with processing what the teacher says, what the teacher writes on the board, and what needs to be written down. Desk work and pencil work can be torture for kids with proprioceptive problems and low muscle tone.

Essential

Your child's preschool teacher may suggest holding your child back a year, or his kindergarten teacher may recommend repeating the year. Don't dismiss this idea without careful thought. Any trauma your child may feel about being left behind will likely be less than the embarrassment of being constantly behind, incorrect, and clumsy at school.

It's not just the schoolwork that will test your child's fragile abilities, though. Even more stressful may be the rising social expectations that his peers put on him. If your child has trouble playing without jostling—or if he screams and cries when jostled—he may be mocked and ostracized. If his play skills are on a different developmental level than those of his peers, he may be called a baby and left out of others' play. As "weirdness" of any sort becomes a social detriment, your child may find it hard to make friends or find inclusion. He may not even be able to understand what is expected of him under the complicated social codes of childhood.

Missing Milestones

Children with sensory integration problems may still be working on milestones from their preschool years, and they may miss additional milestones during these stressful and learning-packed school years. The social, self-control, mobility, and language processing challenges that have been building up explode during this period to present your child with sometimes insurmountable developmental tasks.

The Auditory Sense

Children who have trouble with information from the auditory sense may be unable to achieve such school age milestones as these:

- Socializing through conversation

- Paying attention in a noisy classroom environment
- Understanding social rules
- Controlling behavioral outbursts

The Visual Sense

Children who have trouble with information from the visual sense may be unable to achieve such school age milestones as these:

- Seeing information on a chalkboard
- Learning to read
- Following visual cues
- Concentrating in a visually busy or bright classroom setting

The Tactile Sense

Children who have trouble with information from the tactile sense may be unable to achieve such school age milestones as these:

- Dressing in peer-approved ways
- Tolerating large group activities
- Caring what others think about them
- Understanding appropriate personal boundaries

The Proprioceptive Sense

Children who have trouble with information from the proprioceptive sense may be unable to achieve such school age milestones as these:

- Enjoying playground games and sports
- Sitting still in classroom environment
- Carrying out multi-step instructions
- Imitating adults' behavior

The Vestibular Sense

Children who have trouble with information from the vestibular sense may be unable to achieve such school age milestones as these:

- Enjoying playground games and sports
- Taking appropriate risks
- Finding their way around school and neighborhood
- Going up and down stairs carrying books

Low Muscle Tone

Children who have low muscle tone may be unable to achieve such school age milestones as these:

- Taking notes
- Sitting at a desk
- Eating neatly
- Learning cursive

Teenagers

Along with acne and hormones and physical changes that either don't come when expected or come on too strong, teenage children with sensory integration disorder may still be coping with problems that have plagued them since childhood. Even if your teen has developed skills through therapy and maturity to compensate for his sensory challenges, adolescence presents a whole new array of threats and expectations. It's not fair—but not much about being a teenager is.

Special Concerns

About those physical changes: They may take a real toll on your child's proprioceptive, vestibular, and motor planning abilities. Growth spurts require a complete reorganization of a child's understanding of where her body is, and if she wasn't too sure about that even before the change in height, things will only be worse. You may see the return of problems like bumping into things, general clumsiness, apprehension around stairs and escalators, intolerance of changes in position, and all those other proprioceptive and vestibular hang-ups you may have thought were banished by therapy. A lessening of your child's confidence about her body's position and balance may lead to more reluctance in motor planning activities, just when those are increasing in complexity with the challenges of high school sports and learning how to drive.

If your daughter has trouble with the olfactory sense, she may struggle with the hygiene issues that come with menstruation. If she overreacts to olfactory information, she may be constantly concerned about odor and be overvigilant about checking and changing pads or tampons. If she underreacts, she may not be aware when there actually is an odor to worry about.

All this happens at a time when children are more self-conscious than ever about being different. Fortunately, this means that your child may be especially willing to talk with you about his sensory problems and seek your help to strategize inconspicuous ways to compensate. Remain as open and informative as you can for your child as a sensory integration resource. Part of the job of the teen years is to pull away from parents and establish an individual identity, so you will need to tread carefully. Try not to take charge of your child's environment and routine the way you might for a much younger child. But you may find that your understanding of his challenges and willingness to advise will bring you and your child closer together at the time when he needs a friend most of all.

Missing Milestones

Teens with sensory integration problems may still be working on milestones from their earlier school age years, and they may miss additional milestones during this final tricky stretch of development. The continuing challenges of learning, self-control, social success, and physical coordination become more intense, with less room for variation and plenty of opportunities for embarrassment and failure.

The Auditory Sense

Children who have trouble with information from the auditory sense may be unable to achieve such adolescent milestones as these:

- Listening to peer-approved music
- Talking with friends on the phone
- Following detailed lectures in class
- Tolerating noisy school hallways and lunchrooms

The Visual Sense

Children who have trouble with information from the visual sense may be unable to achieve such adolescent milestones as these:

- Absorbing material from detail-packed textbooks
- Reading novels
- Picking up on visual differences that distinguish peer groups
- Organizing schoolwork, locker, and desk

The Tactile Sense

Children who have trouble with information from the tactile sense may be unable to achieve such adolescent milestones as these:

- Changing for gym class
- Tolerating gym uniform
- Avoiding panic or injury in crowded school hallways
- Understanding appropriate touch

The Proprioceptive Sense

Children who have trouble with information from the proprioceptive sense may be unable to achieve such adolescent milestones as these:

- Succeeding in gym and sports
- Learning to drive
- Adjusting to growth spurts
- Exhibiting increased control of movement and behavior

The Vestibular Sense

Children who have trouble with information from the vestibular sense may be unable to achieve such adolescent milestones as these:

- Finding their way around larger schools
- Finding their way around community with increased freedom
- Learning to drive
- Succeeding in gym and sports

Low Muscle Tone

Children who have low muscle tone may be unable to achieve such adolescent milestones as these:

- Holding large numbers of books
- Writing for long periods of time
- Doing increasingly complicated athletic activities

College and Beyond

By the time your child graduates from high school, a lot of his sensory integration issues may have resolved due to time and therapy. The rest have likely become part of his unique personality. If you've been working with him to strategize ways to compensate, he may be handling things well. Or he may have just decided to go with the flow and take things as they feel right to him. Either way, your job as the administrator of your child's sensory integration program will most likely be coming to an end.

That doesn't mean sensory integration challenges stop at this point. Your child may always need extra time to adjust to new routines.

If she's going away to college, there will be things to deal with that she may not have experienced before—loud music from somebody else's dorm room during study or sleep time, unfamiliar food, a large campus to find her way around without much assistance, long lectures, and lots of notes to take. When your child comes to you with lots of generalized complaints and unhappiness about the college environment, you may be able to use your knowledge of her sensory profile to help her make constructive changes and adjustments.

Fact

If your child has had an individualized educational plan (IEP), that protection will end with high school. But he may still be able to have accommodations in college under a 504 plan. This may be worth pursuing if your child has learning disabilities or significant problems with the physical process of writing.

Being a resource for solutions and a source of understanding is the best thing you can do for your child as she grows up and travels through all phases of development. And it's the best thing you can do for your adult child, as she moves on into her own life. Independence may be just one more challenge your child struggles with, and she may need some final assistance from you even at this phase. When she achieves it successfully, it will be a triumph for both of you.

CHAPTER 23

Explaining Sensory Integration to Your Child

While there's a lot you can do to manage sensory integration needs when your child is small, eventually she will need to understand how her sensory systems work and what she can do to balance them out. Make no mistake—your child will develop her own strategies whether you talk to her or not. However, those strategies will often be disruptive or inappropriate, made not out of understanding but out of self-defense. Giving your child information about her sensory integration problems can help you make appropriate plans together.

Areas of Strength

Sensory integration is rarely all bad. Try to think of a way in which your child's sensory differences work to her advantage. Maybe she has an adventurous taste in food that gives her and others pleasure. Maybe she can do homework in a noisy room because she doesn't process sound well. Maybe she adores roller coasters because her vestibular system doesn't register discomfort, or is an intense athlete because she fears no pain. Talk about how these things make her different from others in a good way. Then explain that, like everyone else, the way she processes the information from her senses makes her special.

You can start laying the groundwork for this when your child is young, even before he is able to really understand about sensory integration. Make sure to praise your

child as much as possible. Recognize when he's doing something he really enjoys or that seems to make his body feel calmer or more alert. Describe what you see when he's being organized or creative or responsible. Allow plenty of opportunity for him to do things that bring him satisfaction and success, and point out when others can't do it as well as he can. Frequent positive comments will make your child feel better about himself, reduce his stress level, and give you a platform from which to start building the concept of sensory integration when your child is old enough to understand it.

What if I can't think of any areas in which my child's sensory integration differences are a plus?
Think harder. It will be very beneficial to your child if you can find positive ways to introduce this subject. If you absolutely can't—or if she won't agree with you over what would be considered positive—then introduce some ways in which your own sensory differences are a minus to you.

Your child will have plenty of opportunities to be aware of the negative side of sensory integration. The main purpose of explaining sensory integration disorder will be to help her understand why some things give her such trouble and feel better about her inability to control her reactions in this area. But you'll want to avoid making your child feel like a victim, beset by a hard-luck disorder that spells nothing but trouble. Instead, teach her to draw on her strengths to compensate for her weaknesses, and enjoy her unique sensory profile for the way it makes her who she is. That's a good way for you to look at things, too.

A good source of ideas for this positive approach to your child's behavior is *Transforming the Difficult Child: The Nurtured Heart*

Approach, by Howard Glasser and Jennifer Easley. The approach includes a constant stream of positive comments toward your child—from simply describing good or neutral things you see your child doing to creating opportunities for him to shine. You'll be surprised how many good things you can find to say when you really concentrate.

Likes and Dislikes

Sensory integration differences often express themselves in terms of strong likes and dislikes, and this is a neutral area in which you can talk about your child's particular ways of processing sensory integration without dwelling on problems. Make a list with your child of the things she absolutely loves—clothes that are bright or soft, tight or loose; foods that are hot or cool, chewy or smooth; smells that are spicy or sweet; loud music or dim lights or active games or quiet reading. Share what you've learned about how hypersensitivity or hyposensitivity in each of our senses governs these strong likes and dislikes. Help your child pinpoint what special thing about her sensory system might cause some of these powerful feelings.

Apply those same understandings to your child's strong dislikes. What does he absolutely hate? The smell of a particular soap? The way his sheets feel when you forget to put the softener in? Certain tastes or textures of food? A noisy house, or a too-quiet one? Discuss how sensory integration differences might figure into those strong negative reactions. Explain that all of these things are reflections of the way he processes the world—not bad, not good, just unique.

Your child might enjoy playing sensory "detective" for other family members, too. Discuss your own sensory preferences, and try to guess about those of other people your child knows. Almost everyone has some strong like or dislike that's well known to friends and family. These can make the basis of an interesting and positive discussion with your child about the way sensory differences affect everyone.

When discussing your child's sensory likes and dislikes, he may say something that hurts your feelings. Maybe he hates your scent or your cooking, or something you've given him sets his senses off. Try to remain positive and not let your feelings get in the way. Your child needs to know that it's safe to share anything with you.

If your child enjoys this, you might make a game of analyzing fictional characters and attributing sensory-related motivations to their activities. When reading a book or watching a television show together, ask your child what sensory issues might be motivating a character. For example, you could ask questions like these:

- Is Goldilocks so oversensitive to touch that things seem too hot or too cold, too soft or too hard?
- Does the princess from "The Princess and the Pea" have a huge tactile oversensitivity problem?
- Does the unnamed character in *Green Eggs and Ham* refuse to eat because of the color, or the smell?
- Does Sam I Am ignore the other character in *Green Eggs and Ham* because of issues with auditory processing?

Have fun and get silly with it. All of this will make the topic of sensory integration less threatening and more empowering for your child.

Sharing Feelings

Your child may never have thought about his sensory integration challenges as anything other than the way things are. Help him connect his feelings of dread or pleasure with his sensory profile. Discuss the way he feels about the things you've noticed make him intensely fearful. What is it like for him? What does he think about? Make it clear that you don't feel the same way about the experience; can he describe it for you? Giving words to feelings helps your child in some way take control over them, and the process may get him closer to finding strategies that will counteract those strong sensory impressions.

Sharing with Your Child

Again, reverse the process by describing something that makes you feel afraid or nervous or stressed-out that doesn't bother your child at all. Try to describe to her the way these things make you feel—the way your body responds, the thoughts that go on in your brain, the actions you take to make yourself feel more normal. You understand her feelings as just normal variations in experience—help her do the same for your feelings. And then talk about the feelings of other people, real and fictional. This idea that other people feel differently about things than she does, and that they, in turn, react according to their feelings without thinking that others might interpret sensory information differently, may be a revelation to your child.

Asking your child how he feels about things can be a good way of getting information in lots of areas. When your child comes home from school, instead of asking what happened or whether the day was good or bad, try asking how he felt at school today, or what three things made him feel good or bad. Besides opening better communication between you and your child, this may give you some hints about sensory trouble spots during the school day.

Sensory Conflict

Discuss with your child some times when the two of you have had a real disagreement or misunderstanding, and see if you can decipher together the sensory preferences and assumptions that might have been behind your difference of opinion. Bring up some common behavioral trouble spots, like refusing to eat certain foods or dislike of hair washing or preference for certain garments, and ask about her feelings regarding those conflicts. Could there be a sensory reason? Does she think you're deliberately trying to make her uncomfortable? Does she realize that you feel differently?

Fact

If your child has trouble identifying feelings, try playing The Feelings Game, which you can find online at *www.do2learn.com/games/feelingsgame*. Your child will view three photos of a child or adult making different facial expressions and be asked to identify the one that reflects a particular feeling.

Be sure to admit when your own sensory issues have been a problem or have bothered your child. Do you have some motor planning problems in the morning that result in late drop-offs to school? Do you put too much spice in food, or not enough? See if he can help you come up with some instances when you do things he just does not understand. Do the same for other family members. Seeing how sensory differences cause misunderstandings between people may help your child come to terms with how his own perceptions differ from the perceptions of others.

Revisiting the Senses

It will help your child to have a good basic knowledge of how her senses work. You don't have to go into great scientific detail. Your child probably already knows about her sense of sight, sound, smell, taste, and touch. Tell her she also has a sense of balance and a sense of where her arms and legs are. Then explain that information from each of these senses travels through nerves to the brain and that the brain uses this data to put together a picture of what the world around your child is like. Each person's picture will be different from everybody else's because each person's senses give different amounts of information.

Exercises to Understand the Senses

To help him understand how the senses work together, try these exercises in which certain senses are blocked:

- Have your child close his eyes and smell some fragrant items, like a lemon, an onion, some cinnamon, and a flower. Can he identify the scent without the sight? Is it more difficult?
- Have your child close his eyes and see if he can identify some items by touch. You can do this with different textures, like rice, sand, cereal, and clay, or with different shaped blocks.
- Have your child taste something while holding his nose. Does the food taste different?
- Watch a movie with your child with the sound turned off. Can you still follow the action? Do you miss some details? Do you enjoy it as much?
- Walk through a room blindfolded or with all the lights off. How does the lack of vision change the way you recognize familiar objects?

A game of Pin the Tail on the Donkey is also great for identifying the way senses work together. First, just put on the blindfold, and see how well your child finds her way to the right spot. Then repeat, but spin her around to make her dizzy. Repeat again, removing the blindfold but making her dizzy. How is her sense of where things are and where she is affected by the loss of sight, of sight and balance, and just balance?

The loss of good information from one sense can make it hard for other senses to do their job well. Too much information can do the same. Talk to your child about how things like loud sounds, strong smells, a head cold, bright lights, a sleeping foot, or other hard to ignore sensations can make it difficult to concentrate on anything else. The information doesn't stop coming in through those other senses, but it can't get interpreted very well when there is so much information from the one overstimulated sense.

Emotion and Memory

In addition to too much information or not enough information, emotion and memory can also make a difference in the picture your child's brain makes. Talk again to your child about the way certain sensations make him feel. What sensory information makes him feel happy—certain colors, movements, types of music, textures of fabric? What makes him feel frightened? Sad? Excited? Silly? Those feelings will cause his brain to make a different picture than it would if he did not have those feelings.

There may be sensory experiences that bring back unpleasant memories for your child. While these will do an excellent job of illustrating the connection between senses and memories, they may be so upsetting that they make it difficult for your child to concentrate on what you're telling her. Use careful judgment in deciding whether to include these in your conversation.

Help your child think of some memories that ride along with sensory information. Have her think of a smell that makes her remember something good—cookies you baked together, the smell of a grandparent's house, movie theater popcorn. Then think of smells that bring less happy memories—a disinfectant used in a doctor's or dentist's office, a food that once made her ill, perfume worn by a disliked relative or teacher. Talk about some of the associations you bring to particular smells and other sensory information. Explain that these memories will also color the picture that the brain makes out of information from the senses.

Putting the Picture Together

To further your child's understanding, you might compare the picture his brain gets from his senses to the way a television works. A television gets information from the air or from a cable, and the information is the same for every television set. But some sets have huge screens and some have small ones, some have color and some are black and white, some have high definition and some don't, some have stereo sound and some don't. The picture on a television set may be too bright or too dark, have strange lines through it, or be beset by static. The sound may need to be adjusted. Maybe the remote doesn't work so well, and you really have to try hard to change the channels. Although the information coming from the outside is the same for each set, the picture that is delivered varies quite a bit, and that affects the viewing experience and impression of what's being watched.

That viewing experience can change, though. There are things the viewer can do to improve the situation. You learn where to aim the antenna. You fiddle with the settings long enough to find the optimum balance of brightness and color. You watch certain shows long enough that you can enjoy them and predict what's going on even if the picture's not perfect. You watch an episode so many times you can say the dialog along with the characters whether you can hear it well or not. You know which shows make you feel happy, and you know which shows scare you so much you avoid that channel altogether. The picture itself is important, but it's never the whole story. What we add to it and how we adjust are important, too.

Keep in mind that children often learn better when they have a concrete example of what you're talking about. Try taking your child on a little field trip to an electronics store or department store, and go to the television department. Have him look at the huge variety of screens, all showing the same program, but with variations in size, color, clarity, reception, and special features. Although they should all be identical, it's hard to find any two that are really giving exactly the same picture.

Areas of Concern

Your child should now have an understanding of how her senses work, how they work together, and what things influence the way her brain makes a picture from that information. When she has a solid understanding of these aspects of brain function, she has a basic understanding of sensory integration. When all the senses work just right and work together well and the picture is clear and reliable, good sensory integration has been achieved, and your child feels confident and successful. When some senses are giving too much information or not enough information, and the senses aren't able to work successfully together, the picture becomes fuzzy and unreliable. This is called sensory integration disorder.

Make sure your child knows that this is not something bad that she's done or an excuse for doing whatever she wants. It's just some words people use to describe the way the brain misinterprets information from the senses. Having a name for something makes it less scary and helps you do something about it. It makes it easier to find other people who have the same problem and get ideas of ways to adjust the picture and make things better.

Now is the time to talk to your child about the things that really concern you and those that have been causing her real difficulty. If she can't stop moving, talk about how you see that causing problems for her at home and at school, and explain that she may be doing it to get more information from her vestibular and proprioceptive senses. If she has trouble getting organized and following instructions, talk about motor planning and what pieces of sensory information might be missing to make that difficult. If she's often accused of not listening, talk about whether she doesn't get useful information from her auditory sense or whether a lack of movement might make her less alert. Work with your child to come up with sensory explanations for behavior that has been causing trouble. It may be a relief for her to know that she's not just a bad person.

Make sure your child knows that the sensory explanation for her behavior doesn't make that behavior okay. But it does offer a way to make adjustments and change the behavior in a way that's comfortable for your child. Your child may not have known why he acts the way he does, and he might have thought there was no other way to act. The reactions to others may have confused or enraged him and made it more difficult to calm down and behave. Your discussions and introduction of the topic of sensory integration will most likely reduce some of the stress your child has been feeling, and that alone will help with control and confidence. The strategies described in Chapter 24 for helping your child manage his own sensory integration needs will do even more to improve his self-image and self-control.

CHAPTER 24

Helping Children Manage Their Sensory Needs

Now that your child has some understanding of sensory integration disorder, you can start to work with him on strategies to keep himself calm and alert. This is not something he'll be able to take over all at once, and you may still have to do a great deal of managing his environment so that he can work on one small area at a time. But your ultimate goal will be to help him find ways to deal with his sensory needs without being disruptive to others.

Recognize What's Working

Your child may be doing a lot of inappropriate actions in order to regulate her sensory system, but she's probably doing some appropriate ones, too. Perhaps she's found some clothing that's comfortable for her, and this has helped her dress herself successfully. Maybe she piles a bunch of stuffed animals on herself at bedtime to get some restful proprioceptive input. She might have found a comfortable spot to do homework or established a routine of jumping on a trampoline before settling down to work. When you really look for them, you may be surprised how many things your child has figured out for herself, often without knowing why.

Keep in mind that things that bring your child comfort and help her sensory system work better may not have an obvious sensory component. She may have a favorite toy or object that has calming abilities just through its familiarity. She may have a particular ritual of movements or words that she likes to do to organize herself. It may be that these things, by being reliable and predictable, give the sensory system a break from having to figure everything out and make accurate interpretations. If it makes her less agitated or more alert, it's worth adding to the list of sensory strategies.

Essential

When you see your child doing something that helps his sensory system without disrupting others, make sure to give recognition and praise for that success. Give your child a sticker or other small reward, such as points on a behavior chart. This will help him understand what's working and motivate him to find other good strategies.

Recognize What Doesn't Work

For your child, the only criterion of whether something works or doesn't work is whether it makes his body and his brain feel better. By that standard, rocking, head-banging, finger-sucking, shouting, and jumping around are highly successful strategies. But teachers and peers are unlikely to regard those solutions so highly. As your child gets older and starts to value friendship and teacher approval, he may realize that the things he does only feel appropriate to him. If he hasn't figured that out for himself, your discussion of sensory integration should have led him to connect the way his senses work and the trouble he gets into.

Your child most likely does not want to be in trouble. She may be puzzled or angry at the reaction others have to her honest attempts to make her body feel right. As much as possible, try to distinguish between the sensory problems that lead to the behavior and the behavior itself that comes as a response to it. While the sensory sensitivities and imbalances may change with time and therapy, the responses can be changed right now.

One Problem, Many Solutions

Play a game with your child in which you think of multiple solutions to a problem. There's a fire: What could you do? You could put water on it. You could use a fire extinguisher. You could try to smother it with a blanket. You could try to blow it out. You could run out of the house. You could call the fire department. All of these might be perfectly valid responses to a fire. Depending on the size of the fire, some might be more desirable than others. Some responses might be dangerous with a big fire; others might be an overreaction to a small fire. One problem, many solutions.

Carol Stock Kranowitz, the author of *The Out-of-Sync Child,* has written a book for children to help explain different types of sensory problems and ways to deal with them. Called *The Goodenoughs Get in Sync,* it offers both pictures and large type for younger readers and more in-depth information in smaller type for older children.

Try another situation. Your neighbor is playing loud music in his backyard: What could you do? You could ask him to turn it off. You could call the police. You could turn up your own music. You could wear earplugs. You could close all your windows. You could join him in his backyard and listen to the music. All of these might be perfectly valid responses to a neighborhood annoyance. Depending on your relationship with the neighbor, some might be more appropriate than others. Some might be unnecessary if you like the music or the neighbor; some might be too polite if the neighbor is deliberately trying to annoy you. One problem, many solutions.

Play this game with your child whenever you have an idle moment—in the car on the way to school, waiting in a doctor's office, at the dinner table. The more nimble both you and your child can be in strategizing multiple solutions, the easier it will be to come up with options for his own difficult situations. Be positive and supportive of any solution he comes up with, no matter how wild or impractical. Sometimes, wild and creative ideas can, with a few tweaks, become the ideal answer.

Another way to incorporate problem solving thinking into your child's life is through reading. When you're reading with your child, make this sort of problem solving part of the experience. If a character in a book has a problem, stop and ask your child what could be done to solve it. Brainstorm a number of different possibilities, and then guess what the character will do. When the character does make a decision, discuss whether you think it was the right one.

Everybody Hurts

You don't have to look far to find people seeking ways to make themselves comfortable. Television commercials abound with examples of items sold to relieve all manner of distress, from headaches and colds to the horror of too-rough toilet paper. Ads appeal to the kind of strong preferences and overwhelming dislikes that your child is all too familiar with. If you can, discuss with your child what sort of sensory need these products might be filling. Let her know that other people seek out ways to deal with their discomforts, sometimes in ways even more disruptive than her own.

Do the same with magazine ads. You might give your child a project of cutting out ads that appeal to people's sense of smell, or of touch, or of proprioceptive comfort. Ask him what sort of ads would most appeal to him, with his particular needs. Which ads seem most off the mark? These are good informal ways to help him see that he's not alone in getting his needs met (and also, along the way, understand some of the manipulation that goes into advertising).

Socially Acceptable Strategies

You've identified your child's most pressing sensory integration–related problems. You've looked at the unacceptable ways she adjusts for these. You've strategized, in the abstract, about other people and other situations. Now, lead your child to apply her newfound skills to solving her own pressing problems.

You'll want to be a resource for your child. You have years of observation to share, and years of changing the environment and manipulating circumstances to contribute to this project. You can help your child examine his ideas thoughtfully and rule out ones that either don't improve the situation or make it worse. But the ideas need to come from your child. He will know best what works for him, and he will be less resistant to strategies that are not being imposed on him from the outside.

Using Words

One strategy your child can concentrate on is finding ways to use words instead of behavior to express discomfort and upset. This can be hard for your child with sensory integration disorder because her responses are sometimes spontaneous and impulsive, and she may not be able to stop and think during times of stress and distress. However, if she knows ahead of time that something may happen that will upset her, she can ask beforehand for a change in her environment. And if a bad and disruptive reaction does occur, she may be able to explain what happened and smooth over potential behavioral conflicts.

It will help if you can practice this strategy with your child so that he has plenty of opportunity to build a "word bank" in his head well before he needs to use it outside the home. Play-act situations where he may become upset and have him rehearse what he could say before or after. Enact the role of a teacher, friend, or other person your child might have a behavioral flare-up with, and give him a variety of reactions to respond to.

Your child will likely still have meltdowns from time to time, even as you're discussing and strategizing and learning together. When this happens, use it as a teaching opportunity. Describe what you see her doing and what you see her reacting to. Afterward, brainstorm on things she could have done instead.

Avoiding Conflict

Walking away from something that bothers or upsets you may seem like an obvious solution, but your child may feel that he doesn't have that option. Sometimes he's right—he can't just get up and walk out of class, or out of the house, or off the playing field. There are times, though, when he will be able to politely avoid something he knows will cause his sensory system to overload. Encourage him to think of situations when avoidance might be a better choice than aggression or overreaction.

As you encourage your child to politely avoid things that bother him, allow him to use those techniques around the house. Let him choose things like what to wear and what to eat. As long as he expresses his preferences appropriately and doesn't cause more work for somebody else, honor his efforts to stay away from overstimulating things.

If your child has been successfully avoiding things that cause her sensory distress, it's likely been by misbehaving—getting sent to the principal so she doesn't have to deal with something in the classroom, dropping a plate on the floor so she doesn't have to eat what's on it, hitting a classmate to keep from being touched, spilling something on clothes she doesn't like, dawdling and arguing to avoid an unwanted activity. Talk with your child about how ineffective those strategies are. Most of the time, she still winds up having to do the hated thing, and she does it under more stress and tension. Have her think of other ways she could reach the same goal. Role-play and practice, using your responses to discourage ways you think would be ineffective and encourage ones that are.

Organization

Your child with sensory integration disorder and motor planning problems may find putting together an organized plan for a particular activity or a particular day to be nearly impossible. He can't find where he put things or remember what he's supposed to do because his brain is as disorganized as his room, notebook, and locker. Your child may not understand that there's a more organized way to be, and if he does understand, he may not think that he can do it. Patterns of organization that look clear-cut and much easier to you may seem inscrutable and unhelpful to him.

Urge your child to focus on one small area that is as annoying to her as it is to others. She may be perfectly comfortable with her messy room and her loaded backpack and her trash-strewn locker. But maybe she wishes she could find things more easily in her closet or her purse or her notebook. Maybe she's frustrated at getting no credit for homework she worked hard on but couldn't find to turn in. Maybe she would like to participate in an activity or help with something around the house but can't put the steps together to do it. Finding something she's highly motivated to do will make it more likely that she'll do what she needs to be successful.

Project Break Down

As you learned to break motor tasks down into small, small steps for your child, teach him now how to do this for himself. Have him practice with situations in books or on television. Cook with him and break down with him what's involved in each step in the recipe—it's rarely just one activity. Even heating the oven involves walking to the oven, finding the right dial, and turning it with just the right amount of force to reach the right number. You can do the same with anything that has steps, from fixing a car to installing computer software to setting up a video game.

Once your child is adept at breaking things down, have her apply that new skill to a small organizational challenge of her own. If it's an activity that needs to be organized, have her concentrate on doing one small broken-down piece at a time. If it's a space that needs to be organized, try to use categories and containers to break a big mess into smaller messes and reduce the amount of decision-making that has to be done. The enormity of an entire task may be too daunting for your child to find her way through, but one small thing a day, or one small thing at a time, may be a challenge she can meet.

Essential

Motivation that comes from your child's own wants and needs will be more successful than motivation you provide from the outside. That doesn't mean that your goals for your child aren't important. The more practice she gets in managing sensory needs, the more she will be able to extend them to things that are important to others.

Practice at Low-Stress Times

Mornings before school, when you're racing around to get everything ready, is not a time to help your daughter work out ways to organize her backpack. Bedtime, when you're both tired and tense, is not the time to tackle cleaning a room. Dedicate an afternoon or a weekend when nothing much is going on to do your strategizing, and transfer that knowledge to higher-stress times only after it's well worked out and well rehearsed.

A school vacation might be a good time for your child to try a new strategy. Organizing the things in her room into bins may take some time, but it will then make cleaning up at the end of the day much easier. Figuring out different purposes for different pockets of the backpack and getting things all set up makes it easier to replicate that in the hectic morning. Going over the steps involved in making a bed or putting together a lunch when there's lots more time to do it makes doing it in a pinch easier (or at least less painful).

Pass on What You've Learned

Your responsibility in all of this, first and foremost, is to pass on the information you've learned about what works for your child and what doesn't. You are the foremost expert in that field. You have been investigating and testing and trying and failing and trying again for as many years as your child has been diagnosed with sensory integration disorder, and probably before that. You are better than any reference book in giving your child an understanding of how his senses and his brain work to give him a picture of the world. Although only he may know exactly what that picture is, you can give him the best idea of how it relates to the world most other people perceive.

Be matter-of-fact with your child about what you've done in the past to help her and why it has or hasn't worked. Remind her of specific incidents in which certain accommodations or changes in environment were successful. Go through this book and remember all the things you decided sounded like your child, and share that information with her. In addition to helping your child have the largest amount of knowledge in devising her own strategies, you will also be turning over the reins of controlling her disorder.

The "How Does Your Engine Run?" Program

One excellent program for you and your child to follow is *"How Does Your Engine Run?": The Alert Program for Self-Regulation*. Devised by occupational therapists Mary Sue Williams and Sherry Shellenberger, the program uses an engine metaphor to help your child understand his state of alertness. He can then do things to slow his engine down or speed his engine up to achieve a maximum state of comfort and function.

As important as the empowerment the program gives children to monitor and adjust their levels of alertness is the way it incorporates parents and teachers into the process. Adults are instructed to identify their own "engine" levels when dealing with children and to model appropriate responses. The understanding this brings will all by itself reduce the level of stress that comes when the adults in a child's life don't understand what he's feeling or dealing with. Everybody's engine runs a little off some of the time, and an atmosphere where that's recognized and handled as just another part of life is the one you want your child to be raised and taught in.

Fact

The Alert Program is designed for children at a developmental age of eight or older. If your child is over eight but has developmental delays that make his functional age younger, you may not be able to fully implement the program. However, you may be able to use parts of it, and it will still increase your own understanding.

Materials for the Alert Program include an introductory booklet; an instructor's manual; a CD featuring excerpts from the manual as well as songs for helping children regulate their level of alertness; and a book of movement breaks and activities called "Take Five." All can be purchased from the Alert Program's Web site at *www.alertprogram.com*, and some are also available from other online booksellers. Your child's occupational therapist may already have this material and be able to train you and your child to use it. If not, you can purchase the books yourself and share the information with your child and with school personnel.

The Alert Program will help you get in touch with your own particular sensory needs, and it will also point out some adjustments you may have been making without even knowing it. In Chapter 25, you'll see how your sensory integration issues can impact your child and maybe even cause some of her difficult behavior.

CHAPTER 25

Sensory Integration and You

Everyone has areas in which sensory integration works less efficiently than others. But as you've seen with your child, understanding where the problems lie is only one step toward pinpointing how they affect behavior. Your behavior is affected by your sensory sensitivities just as much as your child's is, although you've probably developed less disruptive ways of dealing with it. Understanding how sensory responses drive your reactions can help you see why certain areas of conflict keep arising with your child and give you better options for dealing with them.

Understanding Your Own Sensory Integration

You may have thought about your sensory preferences and dislikes in a relatively lighthearted way, in terms of foods and amusements you enjoy or don't enjoy. Now start taking a closer look at how the lifestyle choices you make are affected by the way your senses work. How might your sensory strengths and weaknesses have impacted your choice of career, or your happiness in the jobs you've had? Have they made a difference in where you've chosen to live, what you've chosen to drive, or what sort of exercise you get?

Just as you may suspect sensory integration disorder in your child because he has behaviors that seem to have no logical explanation, your own sensory integration–related behavior may seem to be beyond normal common sense. If you regularly do things that turn out badly and you have no idea why you did them, start looking for possible sensory solutions to the mystery. You may believe you've made decisions for logical reasons, but often there's an undercurrent of sensory need or phobia at work as well.

That's not a bad thing. The way your particular senses work to form your outlook on the world is part of what makes you a unique individual and colors your personality. What can be bad, though, is a presumption that your reality is the same as everybody else's, and that therefore those who see things differently are wrong and you are right. Admitting that others—most significantly, your child—might have their own sensory sensitivities that make their differing reactions just as valid as your own is an important step to being a better and more understanding parent.

While you may comfortably admit that what you taste and smell is governed by sensory preferences, and even what you feel, or how you experience motion or movement, like most people you probably think that seeing is believing. Surely, if there's anything you can trust, it's what your own eyes tell you. But even there, your brain is busy making interpretations that aren't entirely governed by any "real," physical, unequivocal truth. What you see can be influenced by the accuracy with which your brain interprets visual information, how it handles large amounts of new information, and how it integrates the information with feedback from other senses.

Fact

The techniques your brain uses to fill in for your "blind spot"—the area where the optic nerve leaves the eye, which has no light-receiving cells to provide vision—can help illustrate the fact that what you see is not always what's there. Check the exercises at *http://serendip.brynmawr.edu/bb/blindspot1.html* for some good demonstrations of this phenomenon.

You've probably had the experience of looking at a familiar place and noticing something you've never seen before or of not finding something that's right in front of your nose. You may think of this as absentmindedness, but in fact your brain often makes determinations of which things in your field of vision are important enough to be interpreted. Sometimes, things that may in fact be seen with your eyes don't make it to your conscious thought. When you say, in amazement, "I never saw it there!" you're quite right.

At the same time, your brain fills in the gaps for the things you don't see—objects that fall into your blind spot—using memory and generalizations and information from other senses. In most cases, these little visual magic tricks that your brain pulls off are believable enough that you don't even notice any discrepancy. But that doesn't mean what you see is entirely accurate, or that others might not see something different and feel just as sure of their sight.

How Sensory Integration Affects Parenting

If you accept that what you see, feel, smell, taste, hear, and take in through your vestibular and proprioceptive sense is subjectively true and accurate for you but not objectively true and accurate for anybody else, you're going to have to reconsider some of the absolutes you've brought to the project of parenting. How often have you made these or similar statements to your child:

- "Eat it—it tastes fine."
- "You can't possibly be warm enough in that shirt."
- "That's not enough light to see with."
- "You can't concentrate when you're sitting like that."
- "The water's just right."
- "How can you study with that music blaring?"
- "Stop whining. There's nothing to be afraid of."
- "Your room stinks! Can't you smell that?"

It's natural for you to work from your own reality and expect that your child's will be the same. It's hard to imagine how you could keep your child safe, fed, clean, and comfortable without her following the standards you are most comfortable with. But every time you assert your truth as the only truth, you make it harder for your child to come to terms with her own sensory reality without misbehavior and meltdowns. You don't have to suspend all supervision and let your child do whatever feels good, but you do have to be thoughtful and respectful of the fact that she may legitimately feel differently about things than you do.

When you have the urge to make a statement like those above, ask yourself these questions:

- Is what my child doing dangerous?
- Is it going to harm her development in a significant way?
- Is it possible that this offends my sensory sensitivities but is appropriate for hers?

If the answer to the first two are "no" and to the third is "yes," consider letting this be a battle that you choose not to fight.

Mismatched Sensitivities

Having a child who is a temperamental mismatch is a real challenge for a parent. It can be hard to set aside your own strong feelings of self-defense in order to appreciate your child as a different yet delightful individual. Similarly, having a child whose sensory preferences are strongly different from yours can be trying, and you may not even be aware of it.

Think about the things your child does that grate on your nerves. Could they have a sensory integration basis? Is he loud, whereas you prefer quiet? Clingy, whereas you're reserved about touch? Is he slow and careful when you want to keep moving, rough and boisterous when too much movement makes you feel off-balance or clumsy? You probably don't expect your child to be a carbon copy of you, and you may be able to spare some understanding for differences in your personal styles. But when your child's pursuit of sensory comfort sets off your own alarms, it can be impossible to react in a calm and responsible manner.

Hugs and cuddles are such a major part of the parent-child bond, particularly when a child is young. If one or the other can't tolerate that closeness, it may be perceived as rejection. Make sure to find some way to have tolerable tactile contact with your child, even if some forms are too intense for your child or for you.

Of course you love your child. But you may sometimes have the sneaking and unsettling feeling that you don't like her very much. In addition to your mismatch of sensory styles, you probably argue more and have hurt feelings more as you each try to force the other to provide the things that feel so terribly necessary. Although being the adult in this equation means that you have a more profound understanding of what's going on than your child does, and a deeper responsibility to deal with it, that doesn't make it easy to override your strong fears and impulses. Being in the position of constantly subduing your own sensory preferences so that your child can honor hers can cause you—even subconsciously, and against your will—to resent your child.

Don't be afraid to talk with your child's occupational therapist about any serious clash between your child's sensory needs and your own. The therapist may be able to recommend some ways for you to work on your sensory integration challenges that will make it easier to adjust to your child's needs. It may also be possible to adjust therapy to give preference to addressing the trouble spots between the two of you. As your child gets help for his sensory system, he may be better able to adjust to your preferences, and you may learn some tricks to help him to do that.

If you're lucky enough to have a spouse who has different sensory strengths and weaknesses than your own, see if you can split parenting duties in a way that allows you each to tackle the responsibilities that will cause you least distress or match you up best with your child's needs. Maybe the parent with reduced olfactory processing can change diapers, for example, and the one who needs proprioceptive input can do the rough play.

Communicating Your Feelings

Whether your sensory clashes with your child are major or minor, whether they manifest with small disagreements or knock-down, drag-out fights, it's important to let your child know what's going on. Tell your child what you're feeling, what you guess she's feeling, and why that causes a problem. Think out loud about what she could do or what you could do to resolve your differences.

There will always be parent-child disagreements that have nothing to do with sensory issues. It is your job as a parent to know the difference. As you learn more about sensory integration and your child's particular needs, it will become easier to see when behavior and opinions are motivated by sensory issues and when other factors are in play.

For example, you might say something like, "I know singing loudly like that feels good to your ears. But loud noises make my ears feel bad. Maybe you could go in your room when you sing, so that I can hear you more softly through the door? Or maybe I could go to my room? What do you think?" Your younger child may not be able to benefit from this kind of interaction, but as your child gets older, he will most likely come to appreciate that your sensory feelings are different from your feelings of love for him, and he will follow your lead in talking and strategizing about sensory problems.

Using Strategies on Yourself

To help your child deal with her sensory integration problems, you've learned all sorts of strategies and ways to adjust her environment. Now, try using some of those strategies on yourself. You may already be doing that without knowing it—chewing gum for proprioceptive input, listening to music through headphones for strong auditory input, wearing clothes that give appropriate stimulation to your tactile sense. You may read with a bookmark under a line of type to reduce visual distraction, or never go out in bright light without sunglasses, or insist on silence when you need to concentrate, and not think a thing of it.

Now that you've seen some of the tools and exercises used to aid children with sensory integration disorder, though, you may want to try them for yourself. Consider the following possibilities for the tactile sense:

- Try seam-free socks like those offered for adults as well as children by Sensory Comfort (online at *www.sensorycomfort.com*). The catalog also offers bras, tank tops, and bicycle shorts designed with flat seams and comfortable fits for people with tactile sensitivity.
- Keep a fidget toy like a Koosh ball, beanbag, hacky sack ball, stress squeeze toy, putty, or even a homemade item like marbles or rice placed in a sock and sewn shut. These can provide good sensory input when you need it, or they can help relax you if your senses are overstimulated.
- A small hand-held massager or vibrating toy may wake up an underresponsive tactile sense, or soothe an overreactive one by allowing you to pinpoint where and how firmly the input is administered. A shower massager or a vibrating chair cushion may also be good ways to get some calming deep pressure.

Consider the following possibilities for the visual sense:

- Books on tape, now available for an enormous range of fiction and nonfiction titles, are a good option if you find reading visually overstimulating. You can also download recorded books into an iPod through the iTunes store (*www.apple.com/itunes*), or into a wide range of MP3 players, PDAs, and cell phones at Audible.com (*www.audible.com*).
- The bookmarks from Really Good Stuff (*www.reallygoodstuff.com*) with a strip of yellow film that were recommended for your child in Chapter 9 may also be useful for you. Whether you prefer viewing the letters through the colored film or using the bright color as an underlining accent, the visual contrast will help make following lines of type easier.
- Try using bins and boxes to minimize clutter and make it easy to keep things somewhat organized and out of sight. Label them with words or symbols if necessary to help keep similar things together.

Consider the following possibilities for the auditory sense:

- If you have trouble with loud noises, or with tolerating the overamplified sound in movie theaters, concert venues, or your teenager's bedroom, consider a pair of earplugs. The kind designed for hunters, found in sporting-goods stores, might be a good choice.
- Just as your child may have trouble distinguishing your voice from background noise in a busy room, you may not be able to hear children asking you questions from somewhere other than your immediate field of attention. Let your family know that you will probably give a better response if they come directly to you.
- A white noise machine, or one that plays restful nature sounds, may help you relax or get to sleep.

Consider the following possibilities for the vestibular sense:

- While you may not be able to easily sit on the swings at the playground and get the same kind of good vestibular input your child does, a porch swing or similar outdoor swinging or gliding seating may do the trick.
- Indoors, invest in a rocking chair and put it someplace other than a baby's room so that you can rock in it at the end of the day and get some soothing vestibular input.
- A large inflatable exercise ball, the kind you can sit on or lean your body against, can be a very therapeutic and calming item to use as seating in front of the television—the constant work at keeping your body balanced gives a lot of good input to your vestibular sense.

Consider the following possibilities for the proprioceptive sense:

- Wrist and ankle weights used for exercising can give you calming proprioceptive input at times when you particularly need stress relief or concentration. A weighted blanket may improve your ability to fall asleep without tossing and turning.
- You may enjoy jumping on a trampoline as much as your child does. Try a small exercise trampoline with a handle to keep you from jumping right off.
- Air-filled seat cushions can give you some needed movement while you're sitting, while not drawing a lot of attention to it.

Occupational therapy catalogs are full of tools and toys that offer sensory integration stimulation and relief. Browse through the Web sites listed in Appendix B and look for things that seem to fit a need that you feel. You may find solutions you never thought of or knew existed. Sporting-goods stores are also good sources of things that, while not specifically intended for sensory integration therapy, can do duty in that area.

Building a Family with Good Sense

The more you become attuned to your own sensory needs and those of your children, the more you can start implementing changes that keep everybody comfortable, calm, and in control. That may involve something as simple as offering more choices for food or clothing, or as complicated as outfitting a room to offer sensory comfort or stimulation. Follow these tips for increasing family sensory harmony:

1. Give out family chores according to strengths and weaknesses. Apportion careful work, smelly work, and whatever tasks you have to the family member who will be least uncomfortable doing it.
2. Set aside space for therapeutic devices. If you have a spare room, or basement or attic space, consider setting up a room with therapy equipment your child can take advantage of.
3. Set aside space for calming input. Another use of a spare room or space might be a "sensory room," designed to calm and soothe. This could include dim lighting and soft music or a machine that plays nature sounds.
4. Know your limitations. Choose activities that a maximum number of family members will be able to enjoy. Make meals that everybody will like. Set up your family schedule to accommodate your special needs.
5. Stay informed. Children change with time and therapy. Even adults change with age, and new information comes out on sensory strategies. Stay informed on sensory integration by speaking regularly with your child's occupational therapist and consulting sensory integration Web sites.

At best, tolerance for each other's sensory sensitivities can diffuse tensions and prevent conflicts. At the very least, it will provide a framework for understanding why things sometimes get out of control.

Appendix A

Books and Web Sites

Recommended Books About Sensory Integration:

The Out-of-Sync Child: Recognizing and Coping with Sensory Integration Dysfunction, by Carol Stock Kranowitz

Originally published in 1998, revised and expanded in 2005, The Out-of-Sync Child is the book that really put sensory integration on the map. Kranowitz is a preschool teacher, and the book focuses mainly on early childhood.

The Out-of-Sync Child Has Fun: Activities for Kids with Sensory Integration Dysfunction, by Carol Stock Kranowitz

The 2003 follow-up to Kranowitz's popular *The Out-of-Sync Child*, this useful volume offers a wide variety of activities—big and little, messy and neat, involving special equipment or the contents of your pantry—to play with your sensory integration–challenged child.

Building Bridges Through Sensory Integration: Occupational Therapy for Children with Autism and other Pervasive Developmental Disorders, **by Ellen Yack, Shirley Sutton, and Paula Aquilla**

Written by a trio of occupational therapists, *Building Bridges*—originally published in 1998 and updated in 2003—is useful not just for the families of children on the autism spectrum, but for any parent dealing with sensory integration disorder. It offers practical suggestions for a wide range of behaviors, not all of them exclusive to autism.

Sensory Integration and the Child, by A. Jean Ayres

Written by the founder of sensory integration theory, *Sensory Integration and the Child* is the book to reach for when you're really ready to learn about the mechanics of how sensory integration works. Not for the casual reader, the book—originally published in 1979, with a twenty-fifth anniversary edition issued in 2005—rewards the effort and conveys the author's enthusiasm and conviction.

Love, Jean: Inspiration for Families Living with Dysfunction of Sensory Integration, by A. Jean Ayres, Philip R. Erwin, and Zoe Mailloux

Love, Jean, published in 2004, reproduces the correspondence that passed between Ayres and her nephew, Erwin, about the latter's sensory integration problems growing up. Occupational therapist Mailloux supplies suggestions for parents whose children are dealing with the same issues now.

An Introduction to "How Does Your Engine Run?": The Alert Program for Self-Regulation, by Mary Sue Williams and Sherry Shellenberger

Start with this booklet by two occupational therapists; it's inexpensive, gives a good overview of sensory integration and the program for helping kids manage their alertness, and is perfect for passing on to teachers, therapists, and anyone else who works with your child. Then, if you want more detail, you can move up to the *Leader's Guide*. Both are available online at *www.alertprogram.com*, or by calling 877-897-3478.

Brain Gym: Simple Activities for Whole Brain Learning and *Brain Gym (Teachers Edition),* both by Paul E. Dennison and Gail E. Dennison

These guides, available from the Edu-Kinesthetics site at *www.braingym.com* (888-388-9898), give illustrated instructions and explanations for exercises meant to increase alertness, focus, learning ability, and motor skills.

Smart Moves: Why Learning Is Not All In Your Head, by Carla Hannaford

Originally published in 1995 and revised and expanded in 2005, *Smart Moves* focuses on the important effect that movement has on learning. At a time when recess and gym are being cut out of many schools in exchange for more desk time, this book may be more useful and thought provoking than ever.

Answers to Questions Teachers Ask About Sensory Integration, by Carol Stock Kranowitz, Stacy Szklut, and others

Your child's teacher may take this whole sensory integration thing more seriously if you hand him a book like this one, which is written specifically to address teachers' doubts about sensory integration disorder. If he doesn't have time to read it, get one of the audio companion versions from the Sensory Resources site at *www.sensoryresources.com.*

Recommended Books about Behavior Management:

Bookstore shelves overflow with books on dealing with your child's out-of-control behavior, but the following four are particularly well suited to families of children with sensory integration disorder. You may find the best solution is to take what works from each one and develop a plan individualized to the needs of your particular child and family.

The Challenging Child: Understanding, Raising, and Enjoying the Five "Difficult" Types of Children, by Stanley I. Greenspan, MD, with Jacqueline Salmon

Transforming the Difficult Child: The Nurtured Heart Approach, by Howard Glasser and Jennifer Easley

The Explosive Child: A New Approach for Understanding and Parenting Easily Frustrated, Chronically Inflexible Children, by Ross W. Greene

Raising Your Spirited Child: A Guide for Parents Whose Child Is More Intense, Sensitive, Perceptive, Persistent, Energetic, by Mary Sheedy Kurcinka

Other Books of Interest:

An Alchemy of Mind: The Marvel and Mystery of the Brain, by Diane Ackerman

An Anthropologist on Mars: Seven Paradoxical Tales, by Oliver Sacks

The Child with Special Needs: Encouraging Intellectual and Emotional Growth, by Stanley I. Greenspan, MD, and Serena Wieder, with Robin Simons

Freaks, Geeks and Asperger Syndrome: A User Guide to Adolescence, by Luke Jackson

A Mind at a Time, by Dr. Mel Levine

Seizures and Epilepsy in Childhood: A Guide for Parents, by John M. Freeman, MD, Eileen P. G. Vining, MD, and Diana J. Pillas

Steps to Independence: Teaching Everyday Skills to Children with Special Needs, by Bruce L. Baker and Alan J. Brightman

Teach Me How to Say It Right: Helping Your Child with Articulation Problems, by Dorothy P. Dougherty

Recommended Sensory Integration Web Sites:

Sensory Integration International
www.sensoryint.com

The SPD Network
www.sinetwork.org

Kid Power
www.kid-power.org

Children's Disabilities Information
www.childrensdisabilities.info

The Sensory Processing Disorder Resource Center
www.sensory-processing-disorder.com

Sensory Integration Online Workshop
http://snow.utoronto.ca/prof_dev/tht/sensory/

Sensory Integration Dysfunction
http://mywebpages.comcast.net/momtofive/SIDWEBPAGE2.htm

Sensory Diet
www.wash.k12.mi.us/perform/Documents/Sensory_Diet_Yee.pdf

Empirical Evidence Related to Therapies for
Sensory Processing Impairments
www.nasponline.org/publications/cq315sensory.html

About Parenting Special Needs
http://specialchildren.about.com/od/sensoryintegration/

Occupational Therapy Associates—Watertown
www.otawatertown.com

Pediatric Therapy Network
www.pediatrictherapy.com

Come Unity
www.comeunity.com

Sensory Resources
www.sensoryresources.com

Other Sites of Interest:

Adapted Physical Education
www.pecentral.org

Alert Program
www.alertprogram.com

Brain Gym
www.braingym.com

Do 2 Learn
www.dotolearn.com/www.do2learn.com

Eastern European Adoption Coalition
www.eeadopt.org

Floortime Foundation
www.floortime.org

LD OnLine
www.ldonline.org

National Early Childhood Technical Assistance Center
www.nectac.org/contact/ptccoord.asp

NLDline
www.nldline.com

North American Riding for the Handicapped Association
www.narha.org

Post Adoption Information
www.postadoptinfo.org

SchwabLearning.org
www.schwablearning.org

Yoga for the Special Child
www.specialyoga.com

Tourette Syndrome "Plus"
www.tourettesyndrome.net

Wrightslaw
www.wrightslaw.com

Appendix B

Sources for Sensory Integration Products

Therapy Catalogs:

The following Web sites offer products used by occupational therapists. Most allow online orders, or you can call the number listed for a print catalog.

Abilitations
www.abilitations.com
1-800-850-8603

OT Ideas
www.otideas.com
1-877-768-4332

Playful Puppets
www.playfulpuppets.com
1-866-501-4931

PDP Products
www.pdppro.com
651-439-8865

Pocket Full of Therapy
www.pfot.com
732-441-0404

Sensory Comfort
www.sensorycomfort.com
1-888-436-2622

Sensory Resources
www.sensoryresources.com
1-888-357-5867

Southpaw Enterprises
www.southpawenterprises.com
1-800-228-1698

Special Kids Zone
www.specialkidszone.com
1-800-373-4699

Therapro
www.theraproducts.com
1-800-257-5376

Therapy Shoppe
www.therapyshoppe.com
1-800-261-5590

William's Store
www.williamsstore.com/marketplace.html
478-750-7519

Weighted Items:

The following Web sites offer weighted blankets, vests, and other items to provide calming proprioceptive input for your child.

DreamCatcher Weighted Blankets
www.weightedblanket.net
406-642-3253

In Your Pocket
www.weightedvest.com/enhanced.html
1-800-850-8602

MW Sales
www.world-net.net/home/mwsales/index.html
1-877-656-5228

Items for Daily Living:

The following Web sites offer items that may assist your child in eating, drinking, dressing, and other life skills.

Adaptivemall.com
www.adaptivemall.com
1-800-371-2778

Life Solutions Plus
www.lifesolutionsplus.com
1-877-785-8326

Sammons Preston
www.sammonspreston.com
1-800-323-5547

Index

A

B

C

D

E

F

G

H

I

J

K

L

M

N

O

P

R

S

THE EVERYTHING® PARENT'S GUIDES SERIES

The Everything® Parent's Guide to Raising a Successful Child

ISBN: 1-59337-043-1

The Everything® Parent's Guide to Children with Autism

ISBN: 1-59337-041-5

The Everything® Parent's Guide to Children with Bipolar Disorder

ISBN: 1-59337-446-1

The Everything® Parent's Guide to Children with Dyslexia

ISBN: 1-59337-135-7